Praise for
Finding the Fool

"An introspective introduction to tarot card reading . . . each entry includes guidance for reading the card and journal prompts to help readers better understand individual signs. Wall's flexible approach lets readers tailor a tarot practice that works for them."

—*Publishers Weekly*

"In this book, tarot reader Meg Jones Wall (@3am.tarot) invites readers to look past the limitations and exclusions of previous Euro-centric, binary, hetero-normative interpretations of most decks and read tarot from one's own personal story. . . . Wall's book is a likely candidate to join the canon of must-read guides for the serious student of the tarot."

—*Library Journal* (starred review)

"Meg's masterful prose takes us on an experiential adventure where we can channel the essence of the cards and see how they apply to our lives. With *Finding the Fool* by your side, you'll be well equipped as you walk the tarot path to self-discovery."

—Theresa Reed, author of *Twist Your Fate*

"A fresh voice, Meg Jones Wall has written seventy-eight meditative essays that inspire personal transformation. Drawing upon astrology and numerology, *Finding the Fool* is part postmodern primer on tarot and part spiritual philosophy."

—Benebell Wen, author of *Holistic Tarot*

"*Finding the Fool* frees you from meanings tied to specific tarot imagery and invites readers to explore a couple of tarot's underlying principles that apply to any deck. Wall's simple interpretations also expand meaning beyond the personal to an individual's place in and responsibility to community in a refreshing way."

—Mary K. Greer, author of *Tarot for Your Self*

"A beautiful book that drops you right into your tarot cards to experience them for yourself. The author creates a warm, welcoming, info-packed resource for tarot learners at all levels. I absolutely loved this exploration of the tarot. *Finding the Fool* is one of my favorite tarot books I've read, maybe ever."

—Cassandra Snow, author of *Queering the Tarot*

"*Finding the Fool* is the lightning strike that the cartomancy community needs to revitalize its personal and professional readings. Meg Jones Wall reminds us that, by nature, we are perpetual Fools—forever growing, learning, changing, and evolving. She encourages us to earnestly dive into who we are by courageously embarking on the Fool's journey. Wall's clear and concise perceptions are without condescension. As she writes, 'new discoveries give us confidence.'"

—Amber Highland, publisher of *The Cartomancer Magazine*

"Meg Jones Wall's gifts as both writer and teacher shine here in *Finding the Fool*—a much-needed addition to tarot literature."

—Brittany Muller, author of *The Contemplative Tarot*

"This book had me hooked from the very first line! Poetically written and deeply generous, guiding readers through all seventy-eight cards—and their elemental, astrological, and numerological associations—in ways that are accessible and thorough, with plenty of room left for personal exploration. . . . A gentle, yet radical guide."

—Rebecca Scolnick, author of *The Witch's Book of Numbers*

"*Finding the Fool* is like bible study for queer witches. From the first sentence, Meg Jones Wall's voice is firm and comforting—the spicy friend who dommes everyone around her into self-care and spiritual awakening. She reminds us all that magic is a practice and not a lightning strike."

—A. E. Osworth, author of *We Are Watching Eliza Bright*

"*Finding the Fool* is both thought-provoking and a refreshingly unintimidating exploration of tarot. I believe that tarot is supposed to help us strengthen our connection to ourselves and our intuition—not muddle or steer us away from it. What Meg has done with this book is empower people to build an intimate and tailor-made relationship with the cards by challenging tarot's status quo, thereby helping people establish a deep and intimate relationship with themselves."

—Mecca Woods, astrologer and author of *Astrology for Happiness and Success*

"*Finding the Fool* is the warm, gentle hand shepherding us into the needlessly daunting world of self-discovery. This work empowers the reader to own an intentional and personal relationship with the tarot as we build one with ourselves, and it provides infinite opportunities to find importance in this age-old tool beyond traditional definitions. *Finding the Fool* feels like an ascended master on a young diviner's shoulder, reminding them that intuition is built in asking great questions, not having every answer."

—Kendra Austin, writer, diviner, model, and author of *The Realest Oracle*

FINDING THE FOOL

FINDING THE FOOL

a tarot journey
to radical transformation

MEG JONES WALL

foreword by Theresa Reed

WEISER
BOOKS

This edition first published in 2023 by Weiser Books, an imprint of
Red Wheel/Weiser, LLC
With offices at:
65 Parker Street, Suite 7
Newburyport, MA 01950
www.redwheelweiser.com

ISBN: 978-1-57863-787-4
Library of Congress Cataloging-in-Publication Data
Names: Wall, Meg Jones, 1985- author.
Title: Finding the Fool : a tarot journey to radical transformation / Meg Jones Wall.
Description: Newburyport, MA : Weiser Books, 2023. | Includes bibliographical references. | Summary: "This
is a tarot resource, workbook, and study guide that makes space for readers who may not feel represented by
traditional decks. Featuring introductory sections on tarot-related topics as well as clear and contemporary
explorations on every card in the tarot, this book provides the tools and information needed to create a personal,
lasting relationship with the cards"-- Provided by publisher.
Identifiers: LCCN 2022042535 | ISBN 9781578637874 (paperback) | ISBN 9781633412767 (kindle edition)
Subjects: LCSH: Tarot. | Tarot cards. | Self-realization. | BISAC: BODY,
MIND & SPIRIT / Divination / Tarot | BODY, MIND & SPIRIT / Inspiration & Personal Growth
Classification: LCC BF1879.T2 W333 2023 | DDC 133.3/2424--dc23/eng/20221116
LC record available at https://lccn.loc.gov/2

Interior images by Meg Jones Wall © 2023
Cover and text design by Sky Peck Design

Printed in the United States of America
IBI
10 9 8 7 6 5 4 3 2 1

CONTENTS

FOREWORD

When I was a child, I had a lot of big questions. Most kids do. But a lot of my queries didn't have simple answers. While the other kids around me seemed more interested in Star Wars or whatever fad was popular at the moment, I wanted to know about my life purpose.

Who am I? What does it mean to be a good person? What should I do with my life?

No one seemed to be able to provide satisfactory answers.

Instead, the authority figures in my life were more interested in getting me to conform to the norm, and their responses showed that bias. I was told what to do rather than honor my free-spirited nature. Needless to say, I learned early on that most of my answers would need to come from somewhere else.

I immersed myself in music and books for a time, which seemed to quiet the deep ache I felt inside. Hours spent analyzing lyrics provided solace and bits of wisdom. But, oftentimes, they stirred up an urge to walk as far away as possible in search of something better.

Once I reached my teenage years, I was in the midst of a full-blown existential crisis. I didn't fit in anywhere. Instead of proms and pep rallies, I wanted an escape. Then, one day, fate intervened in the form of a fellow misfit, and my life changed forever.

Her mother was an astrologer.

When she explained my astrological chart, the puzzle pieces started to fall into place. Instantly fascinated with the cosmos and my newfound sense of self, I immersed myself in studying the stars. Ultimately, this led to a bookstore and a tarot deck. That was over forty years ago, and I've had a set of cards in my hands ever since.

You probably think this story leads to a neat conclusion where everything instantly worked out, and I was set for my life, right? But the journey isn't quite that simple, and we never remain the same. I'm a different person now than I was at 15 when I purchased my first tarot deck. The path of self-discovery is ongoing, and there is always new terrain to explore.

Tarot is similar. Although it's been around for centuries, it has continued to evolve, sometimes in surprising ways. From a playing card game to a tool for divination or a creative prompt, tarot's journey is a developing story.

Although some old traditional interpretations and divinatory aspects will always remain, new breakthroughs are possible. In *Finding The Fool: A Tarot Journey to Radical Transformation*, author Meg Jones Wall takes the reader on a totally unique path. Instead of going with the standard (and outdated) rules of the road, the reader is encouraged to find their own way of interpreting the archetypes and symbols through a personal lens. This is a wholly modern perspective, one that leaves plenty of room for fresh insights and exciting ways of engaging with the cards.

Like the Fool, you get to take risks, dive in, and see where things lead rather than be told what it all means. Then, it's up to you to write your own story with tarot as your handy guide.

One of the surprises in this book is the choice to not use illustrations. At first, I didn't know what to think about that. After all, tarot IS visual. Readers depend on the symbols to tell the story. But this was a genius move, for I found myself envisioning different iterations of each card as I worked through the exercises in the book. Sometimes, the standard Rider Waite Smith loomed large, while other times, I found my mind drifting to images from newer decks like the Modern Witch Tarot or one of the various cat-themed decks in my collection.

Meg's sage advice throughout the book makes you feel like she's right by your side, guiding you like an old friend who is just as excited about your journey as you are. For example, instead of the usual nudge to pick one of the "classic" tarot decks for your first, she says to "choose a deck that calls to you, that feels good in your hands, that you want to build a relationship with." This friendly advice feels both comforting and radical at the same time.

Her knowledge is vast, which clearly shows her dedication to her craft. Follow along, and you'll go deeper than you thought possible. Astrology and numerology play a significant role in this book, adding nuance and depth to the meanings. Meg's masterful prose for each card takes you on an experiential adventure where you can channel the essence of the cards while seeing how they apply to your life. Journaling prompts throughout the book allow for inquiry and a new understanding of the card and yourself.

Although interpretations for readings are presented, Meg never makes you feel like it's set in stone. You are free to take these meanings and turn them into your own. This approach allows for individuality rather than rote memorization. A smattering of practices and easy-to-use spreads provide plenty of tools for your tarot journey.

With *Finding The Fool: A Tarot Journey To Radical Transformation* by your side, you'll be well-equipped as you walk the path to self-discovery.

As I finished the book, I found myself focusing less on the question of *"who am I"* and more on *"who do I want to become?"* I can't wait to find out the answer.

—THERESA REED
Twist Your Fate: Manifest Success with Astrology and Tarot

INTRODUCTION

The first time I held a tarot deck in my hands, I didn't feel a fucking thing.

I waited breathlessly, hoping for lightning to strike, craving the sparks of magic and power and certainty that so many had described upon handling their first deck. I wanted to be recognized, to feel special, to know in my bones that tarot wanted me just as much as I wanted it. After months of obsessing about the cards, hungry for a sense of connection, I'd finally picked a tarot deck—but it seemed that it hadn't picked me back.

It broke my heart, that first moment. I'd wanted to be chosen, and instead I still felt lost. But after a few moments of sitting in stillness and disappointment, I swallowed my pride and started to shuffle. The tarot may have not chosen me, but I was still choosing it.

If the magic wasn't in the cards, then I'd find it within myself.

. . .

When I was a kid, growing up in a conservative, religious family of pastors and church planters, "magic" was considered a dirty word. Jesus wasn't described as a sorcerer or magician by ministers and teachers—instead he was known as the Son of God, omnipresent and perfect, special in ways that were beyond our comprehension. I was taught that, to be loved, I had to speak and act in very specific way, to twist myself into a particular shape in order to fit the necessary mold. Christians didn't swear, didn't brag, didn't break rank—and they certainly didn't use tools meant for divination or intuition.

I learned early on to hide anything that made me different, especially when it came to my identity. It took a long time for me to acknowledge that I was queer, and even longer for me to confess it to anyone else. In the evangelical church that my parents had helped to establish, one run by a minister who was well-known in the media circuit for being the face of anti-homosexual legislation in our state, it was far safer to stay hidden and follow the rules. Falling in line was a matter of survival, until everything that I was concealing became too much to bear.

Being a good girl meant that I didn't read about magic or sorcery or queerness or anything radical, that I graduated from a Christian college that made me sign a document every semester promising that I wasn't queer, that I married the man I loved on a schedule that my parents dictated. By the time I was in my mid-twenties, I found myself drowning in a tangled mess of lifelong insomnia and major depressive disorder, having lost sight of myself in the fog of purity culture and homophobia and religious dogma. I was suffocating under the weight of my secrets, afraid of the truths that I'd buried inside of myself for so long. And in spite of the freedoms promised by leaving damaging institutions behind, separating myself from the beliefs of my childhood made me feel more lost than ever. I knew that the faith I'd always clung to was hurting me deeply, but going through life without it felt even more traumatic.

• • •

I've been a voracious reader since I was a child, but during those long, sleepless years of struggle and doubt, I read as though all of the answers could be found between the pages of books. As my internal world turned darker, I found myself drawn to stories of magic and wonder, letting myself explore the hidden literary worlds that I'd been kept from as a child. For the first time, I read *Harry Potter* and *The Golden Compass*, lost myself in *The Witches* and *Something Wicked This Way Comes*, revisited *The Lion, the Witch, and the Wardrobe*. Then came *A Discovery of Witches, Practical Magic, Good Omens, Beautiful Creatures, The Witching Hour, Inamorata, The Little Stranger, The Magicians, The Line*, on and on and on—I devoured every story on witchcraft and the occult that I could find, losing myself in those fictional mysteries, craving access to those strange and subversive worlds. By the time I read *The Night Circus* and *The Book of Speculation*, I had become consumed by the desire to personally access this kind of magic, even as it felt out of reach. Yet there tarot was, right in the middle of these pages: a sacred tool used by people of all backgrounds and identities, one that was accessible and affordable, something that anyone could learn. In the pages of these books, I saw people using the cards for rituals of reassurance, enjoying the same peace and comfort that I'd only ever found in prayers.

I had never received a tarot reading. I didn't know anyone who worked with tarot cards. I had never even held a deck in my hands. And yet, learning to read the cards was now my quest, a desperate and all-consuming need that I couldn't ignore. I'd become the Fool, captivated by a vision in my mind, unable to move forward without chasing that new, mesmerizing dream. The only thing to do, the only way to grow, was to get myself a tarot deck.

Of course, it wasn't that simple—acquiring a set of cards doesn't instantly make you a reader—and I was paralyzed by indecision before I even started, uncertain which resources to choose, which deck to purchase. So many of the websites and beginner's guides I found urged tarot newbies to start with the Rider-Waite-Smith deck, citing its long history and traditional, layered symbolism. But as a queer, chronically ill woman, I didn't feel drawn to it in the slightest. The medieval-style imagery, the bright colors, the emphasis on wealthy, cis, heteronormative structures that considered marriage with children as the ultimate version of success—none of it resonated.

Instead, I found myself drawn to the bold, minimalist lines and nature-based images found in Kim Krans's hand-drawn deck, *The Wild Unknown Tarot*. I couldn't stop looking at the gorgeous, stark artwork that was all over Instagram: something in those depictions just clicked for me. And in spite of worrying that I was doing something wrong in buying a modern deck, in spite of a lifetime spent following the rules, I finally surrendered to my instincts and got myself a copy.

It took nearly a year before I felt confident reading tarot without relying heavily on other resources at hand, another six months before I started pulling cards for friends. I didn't know how to trust myself, hadn't been taught that my intuition was something that I could rely on—but working with the tarot, learning to navigate those archetypes and images and symbols, slowly became a part of me. And the person I found while reading tarot was someone who seemed strong and whole, someone I'd been waiting a lifetime to meet.

Tarot is its own kind of magic. And if you pick up the cards and aren't sure what to do with them—if you don't instinctively speak their language or shuffle with ease or know in your bones what Temperance means—that doesn't mean that you can't learn to read tarot, or that the cards aren't for you. It simply means that you need a bit of guidance, like I did.

Learning tarot isn't just about memorizing traditional keywords or relying on outside resources to perform readings: it's about connecting your own experiences and perceptions with broader archetypes, and telling your own story within the cycles and structures of the cards. Tarot can be our companion as we strive for self-discovery, transformation, and radical growth, helping us tap into the wisdom that already lives within us.

$$\bullet\ \bullet\ \bullet$$

This book that you're holding is the resource that I tried to find when I started reading tarot, that I have longed for as I deepen my own practice. Beyond just repeating traditional, familiar meanings or basic keywords, this book offers you a chance to view the cards through a variety of lenses, to discover personal correspondences and definitions that resonate in ways that are engaging rather than limiting.

Tarot is a language, and fluency takes dedicated effort, focus, and determination. This is bigger than memorization, more complex than simply studying standardized interpretations over and over again. Instead, this is about learning to integrate new ideas into your tarot work, to find rich layers and unexpected messages that can transform your relationship with the cards. Within these pages, I will also offer you insights and discoveries that I have found in my own journey, including astrological and numerological correspondences, methods of connecting with the tarot through spiritual and creative practices, and estoteric tools that you can use to explore the cards in new ways. As you work your way through this book, let your understandings of the cards grow and evolve along with you. Stay open to new interpretations and listen to the ideas that come from within yourself when you look at tarot images. Even if, like me, you don't feel lightning strike the first time you pick up the cards, be assured that your path will be lit by the inner spark of your intuition, and that the more you feed it, the brighter your intuition will grow.

In other words, this is an opportunity for you to start fresh, to become the Fool again, to view the tarot through a new set of eyes. Leave your preconceived notions at the door, grab your deck, and allow yourself to get to know the cards once again. In finding the Fool, we also find ourselves.

And I'll be with you every step of the way.

PART ONE

Preparing
Your Way

BEGINNING YOUR RADICAL JOURNEY

Who are you?

I don't mean the version of self that you show to the world, the masks that you wear at work or play or when meeting new people, the methods of protection and preservation that keep you safe in strange or uncomfortable circumstances. I'm not talking about the ways that you've shrunk yourself in order to survive in this difficult, complicated world.

I mean, who are you *really*? Who are you in your fullness, your truth, your bones?

The world is built around systems that attempt to tell us who we are, that seek to categorize us. From doctors who assign our gender at birth to schools that assess our skills to parents who choose our activities to governments that control what we can learn and eat and access—we have so many of our choices stripped away, to the point that true freedom can be hard to recognize or even feel uncomfortable. The structures and institutions that shape our world also force us to paper over our own cracks, encouraging us to prioritize productivity over authenticity, urging us to stay quiet, pressuring us to conform to the status quo. Self-discovery, self-care, self-love—these so often get labeled as selfish luxuries, unnecessary indulgences. Yet the process of breaking free of these systems, and the courage required to interrogate our own beliefs and fears and desires, can fundamentally change what we know about ourselves.

Making the choice to find a path back to who we truly are—*that* is a radical journey.

• • •

This work of self-awareness, of personal interrogation, is not for the faint of heart. It has the potential to be painful, thrilling, awkward, ecstatic, uncertain, pleasurable, disruptive—but it's also a journey that will ultimately answer the question of who you are, and empower you to show up in the world as your most authentic self, without apologies or excuses or shame.

Sometimes, the only way to change our understanding of who we are is to look at our hearts, minds, bodies, and souls from a different perspective. The tarot is the perfect tool for this kind of introspection, giving us multiple lenses through which to explore identity, sexuality, gender, relationship and community needs, desires, and dreams. Each of the seventy-eight cards of the tarot provides a unique opportunity to find new ways of looking at our physical, spiritual, and emotional selves, empowering us to shift our gaze.

Tarot helps us figure out who the hell we *are*, instead of reinforcing who we've been trying to be.

This book is all about putting ourselves into the mindset of the Fool: that figure of desire and purpose, of longing, of knowing that we crave something so deeply and entirely that we're willing to turn our entire world upside down or leap off a cliff in pursuit of it. The Fool is a radical figure, a transformative figure, a courageous figure. They aren't afraid to venture out into the unknown, aren't discouraged by what they don't yet know. Instead, they see the magic in the mystery, are intrigued by all of the possibilities for discovery and experience that dwell around the next corner, over the next horizon.

The only way to fully become the Fool is to be willing to leave behind what we think we know, the ideas and definitions and expectations that may have once offered us comfort. In leaving behind our prior assumptions, in fully stepping into the wide-eyed, eager, curious energy of the Fool, we can approach these cards, and ourselves, in a far more intimate way.

It's so easy to get caught in the web of what we've known, to defer to old expectations or traditions or knowledge. But clinging to the same definitions, the same answers over and over, doesn't invite new discoveries—it just leaves us feeling stuck, struggling to apply conventional answers to modern questions. Human beings are complex and layered. We cannot be defined or captured in a few simple keywords—and neither can tarot cards. The standardized, conventional tarot interpretations that are so often repeated *ad nauseam* rarely allow for personal connection, and we do ourselves a disservice by limiting our analysis of these cards in such a dramatic and stifling way.

By looking at each individual card through a variety of unique lenses, all at once, we can see the cards as they are: as prisms of light and color and emotion and intuition; as new ways of translating old facts, ideas, theories, relationships, or experiences; as points in bigger cycles, sequences, journeys. Instead of trying to force old, impersonal definitions to make sense, regardless of the context, this approach makes space for *you*.

• • •

The Fool has so much to teach us. They serve as "the animating force giving life to the static images" of the other cards, as Rachel Pollack so beautifully writes in *Seventy-Eight Degrees of Wisdom*. This figure sets everything in motion, dwelling not only at the beginning of the journey but also in the in-between spaces of every card. The Fool tugs us forward, considers every possibility with delight and anticipation, invites us to be present and purposeful. With the Fool we learn to dream beyond what we know, to find joy in each stage of growth, to embrace the wonder and awe and potential that live in every single moment.

This book is not going to tell you who you are, but it will offer you tools that you can use on your own journey, revealing a tarot path that you can personalize for your own radical transformation. We will explore the cards in a wide variety of ways and will give ourselves the space to discover new ones. We'll intertwine existing systems of astrology and numerology, and will also layer in prompts, activities, spreads, and questions—because tarot doesn't exist in a vacuum, and neither do we.

As you prepare for this journey, allow me to share a few insights on what this book is, how to use it, and ways to get the most out of it.

No Card Illustrations

There are no pictures of tarot cards in this book.

Many systems that strive to define depend largely on smoke and mirrors, on getting distracted by a fixed, shiny object, on telling you who you are instead of empowering you to discover yourself.

Tarot cards are paper and ink, nothing more. Their weight, their magic, lies in how we use them, the ways we understand them, the power we assign to them. And while you may associate very specific images with specific archetypes, decks always reflect someone else's art, someone else's interpretation and vision. It's easy to get caught up in this and base our definitions solely on the insights of other people, to make these the only interpretation rather than seeing them as one of many possibilities. In doing so, we forget how to observe our own insights. Rather than focusing on any particular deck, rather than forcing my ideas of what tarot is on you or repeating meanings that you may already be familiar with, this book removes that fixed object and starts with a blank slate, offering only hand-drawn glyphs of planets, zodiac signs, and alchemical symbols to reinforce correspondences and connections.

The Empress isn't *only* a beautiful blonde woman sitting on a throne. The Hierophant isn't *only* an old white man yelling about hell and salvation. The Devil isn't *only* a vision of the Protestant notion of Satan, tempting us to a very orthodox definition of sin. You will notice in this book that I do not use gendered pronouns, discuss the gender binary, or explore the divine masculine and divine feminine. This is all done with purpose: not because these cards don't invite that kind of examination, but instead, because they offer us so much more than strict binaries or identities. We can each find ourselves in every card, every archetype, every cycle, and it's not my place to put these massive, infinite archetypes into neat, orderly little boxes.

If we let them, the cards can help us drastically expand our concepts of who we are, what we are capable of, and what our bigger and brighter purpose could be.

On Meanings

Tarot has a long and winding history. Divination tools and sacred decks of cards have been used throughout the world for hundreds of years, and we can trace pieces of the various meanings found within the tarot to card sets created in Turkey and the Middle East, the Eastern tradition of I Ching, Egyptian hieroglyphics, and the Jewish mystical Kabbalah, to name a few. Mutable and fluid, the origins of the tarot are in some ways simple and in other ways impossibly complex—but it's important to acknowledge that the structure of today's decks is based predominantly on European imagery created in the 1400s.

There are thousands and thousands of different decks available today, featuring endless styles, viewpoints, and imagery. Some are based on the Rider-Waite-Smith system, others on the Thoth or Marseilles systems, and still others branch out to create a card set that feels entirely unique. Each of the cards has meaning, concepts that have been passed down through centuries, modified and expanded through use and time. I must mention here that many of the interpretations that have persisted come from centuries-old European, white, cis-gender, binary, patriarchal societies. For those that live on the margins—especially queer communities, disabled folks, and people of color—those meanings rarely include or acknowledge us. This book offers you a chance to reclaim these cards and to discover meanings that represent your heart, your mind, your identity, your life.

As you move through your practice and this journey, I encourage you to pay attention to the keywords and definitions that resonate for you, as well as the ones that don't. Let the cards reflect the language that you use, the beliefs you carry, the perspective that you bring to the world. Sometimes we can find rich truth in the ideas that rub us the wrong way, and in digging into those reactions, we may find new layers of meaning that actually *do* work for us. But if a definition ever feels limiting, incorrect, or harmful, you absolutely do not have to force yourself to use it.

The world is wide enough for many meanings, even—especially—the ones that you create yourself.

• • •

Meanings are personal and may differ wildly from reader to reader. A card that feels positive, healing, and encouraging to you might seem threatening, frightening, or stressful to someone else—and I urge you to see that as a beautiful, powerful thing; don't internalize the idea that your perspective on a particular card is "wrong." Our own experiences and histories shape our viewpoints, and that's a truth to be celebrated rather than avoided. Traditional and classical interpretations can be useful, especially for beginners, but they don't have to hold more significance than your personal definitions. What you see and feel is just as important as the more "standard" meanings, and both hold weight and value in a reading.

With that in mind, resist the temptation to try and find a positive meaning for every card. Tarot isn't merely a tool for positive reinforcement; it offers wisdom for all kinds of situations, challenges, and obstacles, often pushing us to consider new perspectives. Life is not all love and light, not all rainbows and roses, and the tarot can reflect the reality of hardship, pain, suffering, loneliness, disappointment, and grief along with happiness, contentment, satisfaction, joy, abundance, safety, and comfort. While a card that is often associated with more "negative" emotions might feel scary when it appears in a reading, there are times when the cards acknowledge our pain, sorrow, or anger. This can be deeply validating. As you get to know the cards better, as you blend modern and traditional meanings with your own intuitive wisdom, try to see the cards for the magic that they hold, rather than twisting your interpretations around to suit specific queries. Don't let yourself get so focused on what you *want* to hear that you miss what is actually present in a reading.

A loving but firm reminder: the journey toward radical transformation is one of inquiry and discovery, rather than one of finding easy, ready-made answers. This will require you to dig deep, to pull apart the puzzle of you and put it back together again. Falling into the trap of looking for the positive in every card and every reading strips you of the ability to see obstacles, failures, and opportunities for growth, which is why I'm so insistent on this point. Give yourself the gift of acknowledging mistakes or tension points, both within your deck and within yourself. Transformation cannot and will not happen without it.

And if you haven't done so already, I urge you to consider what you believe about this practice and what you are looking for, from your tarot readings and your relationship to the cards in general. Where do you believe that the power and insight within the readings come from? Do you think that tarot readings can reveal destiny, futures, and outcomes? Or are the cards simply providing insights into what is possible? What are our responsibilities when reading, whether for ourselves or for others?

We all have a powerful intuition, an inner sense of wisdom and awareness and drive that guides us forward and nudges us toward certain opinions or choices. Yet for many people, it can be extremely difficult to recognize that voice for what it is, to trust ourselves and our insights. The cards can present truth through another language—a language that you yourself are writing. Be patient with yourself as you learn to listen to that internal voice, as you write this language. Give yourself as much time and space as you need to do this well, rather than trying to do it quickly.

Major and Minor Secrets

There is no hierarchy within the tarot.

Both the major and minor arcana offer their own secrets, their own wisdom, their own perspectives. The Fool's journey through the majors and the individual cycles within the minors all help us find our place within the world, providing insights, encouragement, advice, warnings, clarity, support, and comfort, depending on where we are, what we need, and how the cards emerge.

Many tarot resources focus heavily on the major arcana archetypes—and indeed, these cards hold endless depths, infinite wisdom, an almost intoxicating number of correspondences, connections, and contradictions. But there is also magic to be found within the mundane, the everyday, the expected. In the second section of this book, we will explore every card in depth, considering correspondences and cycles, looking at these cards in context. It may be tempting to focus your efforts on the majors, but remember that the minor cards are essential in your journey to find the Fool—to get to the beginning, to the source, to the essence of your truest self. What you find within the minors will be just as fulfilling, powerful, and transformative as the lessons from the major archetypes.

With the seventy-eight cards of the tarot, we can build countless combinations, exploring important shifts, boundless passions, logical choices, intense relationships, growing careers, and many other aspects of the lives we live during our time on earth. In combination with the majors, the minor cards will provide you with the fullest understanding of how you show up in the world and teach you different ways to discover power, strength, wisdom, intuition, and connection in your daily life.

And in learning to see the wisdom in every single card, you will build a much more intimate, personal, and transformative relationship with your deck.

TOOLS FOR THE JOURNEY

Deepening your relationship with the tarot does not mean that you have to invest in dozens of new decks, books, or tools—but having a few things on hand will set you up for success.

The most important tool you will need is a tarot deck of your own. And while I do believe that committing to one deck can be a beautiful way to build a strong connection with the tarot, looking at a wide range of artistic interpretations is a wonderful way to learn to see the cards through many unique perspectives, particularly ones that are different from your own. You can do this by working with multiple decks, or by looking up various depictions of cards on the internet. Don't limit yourself to only one perspective, only one version of this story: broadening the interpretations that you explore can help you see the cards in so many different ways. Remember the magic of the Fool and the power that dwells in those in-between spaces—I find that thinking about how we get from one card to the next can offer so much food for thought, and so many new opportunities for meaning.

My understanding of tarot, its correspondences and meanings, has come from a wide range of brilliant tarot readers, writers, historians, and artists. For readers who want to learn more about different tarot-related topics, or who particularly resonate with a specific practice, the third section of this book includes a list of resources, centering queer, disabled, and BIPOC voices as much as possible.

Choosing a Deck

Reading the cards can feel intimidating—and centuries of rumors and gate-keeping often keep curious readers from feeling empowered to begin working with the tarot on their own. To quell a few rumors: you do *not* have to be given your first deck, and you do *not* have to work with any particular deck to get started. Choose a deck that calls to you, that feels good in your hands, that you want to build a relationship with. You do *not* have to shuffle in any particular way, do *not* have to store your cards in any particular way, and do *not* have to use the Celtic cross or any other specific spread in your readings. The only truly wrong way to use a tarot deck is to twist readings to manipulate, coerce, or intimidate other people—otherwise, what you do with the cards is entirely up to you. This book is designed to encourage you to trust your instincts and your intuition, and it will guide you in developing rituals for readings that feel right for you.

If you don't already own a tarot deck, this is the moment to choose one (or several) to work with closely, one that you feel naturally drawn to or curious about. For me, that was Kim Krans's *The Wild Unknown*—a minimalist deck that left me a lot of space for dreaming, contemplation, and wonder. But you may be completely different, preferring a deck with more complex images like *The Numinous Tarot*, the *Dust II Onyx Deck,* or the *Shadowscapes Tarot.* You might like a deck that focuses on a particular theme or identity, like *The Black Queer Tarot* or the *Slutist Tarot* or *The Somnia Tarot.* You may also find yourself exploring decks that modernize the traditional Rider-Waite-Smith illustrations, like *This Might Hurt Tarot* or the *Modern Witch Tarot.* This is not a process that needs to be rushed, nor is it one that is the be-all and end-all of your tarot journey—trust me when I say that you can *always* acquire more tarot decks.

If you're just getting started with a new deck, take some time to get to know it. Look at the imagery, the colors, the symbols. See what kind of story is being told, the archetypes that draw your attention, any cards that elicit a strong or emotional reaction. Breathe them in, consider their energy, and be attentive to what they may ask of you. Your relationship with your deck will deepen as you work your way through this book, so you want to select a deck that will both comfort and challenge you, inviting contemplation, reflection, and discovery.

Consider noting the cards that represent different aspects of yourself, the ones that you identify with, the ones that resonate the most deeply—and pay attention to the different ways that various artists depict these cards. Too often in a traditional tarot reading the querent is asked to pick a significator card—one card that represents them—and too often those choices are defined by skin color, hair color, age, gender, or some other narrow identity. This book aims to break through all that heteronormative bullshit and open up a transformative approach that is truly nonbinary, truly expressive, truly authentic. Which archetypes, court cards, pips do you see in yourself? If you were to describe yourself or tell your personal story using only tarot cards, which ones would you choose? And don't think just in terms of people—perhaps you relate to the little dog nipping at the heels of the Fool, or the wickedly sharp blade of a sword, or an abstract type of movement on a particular card. How might the cards you choose change at various points in your life, and what might laying those out and tracing their patterns help you discover about yourself?

Because *Finding the Fool* is a book that focuses on the transformative *energy* of the tarot—rather than on the *images* of the tarot—any deck you choose will work beautifully in tandem with this journey.

Your Tarot Grimoire

One of the best things that you can do in your journey to find the Fool is keep a journal for your tarot discoveries. Think of it as your tarot grimoire: a consolidation of all the notes and insights and questions and knowledge that you glean from this book, and from any other resources, classes, or studies that you explore along the way. This can take several forms, but the purpose is to fill it with your ever-increasing proficiency, to have a reference for yourself that you can return to again and again.

My recommendation is to start with a brand new blank journal (or, if you prefer, a digital folder or document). Create a section for every card in the tarot, and as you find keywords, correspondences, study questions, prompts, observations, and personal experiences tied to this card, write them down. You may want to also collect songs, colors, artwork, scents, flavors, recipes, poems, books, films, characters, or other pieces of media that remind you of this energy. Give yourself room to expand rather than trying to cram everything you know about a card onto one single page.

This is the start of a new habit, not a task to check off a list. Keep your journal nearby when you do readings or meditate with specific cards. If you think of a connection that excites you, inspires you, that shifts something new into place, write it down. Let this be an ongoing project, a place where you can grow. The longer you read tarot, and the more you allow the cards to transform you, the more insights you'll find.

Many people also use a journal or tracker to record their readings, and you may find that recording how often you pull specific cards becomes a beautiful practice. We all have cards that come forward more than others, as well as cards that we rarely draw—and by monitoring our daily, weekly, monthly, and yearly pulls, as well as documenting larger spreads, we can trace those patterns with greater accuracy. How often do you pull your birth card, the card that represents your sun sign, or cards that you have difficult relationships with? Which suits come up the most frequently for you and which ones do you work with less? How do the cards you pull reflect where you are in work, play, relationships, career, creative flow, growth, release, or healing?

In the second section of this book, you'll find journal prompts for every card in the deck. These are meant to be open-ended questions that you can answer again and again, since your answers may vary based on the day, your queries and experiences, or the other cards that come up in readings. The more that you engage with these cards and the questions they invite, the more depth you will discover.

Spreads

In addition to correspondences, keywords, descriptions, and journal prompts, you will also find a chapter in part three dedicated to tarot spreads. A tarot spread—a layout of cards—is simply a way of expressing your inner story, using a framework to provide specific insights and clarity. I've written of learning the language of tarot; think of a tarot spread as an organized way of constructing a narrative. Each card "speaks" in the sentence of the layout. How you interpret those cards and their relationships will take you further and deeper down your path to transformation.

Spreads can be helpful ways of connecting with an archetype that may feel difficult, confusing, or out of reach, which is why this section includes twenty-two spreads that are specifically designed to help you connect with the energy of these cards. I've also included a variety of more general spreads that can apply to many different situations, but these are just a suggested framework to begin with, just a place to begin. Don't be afraid to tweak the spreads, change up structures, add more cards, or rewrite certain positions to be more useful for you. (Just make sure to do that *before* you pull cards for a reading, not afterward!)

I encourage you to record the different ways that you adjust or use these spreads, as you may find a version of a layout that you prefer and want to use again in the future.

Astrology

You were born of stardust.

Astrology is much older than the tarot itself, dating back over 6,000 years. For millennia, people have been studying the stars and planets through various astrological systems, tying those far-off movements to our own cycles of emotion, growth, change, and discovery. Astrology tells us we are all sparks of energy in time and space, emanating from the cosmos, and that planets and timing matter to our fundamental makeup. Your main experience with astrology may be from exploring your natal chart. When we work with the tarot through an astrological lens, we'll specifically look at zodiacal sign and planetary correspondences, elements, and modalities, and ways that those insights can take your tarot interpretations deeper.

Tarot and astrology both include the four elements as a fundamental part of their structure. Fire and wands are connected to passion, drive, motivation, creativity, and spirituality, and fire signs are known for their independence and ambition, as well as an inherent desire to explore and generate. Air and swords represent the intellect, logic, communication, truth, mental cycles, and understanding, and air signs are astute, truth-seeking, constantly questioning, and eager to know as much as they can about people, situations, and topics. Water and cups explore emotions, relationships, self-love, connections, community, and spirituality, and water signs are known for their depth, intensity, empathy, sensitivity, compassion, and intuition. Earth and pentacles deal with the physical world of health, wealth, career, home, family, and sex, and earth signs are responsible, patient, and grounded, able to set long-term goals and find success in a variety of disciplines.

As well as honoring the four elements, astrology also includes three different modalities, or qualities, called cardinal, fixed, and mutable. You can understand these qualities as a cycle: cardinal energy is initiative or beginning; fixed is sustaining or preserving; mutable is refining or transforming. When we look at these qualities in tandem with the four elements and their corresponding actions, you can see that the language of astrology is also about an illuminating and transformative journey.

Cardinal zodiac signs are those that begin each of the four seasons: Aries in spring, Cancer in summer, Libra in autumn, and Capricorn in winter. Each of these cardinal signs brings fresh starts, leadership, and courage, brimming with inspiration and determination. Aries, Cancer, Libra, and Capricorn all usher in new seasons in the calendar year, but they're also forces of nature, offering ideas and plans, setting ambitious goals, and unafraid to be in charge.

Fixed signs—Taurus, Leo, Scorpio, and Aquarius—take the hopes and dreams identified by the cardinal signs and carry them forward. The fixed signs add structure, detail, and a clear sense of purpose to those long-term objectives. Sitting in the middle of their calendar seasons, Taurus, Leo, Scorpio, and Aquarius are known for their endurance, intensity, and stubbornness, preferring stability to constant shifts or uncertainty.

Mutable signs are transformative. They are the most adaptable and flexible, taking the work done by the previous signs and using their creativity to refine and complete projects. Mutable energy transitions from old to new, from beginning to end, and these signs make way for the cardinal signs to begin a new cycle. Gemini, Virgo, Sagittarius, and Pisces come at the end of each of the four seasons. As we see colder weather blowing in or new blossoms slowly emerging, we also see change manifesting. There's a dynamic versatility in Gemini, Virgo, Sagittarius, and Pisces: a desire to explore and understand, a need to always be pushing the envelope and asking questions.

As you progress through the card sections of this book, you'll encounter the astrological correspondences that I've added in, like a faint melody playing in the background. It's another layer to consider—astrology can seem dauntingly complex!—but when you're ready to hear this song, it too will become part of your radical journey. What happens when you weave together the meanings of the archetypes with the energies of your birth chart? How much deeper can your journey go, back to the source, back to *you*?

Numerology

Synchronicities are their own kind of magic.

Numerology is the study of the sacred language of numbers, a methodology of observing the energies and functions of each individual integer. Every digit, 1 through 9, has its own unique fingerprint, its own instincts, its own methods of approaching movement, choice, connection, solitude, progress, work, play, and rest. And by looking at numerological meanings alongside the cards, we can find new layers that expand our perspective on the tarot.

Numbers are built right into the tarot, creating deliberate sequences that we can work within. Each of the twenty-two major arcana archetypes is numbered, 0 through 21. The minor arcana is made up of pips numbered 1 through 10 across four suits. Additionally, when we follow the principles of numerology and consolidate double digits, we find several additional major arcana cards associated with each number. For example, the Devil, arcana number 15, breaks down to 1 + 5, which combine to give us number 6. Arcana card number 6 is the Lovers. And while these two archetypes may feel very different, in considering the different ways that they each express themes of the number 6, we can find some beautiful and important similarities. By grouping the major and minor arcana cards that align with each number, 1 through 9, we find commonalities and connections that reveal greater depth within the tarot and give ourselves new avenues for exploration, depth, and personal discovery.

It is essential to acknowledge that 0, the number of the Fool, is not included in Pythagorean numerology. That is because zero is a cipher, a mystery, a number that isn't really a number. Zero forces us to acknowledge that the absence of something, or the fullness of something, is a thing in and of itself. It simmers with possibility, serving as both a portal and a container, breaking every rule. Zero represents both everything and nothing, the beginning and the ending and the in-between. Sometimes it's hidden and other times it holds necessary space, but zero hovers between worlds, reminding us of the endless possibilities that are always at our fingertips. And in this way, it's the perfect number to represent the Fool in the major arcana.

In addition to sequences and sets of numbers, numerology features several additional groupings. We can first look at the numbers as odds (1/3/5/7/9) and evens (2/4/6/8), noting their energetic differences: odd numbers tend to explore *external* energy or expression, the ways that we allow ourselves to be seen and heard, with themes of leadership, sharing, or connection. These numbers are comfortable acknowledging tension, and use both internal and external conflict to identify desires and create change. Even numbers explore *internal* energy or processing, the ways that we reflect and understand, and themes of personal intention, desire, or exploration. Unlike odd numbers, even numbers crave stability and balance, resolving tension in a way that helps us create solid foundations and grow at a steady, controlled pace. We can also find a second category of groupings when we break the numbers down into three additional triads: 1/5/7 as the mind triad, tied to analysis, imagination, decision-making, and gathering information; 2/4/8 as the manifestation triad, tied to order, discipline, stability, and grounding; and 3/6/9 as the creation triad, tied to compassion, nurturing, expression, and connection.

Grouping the cards together in various ways, and paying attention to the ways that each card builds on the one that comes before it, can help us find our place within the sequence and understand the stories that these cards tell. How does looking at these different groupings help you make new connections within the tarot? What does it mean to see patterns within your own readings, and how does being aware of the numbers in the cards shift the ways you relate to them?

Spirituality & Creativity

We are more than systems, more than structures, more than sequences.

You alone get to determine how you engage with the cards: whether through readings and spreads, meditation, or using them as a springboard for creative projects. The tarot is a tool that you can utilize in hundreds of different ways.

Beyond sharing keywords, descriptions, correspondences, sensory depictions, journal prompts, and spreads, this book will also offer a number of suggestions for ways that you can explore these major and minor secrets. The third and final section of this book contains ideas for alternative methods of connecting with the tarot, including creative prompts, spiritual practices, and additional tools such as pendulums and Lenormand cards that you can use in tandem with your tarot deck.

So much of your work with the tarot is about broadening your experience, allowing yourself to play and dream and see what comes forward when you step beyond binaries and boundaries. Resist the temptation to see the cards only through my lens, to work with them only in a few deliberate ways. What does it feel like to take a walk with the Empress, to cook with the Wheel of Fortune, to pray with Temperance? How do you see the court cards show up in friends, characters, music? When do you deliberately harness the power or intention of a certain archetype, and how does that shift your perspective on what you believe, imagine, create?

• • •

Now it is time for the journey to commence, to begin finding the Fool, and to write our own transformative story.

PART TWO

Finding
the Fool

THE MAJOR ARCANA

The major arcana is a collection of twenty-two archetypes that explore creation, discovery, stability, choice, pursuit, loss, stagnation, release, community-building, solitude, clarity, healing, surrender, and transition. These cards interrogate ideas, events, and turning points in our lives, giving us a framework for processing and understanding the ways that we move through the world. The Fool is the catalyst, the hero, the figure that sets all of this change in motion. As they pursue their dream and are gradually, radically transformed, we see ourselves reflected and learn so much about who we are, what we want, and where we can go.

While there are established elemental correspondences for these cards, I prefer to leave these archetypes open to interpretation and to intentionally uncover aspects of each element within every single archetype, as well as to seek out glimpses of the elusive fifth element, known as spirit or *akasha*. Each of these cards has specific astrological and numerological correspondences, which can help us see them through different lenses and find greater depth in their meanings.

There are several methods for understanding the figures that the Fool meets along their journey. Some interpret the major arcana as a set of interactions with figures of wisdom and mystery, slowly shifting into specific experiences, transformations, and evolutions. Others see the Fool actually *becoming* these figures: the Fool shifting into the Magician, the High Priestess, the Empress, changing and growing and gaining new levels of expertise as they progress. You can also understand these archetypes as forces in the universe, energies or happenings that push us forward, pull us back, or encourage us to stand still. Depending on your questions, your spread, and your interpretations, your relationships with these cards will change as you grow in your tarot practice and will likely surprise you with the secrets they reveal.

The major arcana is one long and winding story, but it can be useful to break it up into different, smaller cycles. The Fool stands apart as card zero—the spark that starts the fire—and in setting this card aside, we have twenty-one remaining archetypes, which divide into three groups of seven, or into seven groupings of three. You may find it helpful to pull all of the majors out of your deck, and to lay them out in sequential order, organizing them into three horizontal rows of seven cards each.

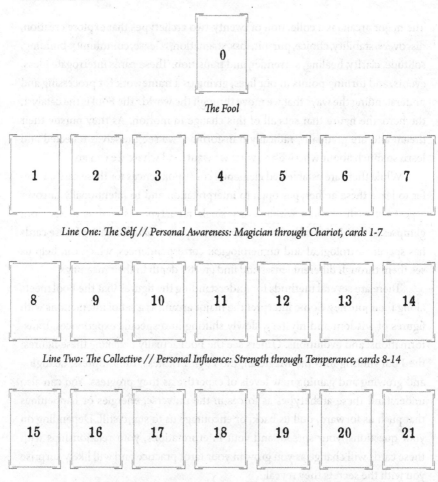

0

The Fool

1 **2** **3** **4** **5** **6** **7**

Line One: The Self // Personal Awareness: Magician through Chariot, cards 1-7

8 **9** **10** **11** **12** **13** **14**

Line Two: The Collective // Personal Influence: Strength through Temperance, cards 8-14

15 **16** **17** **18** **19** **20** **21**

Line Three: The Cosmic // Personal Evolution: Devil through World, cards 15-21

Each of these three horizontal lines highlights a different stage of growth as we learn about ourselves, our world, and our contributions. In the first row, the Magician to the Chariot, we learn more about who we are, what we want, and which impulses and experiences drive us forward. This is a time of self-discovery, of exploration and awareness that helps us find our place and purpose in the world. In the second row, Strength to Temperance, we tap into a deeper understanding of collective consciousness, considering how our actions, choices, and ideas impact the people and systems around us. We recognize our place in society and the world, understand the influence we can have, and learn to navigate different methods of belief, movement, and change. The final row, the Devil to the World, expands beyond the individual, acknowledging forces larger than us and focusing on larger cycles of evolution.

These cards are broad and deep, expansive, and elastic: they push us to consider the ways that we embrace transformation, the times that we grow in response to our experiences. As you journey through the major arcana, think about the larger context of each card, paying attention to how these archetypes offer wisdom and experience while also setting you up for the next stage of the journey. How does each card serve as a bridge from the card that comes before to the card that follows? When in doubt, zoom out.

In the same way, we can look at the vertical lines that are formed by this arrangement and consider what these smaller trios have in common. The first group of Magician / Strength / Devil shows us potential—for expansion, for steadiness, for destruction. What we choose to do with that potential is entirely up to us, for better or worse. High Priestess / Hermit / Tower are all opportunities for choice and interrogation: will we reflect, will we isolate, will we flee chaos, or will we find freedom within change? How do we handle multiple options, and what happens to our dreams when are we forced to adapt? Empress / Wheel / Star are expressions of deep awareness and hope as we understand how we show up in the world and allow ourselves new perspectives on what we have to offer. Each of these cards gives us a glimpse of abundance, of possibility, of connection. Emperor / Justice / Moon examines existing systems and challenges what they can be; this trio suggests that we leave some behind entirely. How do structures protect us, and when do they stifle us? How much power do we really have over the foundations we build on? Hierophant / Hanged One / Sun asks us to be entirely present and to consider how growth, stagnation, and celebration occur through understanding. What do we learn about ourselves when we simply observe? How does perception change us? Lovers / Death / Judgment represents periods of permanent shift, when our consciousness evolves and we begin to see the world through an entirely new lens due to connection, loss, or forgiveness. Each of these cards offers us a different kind of freedom. Chariot / Temperance / World, our final trio, reveals what can happen when we learn from what we have endured, the serenity that we can establish when we take everything into consideration and honor boundaries, contradictions, and self-love.

• • •

As you work with these complex archetypes, consider their many correspondences and contexts along with keywords, meanings, and interpretations. There are so many different ways to view these cards, and as you get to know them better and build relationships with them, stay open to the new lessons that are being offered to you. Every reading is an opportunity for discovery, for connection, for transformation. Listen to your cards, pay attention, be open. You never know what secrets the cards may have for you.

When it comes to the interpretations that I share in these pages, take what resonates and leave anything that doesn't behind. These descriptions are in no way definitive or exclusive, and are meant to offer you a place to start, with plenty of room to grow. Record your discoveries in your journal, ask questions, and remember the energy of the Fool, and the magic of discovery.

You are writing your own language: let your intuition be your guide.

0. The Fool

URANUS // Innovation, revolution, rebellion, change

ZERO // Infinity, freedom, possibility, the beginning and the end

KEYWORDS // desire · profound trust in self · fearlessness · intuition · new beginnings · taking a chance without a full plan · moving into the unknown with joy · seeing endless potential · a fresh start · an unknown journey · inexperience · freedom · aspiration · risk

Some dreams stay with us even after waking. Our eyes slowly open and we come back to the physical world, yet our hearts linger in a fantasy that captivates our imagination—a spectral prospect that steals our breath and demands our focus. We may emerge slowly from slumber into our day, but pieces of our mind, heart, and soul have been left behind, continuing to explore this new possibility. Weeks slip by but the mirage remains, coming into richer clarity, distracting us from our usual patterns and routines. What started as a vague whisper becomes an insistent obsession. We abandon any thought of leaving this yearning behind, and instead embrace new details as they emerge, letting potential grow. Complicated desires manifest, and we consider ways that we could adjust our current path to start moving in this unexpected but promising new direction. Optimism floods us, hope begins to grow, even as that vision feels so far out of reach, so unrealistic, so uncertain. There's no promise of success, no guarantee that we'll reach that shimmering, far-off horizon. We're considering rearranging our entire life to chase after something theoretical, something unsettled, something that we desperately want—but we aren't sure how to accomplish such a thing and don't even know where to start.

That moment when we decide to throw caution to the wind and chase the fantasy anyway, when we begin to actively move toward that vision that has manifested in our mind and begin a radical journey—that is the brilliant, wide-eyed, aspirational energy of the Fool.

• • •

It takes strength to hope, to dream. There's an inherent idealism in the Fool, a belief that our wildest ambitions and richest fantasies are not only possible but also worth pursuing. And rather than seeing the Fool as a naïve figure of fearlessness, as someone with no concept of pain or struggle or disappointment, we should give the Fool credit: they acknowledge their doubts, their lack of experience, yet choose to act in spite of the unknowns anyway. This is the energy of the radicals, the rebels, those that exist outside the binary and are willing to break the rules. The Fool knows that their calling is unconventional, but they also understand that this wish has become so central to their identity that they simply have to reach for it, have to act. Their desire pulses in every heartbeat; it cannot be ignored or denied.

There's a leap of faith involved in this choice, a confidence in instinct and intuition. But the Fool is also deliberately choosing the road less traveled, deciding to break a new trail and follow their own personal arrow. Every step is important, leading the Fool away from the life that they have known and into something beautiful, a future glittering with promise. They are chasing authenticity, being as true to themselves as they can possibly be, and are brave enough to wish without limits.

Astrological correspondence: Uranus

Uranus is connected to innovation, revolution, and lasting change. It's within Uranus that we find our eagerness to rebel against established systems, to go our own way and carve our own path, to dream of a different kind of future. This is a planet of breaking through old structures, of powerful shifts that have a lasting impact. The Fool acts as the embodiment of this energy, a figure eager to start a new cycle of growth, transformation, and evolution, regardless of what it may cost. And while the Fool in many ways is deeply independent, Uranus reminds us that nothing happens in a vacuum, and that the chances we take can change the world.

JOURNAL PROMPT: *Where does Uranus fall in your chart? In which house? In which sign? Think about how the energy of the Fool intersects with the energy of that Uranus placement, and with Uranus energy in general. How is the Fool radical, transformative, revolutionary? What do you admire about the Fool's willingness to try new things? How do you believe in yourself, and when has trusting your desires paid off?*

Numerological correspondence: Zero

Zero is a number of freedom, infinity, nothingness. It stands apart from the other nine digits, living outside of restrictions and rules. This number represents the beginning and the end, eternity, endless cycles, letting us step away from everything we know and simply exist. And in the same way, the Fool sits outside of the major arcana: a figure of possibility, endlessly leaping forward into the unknown, representing both the beginning and the outcome. The Fool lives in the in-between, bridging the gaps between cards, bringing desire and completion to every step of the journey.

JOURNAL PROMPT: *Think about the meanings of the number zero and consider the places that it appears in your life. Journal your insights, questions, and thoughts. What does it mean to be the beginning and the ending? How do you see zero as taking up space, and when does it disappear? How does the Fool embody this energy, and where do you see this energy echoing throughout the tarot?*

In Readings

The Fool lives in moments of risk, movement, and personal choice. When we stop caring what others think about us, or when we are willing to endure judgment or ridicule in order to be true to ourselves, we embody the Fool's unusual, subversive magic. This is disruption, courage, a willingness to fail. In spite of how things may turn out, in spite of all that they don't know, in spite of all of the ways that this journey could go wrong, the Fool decides to try anyway. And in trying, the Fool begins an adventure that will fundamentally change them, that has the capacity to change the world.

Depending on the subject of a reading, the Fool can indicate different courses of action—but the lesson here is always one of optimism, in both the self and the universe. Where does our sense of hope and purpose come from? How can a drive to discover something new eclipse the life we had previously built, and what does it mean when we instigate movement, when we break free of the old ways? What do our secret, lofty aspirations tell us about ourselves? How much are we willing to risk to achieve the things we're longing for?

1. The Magician

MERCURY // Communication, information, travel, speed

ONE // Motivation, confidence, independence, vision, trail blazing

KEYWORDS // spark · potential · high energy · belief that anything is possible · gathering resources · courage · visionary · trail blazing · optimism · self-confidence · healthy ego · expansion · brainstorming · dreaming · imagination · sky is the limit · capability · exploration

Committing to the pursuit of a dream is a heady, intoxicating, endlessly exciting sensation. Our blood thrums beneath our skin, heart pounding, lungs rushing, skin tingling. It feels like the very air is crackling with energy: the sharp smell of ozone, bright sparks of electricity. That thing that we've been craving, obsessing about, has finally taken up enough space within us to demand that we make it a reality. All we want to do now is get started with the process of creation. Everything in us feels coiled with delicious tension and desire as we survey the roads ahead, gather our resources, and imagine all of the ways that we could achieve those lofty, magical goals. There are so many paths stretching out before us, and every breath is charged with awe, eagerness, anticipation. This is a moment of pure potential, as our soul cries out in affirmation. Absolutely anything we can imagine is possible, and the question becomes: *what will we do first?*

So exhilarating is this sensation that we find it hard to sit still; it's challenging to focus on any particular detail. The sky's the limit, everything is at our fingertips, the world is our oyster. This internal building, the confidence and courage that come with a brand new start, is the bewitching, intoxicating, overwhelmingly bold energy of the Magician.

• • •

There is joy in discovery, wonder in imagination, power in validating our own desires. With the Magician, we begin directing our will, making space for what we want, allowing our goals to take up room and resources. This is the time for breathless visualization and extravagant fantasy, for putting absolutely no limits on what we can accomplish, where we can go, who we can become. The Magician brings confidence, vision, and clarity to the Fool's dream, pointing out proposals and strategies that are available, all while affirming everything that the Fool already has access to. Instead of fretting that this dream is foolish, the Magician doubles down, making it real, providing answers and options. With the Magician, we don't just believe that magic is possible—we know it in our bones. Magic is ours to wield. The Magician invites excitement and possibility to bubble up within us.

There's a thrilling combination of connective brilliance and independent daring in the Magician. We are in the right place at the right time, doing what we're meant to do. Nothing is out of our reach, and the visions that we hold within ourselves will keep expanding forever if we let them. This can be an electrifying energy, a rich and endless potential that builds on itself. The Magician offers validation, audacity, fortitude: the kind of swagger and conviction that stop doubts in their tracks. And while we may still feel alone in this exact moment, we trust that, eventually, others will find us to offer skills, wisdom, infectious energy.

But the Magician doesn't want us to only live in a fantasy world—this archetype is pushing us to envision things the way that we want them, and to then harness the power and magic that we hold to make those dreams a reality. Their sense of hope is so strong, so certain, that it erases any possibility for failure. Anticipation, excitement, and imagination are balanced by a deeply practical analysis, a realistic assessment of the various approaches available. The Magician takes the Fool's questions and provides solutions, throws open doors, points to distant horizons, pulls out books and tools and every possible resource. Momentum is building, strength is gathering, everything is crackling with light and intention and brilliance. There are no limits on what we can do, who we can be. We *will* change the world.

Astrological correspondence: Mercury

The smallest and quickest planet in our solar system, Mercury is connected to communication, intellect, and the ways that we process and share information. Ruler of the mind and hands, we see here a deep awareness of the weight that words and ideas can carry, the ways that our dreams can manifest into the physical world. Similarly, it's with the Magician that we embrace changes on the horizon, harnessing our ability to make things happen and to imagine all of the best possible outcomes. We anticipate all that we could do, could build, could offer, and find magic and passion in watching our dreams expand and evolve. Both Mercury and the Magician are tied to self-awareness, to recognizing the brilliance we carry and deciding how to utilize it fully.

JOURNAL PROMPT: *Where does Mercury fall in your chart? In which house? In which sign? Think about how the energy of the Magician intersects with the energy of that Mercury placement, particularly when it comes to the element that your natal Mercury is in. How do you explore the Magician through the four elements? Which one feels most comfortable for you, and how does that element relate to your natal Mercury placement?*

Numerological correspondence: One

Ones are powerfully present, motivated, strong-willed, and confident, ready to take on new challenges while staying focused on their bigger goals and dreams. With passion and dominance, the number one is independent and assertive, a pioneer that is ready to push forward and create impactful change. Similarly, the Magician asks us to dream as big as possible, to let our imagination expand, to tap into the vast resources that we have both within ourselves and in the world around us. There's an originality and confidence within this archetype that make it seem that anything is possible. We connect with our personal magic and accept an irrefutable *yes* from the universe, dreaming about what to do with all of this positive energy.

In Readings

When the Magician arrives, we tap into a deep well of self-assurance: an overwhelming sensation that all is right with the world, that anything we can imagine is within reach. We are strong enough, brave enough, supported enough, to chase after our biggest wishes, our brightest ambitions. The Magician wants us to own our power and our potential, to rejoice in all that lies ahead.

Now that you have been reminded of your magic, what will you do next? What do you truly crave? What does it look like to let your needs take up space, to visualize getting everything that you covet? If the future could be anything you wanted, if all the hopes in your heart were possible, what would you manifest? Where would you start?

2. The High Priestess

MOON // Cycles, wildness, emotions, embodiment

TWO // Sensitivity, intuition, psychic wisdom, choice, awareness, duality

KEYWORDS // crossroads · stillness · inner wisdom · stepping back from movement · trust in the self · awareness · personal magic · intuition · deliberation · thoughtful decision-making · mystery · choices · checking in with the self · psychic power · balance · receptivity

A sense of calm washes over us. After the blaze of magic and possibility that set us aflame, after opening our eyes wide to take in all of the options before us, now is a time of gentle reflection, of deep awareness, of checking in with the self. Our skin cools, our breathing slows, we hear water lapping at a distant shore and feel the gentle kiss of wind ruffling our hair. The potential that crackles at our fingertips is ours to wield, but there's no rush, no timeline, no one who can force our hand. Instead, this is a chance to observe, to be still, to heed the wisdom and experience and intuitive wonder that settle within us. When we embrace our unique brand of magic, when we rely on our mind and spirit to guide us, when we step away from the rush of the world and listen only to the steady beating of our hearts, certainty becomes easier to imagine, to feel, to grasp. As we prepare to take our first steps toward our future, what feels important to remember, to hold fast to? As we acknowledge all that we do not know, which truths offer us comfort, sovereignty, assurance?

This period of questioning, this time of checking with the self, this stillness that makes space for contemplation, is an essential and extraordinary part of the evolutionary process. Mystery is balanced with serenity, trust in the self is affirmed, and a rich sense of personal magic and wisdom is celebrated. As we commit to the future we have glimpsed, we step into the grounded, thoughtful, self-assured energy of the High Priestess.

• • •

There's something sacred about an intentional, purposeful pause. Not just for the stillness, for the opportunity to observe, but also for what we hear in the silence, for what our heart whispers when we slow down and take notice. The High Priestess brings composure, serenity, a different kind of confidence. This is an invitation for awareness, a chance to let our intuition speak, a time for checking in with the self and seeing if any of the paths that the Magician laid out for us resonate. In sitting with silence, in monitoring our breath, in stepping back from the rush of movement to simply be, we see our reality clearly, recognize what energizes and inspires us the most about the path that we are on. The High Priestess makes space not only for our hopes, but also for our fears.

Sometimes we keep secrets from ourselves, intentionally or otherwise. We tuck things away in a quiet corner of our spirit and try not to examine them too closely, perhaps even forget that they're there. And when we're caught up in a heady dream, when we're rushing toward something new with passionate fire and joyful intention, it can be easy to let the momentum carry us forward, to get caught up in the excitement of it all and never question where we're really going, what we're really doing. But the High Priestess wants us to recognize the progress that we've already made, to honor the steps that we've already taken and the choices that we've already committed to. And sometimes, this figure reminds us that we have room to reconsider, to adjust, to make a change or even go back to the drawing board.

When we create opportunities to acknowledge the things that lie beneath the surface, we empower ourselves to reclaim any magic that we may have forgotten along the way. We are reminded that we are in control of when, where, and how our dream begins to come true. We honor our emotions, allow ourselves to be in tune with our deepest, most internal stirrings. Our shadows are part of us, and even if we don't fully understand them yet, we can still show them respect. This is solitary magic, trusting ourselves, recognizing our agency in this journey. We don't have to keep going if we don't want to, don't have to follow any particular path, don't have to operate on anyone else's schedule. The High Priestess reminds us that we are the driving force, that we have ownership and sovereignty over our movements, and that we are allowed to dictate the terms of our progress.

Astrological correspondence: Moon

The celestial body closest to the earth, the moon rules emotions as well as embodiment, helping us connect with and understand our own natural cycles of creation, growth, decay, death, and rebirth. The moon reckons with our light as well as our shadows, understanding our patterns and desires and emotions in a way that is empowering rather than stifling. In the same way, the High Priestess urges us to utilize reflection, intuition, and stillness, giving us the necessary time and space to make a decision that feels authentic. There's a mysterious quality to this archetype that we see captured in the moon, a sensation of wildness and unpredictability that sits at odds with the moon's measurable movements. The moon empowers us to consider the wisdom that can be found in fantasy, imagination, uncertainty. And when we take the time to sit under the moon's gentle glow, to see the world through this dimly lit and strangely beautiful perspective, new truths are often revealed.

JOURNAL PROMPT: *Where does the Moon fall in your chart? In which house? In which sign? Consider the ways that you are contemplative, the time and energy that it takes to make choices, and the things that you need in order to feel secure in your decisions. How does that connect with the element that your Moon is in? How do you understand the High Priestess through this lens?*

Numerological correspondence: Two

The number two is tied to choice, consideration, and careful reflection, brimming with a deep desire to understand and be aware of all of the layers involved in a situation before making a decision. Twos are sensitive, intuitive, even a little psychic—they trust themselves implicitly and rely on their instincts and innate sense of self to make choices or form opinions. In the same way, the High Priestess takes all of the ideas and magic from the Magician and internalizes them, looking within and making sure that the chosen path forward resonates. There's caution with twos, a desire to be sure about what we want and feel before moving forward—and in the same way, the High Priestess reminds us to trust ourselves completely.

> **JOURNAL PROMPT:** *Consider the role that the High Priestess plays in the Fool's journey, and how this energy differs from the Magician's. What do they each offer? How is the Priestess unique? Where do you see the 2's energy of dualism, partnership, and integrity manifest in this archetype? How can making a big decision lead to peace?*

In Readings

In working with the High Priestess, we turn inward, make space for mysteries and uncertainties. We all have inner wisdom and sharp instincts, but we don't always take the time to listen and trust ourselves. When this card comes forward, it asks us to slow down, pause, and pay attention.

What can we discover beyond the veil, within our own inner sanctum? Which doors are we opening, and which have we been avoiding? Does this path we're on feel right? Is our intuition still guiding us forward, or is it buzzing with warning? Are we ready to take this next leap, to start manifesting our dreams in a real and tangible way?

3. The Empress

VENUS // Pleasure, beauty, balance, relationships, unification, values

THREE // Innovation, creativity, expression, growth, manifestation

KEYWORDS // abundance · creativity · turning dreams into reality · joyful manifestation · growth · tangible progress · community & collaboration · momentum · expansion · joy · being present · pleasure · connection · wellspring · movement · love · belief in the self

Abundance bursts forth in every possible direction. The seeds that we have planted begin to bloom, the storm that we have summoned soaks the earth, and all around us is bounty, excitement, progress. New life emerges in a riot of movement, and we raise our faces to the sky, enjoying the rain and the wind and the warmth that surround us. Creativity overflows from our heart center out into the world, and all of the visions that have been dancing in our heads begin to take up space, becoming tangible. This is a time of beauty and radiance, of sparks catching fire, of procreation and manifestation. Dreams become reality, fantasies find their form, and the work that we have begun attracts the attention of those around us. We own and share the creative vision that we've been carrying, and our community offers their support, their ideas, their unique talents and gifts. There is more than enough magic to go around, and as collaboration births even more new threads of invention and inspiration, our energy expands at a breathtaking pace.

It's here that our dreams come to life, taking shape in a way that others can see and understand. And as our momentum builds, as new surprises saturate our world with light and color, we're filled with optimism and hope. We're finally doing it, finally demanding that others see our visions for the magic that they are, and it feels incredible. That sensation of growth and power—as we express our rawest, most authentic feelings and desires—lives within the lavish, generative, profound grace of the Empress.

· · ·

Action is a kind of affirmation. We express what we crave through movement, creation, construction. The Empress delights in letting ourselves see and be seen, in taking up space, in demanding attention. Visions become realities, fantasies become corporeal, wishes become truth. What was once a twinkle in the Fool's eye is now a real thing, with shape and texture, weight and meaning. And as our dreams take up physical space, as we utilize the resources we have gathered and the wisdom we have uncovered, there's satisfaction, even a bit of awe. We are making something incredible, doing something special, bringing our vision to life. It's pure, intoxicating magic, and it's coming from deep within. It's *ours*.

The Empress is a wellspring, a source, a flow state. But this isn't the part of the journey where we pick everything to pieces, point out every flaw, strive to make it better. There's no real regard to detail here, no expectation of perfection or completion—instead in this archetype we discover the true joy in letting ideas and magic emerge naturally. The Empress gives us permission to find gratification in these early, messy stages of creation, to celebrate the measurable progress we've made, to get caught up in the excitement of what we're doing. This isn't about wholeness; instead it's about wonder, awe, delight. It's about taking real pleasure in what we are doing, about finally getting to show our wildest dreams to those around us.

Part of the process of creation includes allowing other people to observe and engage with what we're building. Our hearts are on display, a vulnerable and exhilarating experience. And as those around us begin to interact with our designs and concepts, opportunities for collaboration and collective work emerge. Rather than being precious with our work, feeling a need to jealously protect or hoard our ideas, the Empress teaches us to overflow with rich abundance, to share what we have, to offer our discernment to others. There's a serene and generous wisdom here, a faith that those who are drawn to us are meant for us, a recognition of our own inherent wealth. And in feeling the energy and excitement generated by those that connect with our vision, we are empowered to continue our trajectory, to keep growing.

Astrological correspondence: Venus

The planet of beauty, love, connection, and spiritual treasures, Venus rules values and pleasure, as well as the signs of resilient Taurus and balanced Libra. Within a birth chart, our Venus placement corresponds to the ways that we express and experience love, how we attract others, what we care about, and the ways that we bond and caretake. It's a luscious pairing with the Empress, the archetype of bountiful creation and brilliant, personal expression—an urge to use our senses and sensuality, to embrace the things that we love and allow them to move freely between our imaginations and our realities. Just as Venus gives us the space to create bonds of union and connection between ourselves and the things that we love, the Empress helps us establish a presence on earth, allowing our desires to take up space and grow into beautiful new creations.

JOURNAL PROMPT: *Where does Venus fall in your chart? In which house? In which sign? Think about the ways that you experience abundance, the ways that you connect with other people, the ways that you express strong emotions, desires, or fears. How do you experience the Empress, and what does that have in common with your natal Venus placement?*

Numerological correspondence: Three

Innovative, creative, and brimming with joy and positivity, the number three is powerful expression and brilliant promise. There's a sense of raw possibility here, an ability to create with abandon and share ideas and artistry with the world, making everything more beautiful and inspiring. And while this energy can be expansive and joyful, it can also be a bit unfocused, even impatient: eager to move but sharing ideas that may not be fully complete yet. We see this kind of effortless manifestation in the Empress, where the vision of the Magician and the inner wisdom of the High Priestess explode into the world, becoming tangible, taking up space. This card is about beginning the process of external connections, as our ideas shift into actions and others are able to see us in a brand new way.

Meditate on the number three, and themes of connection, creativity, and expression. How do you see these concepts manifest within the Empress? In what ways is this archetype a physical expression of the Fool's desire? What does it mean to create without expectation? How does this figure help you to expand?

In Readings

Working with the Empress allows us to release all of the desire that we've been carrying, to celebrate wild and raw creation, to share our ideas with those we trust and love. There's a kind of nourishment that happens when we let others in, a mutual exchange of energy that feeds us on a spiritual level. The Empress nurtures and encourages, reminding us of how good it feels to take our fantasies seriously, to put in the work to make a personal vision come to life.

What kind of magic lives in those first strokes of a paintbrush, those early drafts, those initial lines of code, and what value do we place on those opening expressions? How do our biggest dreams look when they start to find shape in the world? How do we describe our vision, begin to invite others into our new understanding of what we crave? What does it mean to share our joy with those around us?

4. The Emperor

ARIES // Independence, motivation, determination, ambition

FOUR // Structure, organization, systems, progression, foundations, stability

KEYWORDS // control · discipline · organization · long-term planning · solid foundations · feeling worthy · knowledge of personal strengths · rules & regulations · leadership · experience · authority · caution · adaptation · challenging · taking ownership · ambition

In surveying the raw creative energy that we have released, in thinking about our next steps, we recognize a need for order, crave a framework that will help us stay true to our purpose and intent. Our ideas clarify and sharpen, a refining fire transforming wild magic into foundations rooted in steady, stable earth. The seeds that have germinated must be protected, sheltered, organized into systems that make their care routines simple and clear. As we continue to create, as our ideas take up space and our future finds its footing, we protect what we have made. We combine intellect and observation with hard work, awareness, a deep understanding of existing structures that we can utilize as we think about how we want these seeds to grow and blossom. This is blueprints and budgets, long-term planning, careful collaboration: moving plants from the greenhouse into orderly field rows, organizing notes and scribbled ideas into a novel's rough draft, writing out a favorite recipe after tweaking and tinkering over time. Rules and boundaries help us to categorize and define what we are building—and through this process of establishing procedures, we also learn about existing organizational formats, finding context for what our work is accomplishing and contributing. In getting our hands dirty, in thinking about the big picture, we allow for progress, exercising enough control to stimulate new kinds of growth.

Discipline helps us build with purpose, hone our strengths, create the best possible chance for success. And this energy of planning and evaluation, of assessing strengths and weaknesses, of getting organized so that we know exactly how to execute our vision, is the bold pragmatism of the Emperor.

• • •

There is pleasure in good work done well. When we embrace our natural authority, when we claim ownership of our ambitions and our happiness, it empowers us to take our dreams seriously, to dig into the underlying meaning of our creations. Acting with purpose, protecting our intentions, letting ourselves be captivated by every stage of the process—these are all hallmarks of the Emperor. This is a patient, focused, detail-oriented figure who understands control, who knows how to develop systems of organization, who uses discipline and order to accomplish big goals—not because they're power hungry or desperate to micromanage, but rather because they recognize the many gifts that procedures can provide. After the wild outpouring of the Empress, the Emperor helps us look at those early expressions and make sense of them, creating a plan that will empower us to keep going.

Restriction is a useful tool, one that the Emperor understands. Rather than stifling ideas or productivity, boundaries can enable creativity to thrive. If we rush into a new project with only our inspiration flowing, with our hearts in our hands, and don't spend some time getting organized or building a budget or defining the parameters of our work, it can be easy for all the passion and excitement and energy to quickly fizzle out. In creating a safe container for our ideas, we can thrive, play, experiment, even make mistakes. We take bigger chances when the risk is low, when we know we're on schedule, when expectations are clear.

Taking the time to make a plan does more than set the stage for success—it is also a way of declaring to ourselves and our communities that this vision matters, that this dream has value. We are investing in our future, making plans for long-term stability and pleasure, establishing our legacy. There's such potency in claiming a bit of the world for ourselves, in not apologizing for wanting things, in demanding space for our own growth. The Emperor urges us to take ownership of our own happiness, to protect ourselves and our ongoing expansion, to act with intention and purpose. We are allowed to take control of the narrative, to tell the story we want to tell, to build the future we want to build.

Astrological correspondence: Aries

The first sign of the zodiac, fiery cardinal Aries ushers in the spring and is known for passion, independence, and influential leadership. Aries are go-getters and idea-havers, always ready for the next adventure. They brim with confidence, are bold and self-assured, and the Emperor, an archetype with a certain degree of fearlessness who knows exactly what to do and how to do it. The Emperor comes in and makes decisions, putting together a plan for the future and giving us the resources to execute it brilliantly. In this card we lay a foundation, find our inner authority, make choices about what's to come and what we want. And during Aries season, we set long-term expectations and boundaries, firming up our ambitions and deciding how to make our dreams a reality.

> JOURNAL PROMPT: *Where is Aries in your natal chart? Which element does it live in? Do you have any placements in Aries? Think about the ways that you do or do not experience this energy, and what cardinal fire might mean for you. How do you understand passion, and where does that concept intersect with control, discipline, intention? What does it look like when you protect your dreams?*

Numerological correspondence: Four

Fours are detail-oriented, systematic, focused, and driven, eager to create structure and patterns that allow them to build and maintain organization. Accomplished and steady, four is connected to both progress and perfection, constantly striving to improve every aspect of a project, dream, or goal. Four is a number of deep confidence and strives to do things in the best possible manner, adapting where necessary but preferring to stick to the plan. Similarly, the Emperor takes the creations offered by the Empress and organizes them, helping to lay a foundation that can offer discipline to a project. Fours and the Emperor empower us to find focus, shaping our ideas into more tangible goals and allowing us to create a plan for success.

But four also can settle into routines that invite complacency or boredom, setting the stage for tension, disruption, or change.

JOURNAL PROMPT: *In building a foundation for future growth, the number four creates an atmosphere of stability, safety, and protection. How do you see this demonstrated within the Emperor? Which other names for this archetype resonate for you? When have you relied on structure or limits to help you focus on a bigger goal? What is your relationship to power, control, and evaluation?*

In Readings

When the Emperor comes forward, it's a call to claim your power, your agency, your dominion. Your ambitions are worth tending, not just with creative output but with discipline, organization, command. And by making a plan for the future, by investing in your biggest dreams, you ensure that every step can be taken with confidence.

Which frameworks give you freedom? What helps you guard your pleasure, protect your inspiration, ensure that you will reach your goals? How can you build the structures that you need, the milestones that will keep you on track? How are you assessing your progress, and how do you define success? What are you discovering about your own process, and how can you use that knowledge to shape routines of creation?

5. The Hierophant

TAURUS // Abundance, industriousness, security, pleasure

FIVE // Change, freedom, exploration, tension, growth, adventure, balance, transition

KEYWORDS // education · keeper of knowledge & wisdom · gathering information · exploration · examination · questions & interrogation · ritual · tradition · history · finding community · testing limits · spiritual & physical worlds · understanding magic · adventure · humility · esoteric insights

A new curiosity begins to awaken within us. Through implementing structures, we are reminded that our world has a deep and complex history, one that we long to learn more about. We have always had teachers, elders, mentors: wise ones that hold knowledge, share and educate, offer instruction and direction. And even when we are embarking on a new journey, even if we seek to transform the world with our artistry and brilliance and magic, there is still power in surveying what has always been, the old ways, the traditions. This is the turning of weathered pages, the aromas of incense and beeswax, the intersection of deep knowledge and rich insight: questions and answers, seeking and finding, expanding wisdom, and unpacking ideas. As our dreams continue to grow and clarify, learning communities emerge, and we find footholds in both the physical and spiritual worlds. We establish rituals of comfort and routine, experience friction and uncertainty, interrogate our existing beliefs and open ourselves to new ones.

Both intellectual and spiritual, this moment represents the bridge between mundane and magical, a shift where we recognize what we know and what we don't. We honor where we have been and where we are now, giving ourselves the information we need to look toward the future with new clarity. This period of scrutiny, this exploration that can lead to both drive and doubt, is the complex, endlessly seeking energy of the Hierophant.

· · ·

There is a natural, necessary tension between the allure of mystery and the desire to understand. When we deliberately engage with the unknown, when we embrace our most inquisitive self, when we refuse to accept anything at face value, we embody the spirit of the Hierophant. This figure is a teacher and holder of knowledge, but they are also an eternal student. The Hierophant instructs with a deft hand and an open mind, showing us how things have been done before without necessarily restricting us to those same choices.

History has its place, practices have purpose, and tradition is not a dirty word. There is deep, strange, wonderful magic that dwells in repetitive rituals. We tap into something beyond ourselves when we echo words and actions that are older than we know, create and reinforce connections to past communities, bind ourselves to sacred threads that were woven long before we were born. There's a particular kind of fellowship in following the spiritual footsteps of those that came before us, a holy gnosis we discover in retracing old lines.

But beyond echoing the sacraments of the past, we also have the power to create our own ceremonies, our own rites, our own customs. It's essential that we learn to clarify what we believe, to ask questions and dig deeper. We do not have to confine ourselves to what came before, particularly when those are structures that have historically done harm, taken advantage of the marginalized, knocked some down while elevating others—with knowledge of the past we can build on the now, generate for the future. There are curiosity and loyalty here, acknowledgments for what has come before paired with eagerness to learn, to evolve, to change the trajectory of the world. In understanding the mistakes of our collective past, we can make the effort to avoid repeating them.

At their heart, the Hierophant seeks to create an environment for individual and collective evolution. Reflection and engagement in equal measure facilitate the discovery of truth and help us recognize what we are truly devoted to. We're shown where we might be going through the motions, participating in inherited beliefs without truly dedicating ourselves to them. In stepping into this energy, we are encouraged to ask others these same questions, to search for our people among the students. The Hierophant helps us to find existing communities that will support and challenge us, but this figure can also empower us to consider establishing our own groups, to develop places where we will intellectually and spiritually thrive.

Astrological correspondence: Taurus

Utilizing fixed earth, Taurus is a sign of determination and stability, moving with patience and care toward set goals. This sign is thoughtful and focused, with ambitions carefully defined, balancing pleasure and practicality. There's an appreciation for history in Taurus, a respect for the ways that things have always been done, and we see a similar desire for structure and tradition in the Hierophant. This is an archetype that bridges the physical and spiritual worlds, helping others create frameworks for knowledge while also making space for questions and exploration, for honoring the unknown. And while this archetype does include a bit of stubbornness, even skepticism, there's also a desire for understanding that can inspire change and growth.

JOURNAL PROMPT: *Where is Taurus in your natal chart? Which element does it live in? Do you have any placements in Taurus? Think about the ways that you deal with tension, the rituals that ground you, and the questions that you wrestle with regularly. What does it mean to interrogate your beliefs? What is your relationship to change? In considering the energy of Taurus, how do you find both joy and frustration in asking hard questions?*

Numerological correspondence: Five

Inquisitive, adventurous, and loyal, the number five represents dynamic energy and a desire to understand and explore. Endlessly curious, five can be a bit restless, conscious of change, and eager to see the shifts and growth both within and around them. This energy can feel unstable or unpredictable, which is why the Hierophant is often a difficult archetype to pin down. There's a natural tension to this number, a need to stay in control that's at war with a hunger to keep questioning, to let the things that we are discovering change us and free us. Intellectual curiosity is a powerful thing, and even as we may cling to the familiar and comfortable, we also desire growth, progress, possibilities.

The number five is often described as impulsive, bold, and unpredictable—do you see any of those qualities in the Hierophant? How do the Hierophant and the Fool each express and explore their natural curiosity? When do themes of learning, study, and exploratory communities create space for adventure, growth, and change? What does it mean to know and not know at the same time? When does the Hierophant urge you to conform, and when do they push you to transform?

In Readings

The Hierophant holds space in that endless in-between, hovering between the tangible and the dazzling spirit beyond understanding. This card lets us ask our questions and offers possible answers. It's not about finding the one single, universal key to the universe—it's about finding a key that fits in our hand, using it to open a particular door, and being brave enough to pass through.

What do you believe, and why? Which daily, weekly, monthly, yearly rituals have you developed that feel right for you? Are those rituals associated with religion or spirituality, or were they developed with your own natural, internal magic? What do you feel empowered to question, and what do you accept at face value? What keeps you rooted in times of spiritual questioning? How do you learn from your own experiences, and how does broader, collective history either support or challenge those lessons?

6. The Lovers

GEMINI // Duality, communication, information, collaboration, curiosity

SIX // Harmony, nurturing, community, caretaking, movement, pride

KEYWORDS // expansion · partnership · exploration · community · being seen · balance & harmony · freedom · self-discovery · dreams & desires · experimentation · gathering information · taking changes · opening the heart · acceptance · finding our people · nurturing the self

After studying the traditions and foundations that already exist, after examining the ways that the world has always been, we feel the drive to blaze a trail, to make our own way, to unfurl. There is such expansive freedom in gathering information, in making decisions based on what resonates rather than what everyone else is doing—and now that we understand the rules, we can decide which ones to follow, and which ones to break. We are not alone in this impulse, and as we recognize our craving for both individual freedom and supportive harmony, we find others like us: kindred spirits, soulmates, partners. We let ourselves be seen, celebrate what makes us unique, feel love and connection in a joyful and exciting way. This is studying a road map only to throw it out, packing up the car with the music blaring and the windows wide open, feeling air rush over and through us as we race down an exciting and unfamiliar road, exploring the world with someone we love deeply, completely. This kind of collaborative confidence is energizing, transformative, and teaches us to blend self-sufficiency with earnest trust in other people.

Partnership and community are profound and beautiful gifts, offering us a sense of belonging, agency, and magic. We find freedom in being loved for exactly who we are, celebrate the things that set us apart, and move forward with sincerity, empowered to explore in our own special way. This mingling of curiosity and connection, this intoxicating tangle of hearts and minds, is the inquisitive, affectionate, effervescent spirit of the Lovers.

• • •

The world is full of wonder, beauty, pleasure, delight, curiosities. We have our own dreams to fulfill, our own path to follow—but there is also so much to see, to do, to experience. The Lovers asks us to explore everything that matters to us, to not be ashamed of the things that rouse our passions or drive us to deeper growth. Our interests, desires, and longings reveal so much about who we are, create threads that connect these different aspects of our lives into a larger, more complete picture. And when we embrace all of those distinctive parts, let them take up space and recognize their inherent value, we can take authentic pride in ourselves and move forward with boldness.

No matter what we crave, what we're drawn to, there are others out there who feel the same way. We are not the only Fool in the world. The Lovers gives us the space to build harmony within ourselves, to find balance between the natural tensions and contradictions that make us who we are, and to discover places where we feel accepted, whole, and cherished. There's liberation with this archetype: a breaking free of assumptions, an embracing of all of our quirks and oddities, a delight in our strange kinds of magic. We fall in love with ourselves, even as we also find our people within the world—friends, partners, collaborators that cherish and celebrate us for all that we are. These are the people that we can share our dreams with, who encourage us rather than stifle us.

In many ways, the Lovers is about testing the limits that we established with the Emperor, about making our own way after studying rituals of belief with the Hierophant. We make choices about what to pursue and what to leave behind, about which parts of ourselves to embrace and which ones we may not be as satisfied with. When we know what feeds us, what excites us, what challenges us, we can be more deliberate in our actions and can pursue ambitions and objectives that reflect those values and desires.

Astrological correspondence: Gemini

 Airy, mutable Gemini is known for impressive communication, a desire to collaborate, and an ease in gathering and distributing information. With dazzling energy and quick movement, Gemini loves indulging their curiosity and prefers to be able to move from project to project, constantly expanding their intellectual understanding of the world around them. In the same way, the Lovers card brings open expression and intentional partnership, with couples or groups encouraging each other to explore. We often think of this archetype and this kind of duality as existing between multiple people, but the Lovers also speaks to the various aspects we all hold within ourselves, a desire for freedom and understanding along with a need for stability and ambition. We find free and open expression in both Gemini and the Lovers, a desire to be understood as well as the independence to move at our own speed.

> JOURNAL PROMPT: *Where is Gemini in your natal chart? Which element does it live in? Do you have any placements in Gemini? Consider how trying new things, meeting new people, and absorbing new information feel for you. Do you think of yourself as someone curious, or do you prefer to stay in your comfort zone? How do you nurture yourself, and those you love? What does it take for you to feel connected to a person, place, or thing?*

Numerological correspondence: Six

Six is associated with harmony, movement, celebration, and partnership. We see a shift in focus toward goals here, pride in accomplishments as well as a desire to keep reaching for bigger ambitions and more personal objectives. Present and attentive, sixes often bring healing and solutions, as well as a sense of protection. In the major arcana, the Lovers explores harmonious connection, finding acceptance and joy in personal identity. The partners and communities in this archetype are so well matched because they work at it, helping each other to responsibly grow and celebrating the people that they are. Rather than looking for someone perfect, the Lovers and six are about finding the people that are perfect for *us*.

> JOURNAL PROMPT: *Consider the idea of nurturing, and the ways that the number six explores this theme. How do you see partnership, pride, and connection manifest within the Lovers? How does compassion show up in this archetype? In what*

ways does this card connect to the abundance of the Empress, and how does it set the stage for the Chariot? How do self-love and love for others intersect?

In Readings

As we find freedom in being ourselves, as we fall into love and friendship and community with people that appreciate who we are, our confidence grows. There's so much to learn about ourselves, and with the Lovers, we explore those new roads with joy and anticipation, free from shame—there's a hint of the Fool's curiosity and wonder here, but now, the Fool gets to wander arm in arm with someone who really gets it, who really sees them.

How do we choose ourselves? What does it mean to find our place within a community that fully appreciates and understands us? What are we ready to invest in? How do we live in alignment with our values? Whom do we want by our side as we pursue our big dreams, as we make our mark upon the world? Whom are we willing to care for, and whom do we allow to care for us?

7. The Chariot

CANCER // Caretaking, security, nourishment, sensitivity, privacy

SEVEN // Intelligence, duality, movement, determination, protection, responsibility

KEYWORDS // seeking · triumph · victory · intentionally breaking boundaries · self-protection · focus · achievement · determination · independence · reaching a finish line · power · pride · self-confidence · courage · perseverance · moving into a new chapter · nourishing work · finding meaning

In recognizing exactly what we crave and vowing to pursue it, we find a sense of personal power that allows us to set new boundaries as well as break through old ones. But after embracing our human needs and desires, the structures and traditions that once grounded us now grow restrictive. They start limiting our ability to set our own course. We're filled with purpose, putting our energy and drive and focus into pursuing that goal with single-minded perseverance. Wandering was a necessary part of our journey, but now our destination is becoming clear, and we chart an intentional course: driving toward that ambition with steady attention and overflowing excitement, reaching that destination with joyful triumph and pride. We believe in ourselves fully and move in a way that balances self-protection with dignity, satisfaction, and delight. And in pushing through old limits, in asserting our knowledge and experience, we're free to take calculated risks and to keep making space for our dreams to grow and thrive.

We are hurtling toward the finish line, knowing that we are exactly where we are meant to be, finding success and magic as we complete a major milestone. This is victory, confidence, a necessary conquering—and whether what we have conquered is internalized self-doubt or a more external kind of obstacle, our success and satisfaction in this moment cannot be denied. This sense of personal expansion, this ability to fix our eyes on the prize, this thrilling momentum and drive toward our goals, is the riveting, dynamic, commanding energy of the Chariot.

· · ·

Sometimes we can feel pieces falling beautifully into place. Momentum is building, our gaze is focused, our energy is high. We're protected and passionate, and an important milestone is within reach. And as we barrel down our chosen path, gathering our strength and moving past obstacles with ease, we find the Chariot. This is a triumphant archetype, one that gives us space to celebrate achievements, to recognize the courage and perseverance that it has taken to get this far. And while the Chariot represents reaching a particular finish line, bringing us to the end of the first line of the major arcana, our journey is far from over.

Movement can both sustain and deplete us, especially when we are working hard to control every step, every breath, every heartbeat. The rush of excitement, the knowledge that we are accomplishing something incredible, the pride in ourselves, all feel like magic. The Chariot helps us to find balance between a healthy ego and humility, between experience and discovery—and in harnessing this energy, we find stability in movement, temper our expectations with reality, keep safety and stability as priorities. We may focus on advancement and intention with this archetype, but the Chariot also reveals the ways in which we show up in the world, the things we stand for, the pride we hold in our individualism and uniqueness. In following our hearts, in trusting our instincts, sometimes we have to break some rules.

When our energies align, when we believe ourselves capable and trust in the influence we wield, it can inspire us to harness our willpower. Fears and doubts are soothed by fierce hope, and our goal becomes crystal clear. Confidence creates space for us to explore restrictions—ones that we have previously set for ourselves, and ones that were set for us by society. We know that we are experienced enough to push our own limits a little, that we can take calculated risks and make cautious explorations without all of our progress crumbling into dust. From the outside, it may still look like we're following that chosen path, but internally, we find ourselves stretching, seeing how hard and fast we can really go. And after finding intellectual community with the Hierophant and heart-centered community with the Lovers, the Chariot offers the support we need to begin a new chapter of growth, change, and evolution.

Astrological correspondence: Cancer

Cancer is the first water sign of the astrological calendar, a cardinal sign that ushers in the summer and embodies a spirit of protection, intuition, and focus. This energy is emotional and introspective, with strong boundaries along with a deep desire to utilize natural creativity and ambition. Similarly, the goal of the Chariot is to expand in a practical and controlled way, to make space for spiritual and emotional exploration with a clear expectation of returning home. There's a necessary grounding here, and with so much sensitivity and emotion, Cancer knows that they need to have a safe space to land, even after working so hard to build something new.

> JOURNAL PROMPT: *Where is Cancer in your natal chart? Which element does it live in? Do you have any placements in Cancer? Think about what makes you feel safe and protected, and the things that you're willing to take risks for. What nourishes you? Do you find comfort in stability, or does it make you frustrated, edgy, restless? What are you willing to fight for, and how does thinking about those values help you understand the Chariot?*

Numerological correspondence: Seven

Driven, observant, and intellectual, the number seven is associated with experience, intelligence, and seeking. Seven embraces awareness and is eager to understand movement, wanting to discern the deeper meanings underneath our desires. The Chariot is a card that we often associate with intense drive and rapid movement, but this archetype is also one of deep strength, brilliant focus, and a willingness to consider and even challenge our own limits. This archetype offers an opportunity, a chance to succeed. It urges us to consider how we want to reach our destination. There's a need for control within this card and the number seven, and our ability to navigate new paths without getting lost or losing sight of our goals is an important part of harnessing this energy fully.

Wisdom and spirituality are major themes of the number seven—how do you see these ideas show up in the Chariot? In moving toward a goal at a rapid pace, in pursuing victory, how do we seek, quest, discover? Does the Chariot feel like a card of conquest to you, or a card of movement? How do we change through our experiences?

In Readings

In working with the Chariot, we take the confidence that we have found and put it into practice, letting the world see us succeed, earning our place among the champions. This kind of breakthrough can generate a tremendous amount of energy, but it also requires immense control and expertise.

What makes you feel powerful, resilient, courageous? What inspires you? Where do you find your strength? What boosts your willpower, and how do you keep your eyes on the prize? What feeds you, keeps you moving with courage and confidence when you're nearing the end of a major project, ambition, or goal? How do you see the courage of the Fool in the Chariot?

8. Strength

LEO // Courage, independence, leadership, ego, creativity

EIGHT // Power, momentum, discipline, assurance, control, practicality

KEYWORDS // patience · wisdom · self-awareness · confidence · restraint · adaptability · stamina · observation · balance · personal power · waiting for the right moment · resilience · pride · maturity · trusting in our experience · knowledge

After a blaze of triumph, we find ourselves slowing our pace. We're settling into a rhythm, allowing our brilliance and power to shine in a way that is impossible to ignore. We've conquered a particular milestone and now are exploring a new position, confronting new challenges, assessing new risks. We feel our hearts beating steadily, our breath coming slowly and deeply, our minds focusing on the tasks at hand. Our confidence has been building, our sense of self is bolstered, and our satisfaction continues to intensify, igniting us in profound new ways. The experiences that we have enjoyed and the challenges that we have endured have given us renewed poise, the kind of wisdom and capability that comes from overcoming adversity. And while obstacles may once again enter our path—while others may push us to follow their lead or present us with new problems to solve—we know our worth, understand our value, rely on our own fortitude. We appreciate that strong emotions have their place, understand that our ability to express ourselves is a gift rather than a burden. We know for certain that using all of the tools at our disposal is the best way to navigate complex situations.

In recognizing our internal steadiness, in believing in our own stamina and resilience, we are able to make choices with precision, to trust in our actions. This ability to practice patience, to gather information before acting, to balance our wildness with our wisdom, is the bright hope and bold resilience of Strength.

• • •

Power isn't always loud. Often it's patient, quiet, composed, manifesting as discipline, courage, or subtlety. Strength is not simply a tamed animal, not someone who has been stripped of all of their wildness or deprived of their primitive instincts. Rather, Strength understands the persistent threads of magic that live beneath their skin, knows the complexities and cleverness that they have at their disposal. They don't see emotion as a curse, as something to be struggled against—instead they understand the weight of desire and are willing to be patient in order to have those desires fulfilled. As we move into this second line of the major arcana, we find Strength in restraint, in grace, in quiet wisdom. We move into a cycle of personal influence and collective awareness. We're being thoughtful about what we project into the world.

The last few archetypes explored boundaries in different ways, setting them, stretching them, even breaking or changing them. With Strength, we feel steady in where we are, protected but still able to grow, supported in all that we do and say and long for. As our personal gifts continue to manifest and reveal themselves, we treasure them, cherish them, celebrate this magic that flows through our veins. We know how valuable we are and are able to harness our skills with discernment rather than jumping recklessly into every new opportunity or invitation. There's a deep trust in the self, an awareness of power, that radiates from this card. Even in difficult times, Strength is an archetype that can be relied on for poise, maturity, and wisdom.

We all have trauma, fears, and wounds that run deep. Sometimes these things are painful to examine, truths that we would rather bury and avoid. But Strength does not shy away from those tender, injured facets of self. Instead, Strength regards themselves and others with empathy, kindness, and respect. This is an energy of observation, of waiting for the right moment to act, of treating the various gifts and talents that we possess with respect. There's a stately composure to this archetype, a regal deftness, the kind of precision that we don't always find with the cards in the first line of the major arcana. We have adventured, conquered, triumphed, and we stand proud in our victory. We know who we are and what we have to offer. In taking ownership of these gifts, we also accept responsibility for the ways that we wield them and take on a mantle of leadership. Strength encourages us to acknowledge the authority we carry and to be thoughtful about the impact that we have on those around us.

Astrological correspondence: Leo

Our fixed fire sign of the zodiac, Leo is known for confidence and charisma, independent powerhouses who are willing to fight for the things that matter and honor their deepest desires and needs. These lions know where their talent lies, understand how to utilize their inner magic to the best of their ability, and often shine brightly when doing the things they love and care about. Leo has much in common with Strength—many tarot decks even feature a lion as part of this archetype—but rather than a roaring beast, this card represents fortitude and awareness, someone waiting for the right moment to act. Strength asks us to remember our experience, to wield our wildness with precision, to observe as much as possible before acting, and to be brave enough to trust in our own discernment.

JOURNAL PROMPT: *Where is Leo in your natal chart? Which element does it live in? Do you have any placements in Leo? Think about the situations where you feel calm, patient, able to stay in control. Are you a natural leader, or do you prefer to stay in the background? How does it feel to know that people are listening to you, or relying on your experience, wisdom, and knowledge? What connections do you see between the energy of Leo and the archetype of Strength?*

Numerological correspondence: Eight

Eights are powerful, levelheaded, and headstrong. With eyes on the prize and a determination to succeed, the number eight is associated with hard work, resources, and discipline. And while they are willing to take some calculated risks to achieve their goals, this is all about doubling down, putting everything that we have into our ambitions and objectives. After assessing our options with seven and the Chariot, Strength moves forward with balance and assurance, committed to their path and trusting in their own experience. Eight and Strength both encourage us to celebrate our power, to move with boldness and poise, and to believe in our ability to get shit done.

Eight is deeply tied to power, a concept which can manifest in many different ways depending on how it is wielded. What kind of power do you see in Strength? What does it mean to be well-resourced, to create systems of abundance? How does this kind of success and pride feel different from that of the number six?

In Readings

When we embrace the energy of Strength, it's essential that we act with dignity, that we use our power with intention, that we listen and observe and make decisions with care rather than haste. Yet there's joy, pride, satisfaction in this kind of practiced, purposeful effort, in believing with every facet of our being that we will succeed.

How can you lead with patience? Where are you being called to take your time? Which fears or obstacles are you facing? What personal magic are you uncovering, and when might the Fool have felt flickers of this confidence at the start of their journey? How do you balance movement with stillness? When do you let your wildness out? Where are you being asked to show grace, and can you show yourself the same compassion that you offer to others?

9. The Hermit

VIRGO // Service, ideals, precision, organization, healing, purification

NINE // Observation, personal responsibility, collective growth, expansion, clarity

KEYWORDS // spirituality · wisdom · stepping back · solitude · observation · examination · care · authenticity · reflection · peering into shadows · patience · interrogation · attention to detail · new routines · secrets · honesty · intentionality

Our light has been shining so brightly, visible to all. Yet after allowing ourselves to be seen and celebrated we feel an urge to sink into the shadows, to break away from our established routines and experimental trail blazing, to focus our attention on our innermost selves. We find a place where we can be alone and take the time to dim our glow, light a lantern, and appraise ourselves and our world with deep care and patient attention. We look into every nook and cranny, interrogate and inspect, probe the ways that we have grown and evolved. We ask questions and take all the time and space that we need to answer them thoroughly, fully, authentically. As we retrace our steps on this journey, as we think about the choices that we have made and the victories that we have won, we recognize what we're proud of and what we are still pursuing. We evaluate, reflect, consider. Our hidden places sometimes hold our most magical aspects, and in taking the time to get to know them, we find a new sense of self, a new belief in our own power, a new feeling of empowerment around our magic.

This peering into the darkness, this willingness to retrace our own steps, leads to deeper self-awareness. In intentionally stepping into our shadows, in focusing our attention on what lies beneath, we can see our full selves more clearly. And in these moments of stillness and reflection, we give ourselves over to the thoughtful, sensitive, probing energy of the Hermit.

• • •

Self-examination takes patience, bravery, and honesty. In the pursuit of truth, in interrogating our own motives and desires and fears, we need to become comfortable with mystery. We need to be willing to slow down and feel our feelings. The Hermit reminds us that not every question will be answered, but that in asking, we can develop sharper, more precise insights, uncover new internal layers, and dig more deeply into our own secrets.

In stepping back from life's daily routines and regular cycles, we can observe our own habits and tendencies through a more discerning lens. We give our various aspects of self the room to breathe, using active energy to seek, discover, clarify. This is getting to know ourselves in a new and profound way, being brave enough to be completely honest. If we've been avoiding truths within us that feel ugly or uncomfortable, realities that we're ashamed or afraid of, then taking the time to come to terms with who we are can be deeply, profoundly liberating. And even if this process is troubling, the conclusions we draw when we drag everything into the light can rarely be denied.

Healing is not always a sweet, gentle process—sometimes it requires deep meditation, intense scrutiny, going over our souls with a fine-toothed comb. Identifying what we are enduring, excavating everything that we find within ourselves, can be a grueling, painful undertaking, demanding intensive amounts of time, energy, and courage. Yet it's important to remember that the revelations of the Hermit can also bring legitimate relief, powerful healing, and rich beauty. In our isolation, we have nothing to prove, nothing to hide—we can be completely, brutally honest with ourselves; we can ask the hard questions and gather the courage to answer them truthfully. Instead of continuing to let old wounds fester or worrying about unwanted exposure, the Hermit gives us some of that control back, dictating the terms of our most intimate confessions. We have the chance to breathe through pain and fear, to embrace deeper desires, to accept all of these parts of ourselves. The Hermit sets the stage for absolute authenticity, clearing the way for another new beginning.

Astrological correspondence: Virgo

A sign of mutable earth, Virgo is often associated with organization, structure, and perfection. It's in this energy that we slow down a bit, regroup, assess our progress, and consider where we're going. Virgo is thoughtful and patient, creating a structured yet flexible, service-oriented plan that helps us reach those ever-important goals and ambitions. Harboring that same determined and patient spirit, the Hermit is a card of retreat and solitude. There's a gentle care within both the Hermit and Virgo, a desire to understand fully, to not make changes or move forward until we are confident of what our next steps should be.

JOURNAL PROMPT: *Where is Virgo in your natal chart? Which element does it live in? Do you have any placements in Virgo? Consider the natural solitude present in the Hermit and the ways that this may manifest with the energy of Virgo. How does thinking about concepts like flexibility, perfectionism, or focus help expand your understanding of this archetype? What does it mean to examine the self, and how does looking at your deepest secrets through a critical lens help you grow?*

Numerological correspondence: Nine

Connected to isolation, individuality, and anticipation, nine is a thoughtful and observant number, with humanitarian awareness and acceptance of deep personal responsibility. There's a notable sense of consciousness in this card, a willingness to dive deep and create rich connections among people, goals, and ideals. We find strength and compassion in these explorations, an expansion of our own consciousness that prepares us for coming changes, a growing need for something new. And many of those themes also exist within the Hermit, an archetype who asks tough questions of themselves, always looking for the deepest truths and most hidden realities. This quality makes them both solitary and connected in unique ways to the world around them, always aware of the ways that this internal exploration will eventually manifest externally. Brimming with anticipation and transition, with the Hermit we see intentional moments of stillness, the deep breath before another major leap.

JOURNAL PROMPT: *Nine as a number is deeply associated with care, humanitarian systems, and creating a better world for all, but it also serves as the final number in the numerological sequence of 1-9. How do retreating into the self and studying your*

internal fears, desires, and ambitions help you come back to the world in a new way?
Do you believe caring for the self makes you better at caring for others? As the last
number in the sequence, how does the number nine set you up for a new beginning
and point you back to the number one?

In Readings

In stepping into the energy of the Hermit, we may find things we don't like. We may need time to grieve or cry or scream, may need to come to terms with wounds we thought had healed or hurts we didn't realize we'd been carrying. But that work, difficult as it can be, is essential for evolution. The Hermit wants us to know ourselves intimately, to understand all that is inside of us, to own and respect all of our facets and joys and fears.

How does the Hermit carry on the work of the Fool, the Priestess, and the Hierophant? When we take off our masks, when we look at the core of who we are, who do we see? What gives us the strength to carry on, and what makes us feel defeated? Which boundaries are necessary in this kind of work, and how do previous archetypes teach us about setting, maintaining, and adjusting those boundaries? Which emotions manifest when you confess your deepest truths, and how does sitting with those feelings impact the goals you set, the dreams you chase, the relationships you pursue?

10. The Wheel of Fortune

JUPITER // Expansion, abundance, growth, stabilization, belief, ideals

TEN & ONE // Unity, vision, pride, independence & community together,
trail blazing, confidence

KEYWORDS // a new spark · destiny · larger forces · fate · karma · control · vision · essential change · patterns of movement · routines · luck · understanding our purpose · cycles · transitions · responsibility · rapid change · positivity · trust · faith in something bigger

We've been focusing on our own journey, our own dreams, our own understanding of who we are. But after spending so much time in solitude and reflection, we rejoin the world, newly sensitive to the ways that our unique magic, wisdom, gifts, and skills contribute to the cycles and patterns of the universe. Like sliding from the driver's seat into the passenger side, like getting strapped into a carnival ride that restricts our movements, this sensation can be topsy-turvy, our stomach dropping and our breath catching in ways that are surprising, unexpected, exciting. Luck and fate and destiny form a tangled web of movement, stillness, growth, and destruction, and as we slip back into the currents of society, we see how the choices that we make impact those around us. Our lives do not exist in a vacuum, and the things that we create, the vision that we have for the future, have the capacity to make lasting, permanent, significant change. Bigger cycles are always at play, and there will always be forces that are beyond our control. But we find an undeniable sense of empowerment here, begin to celebrate the things that we can influence, and emancipate the things that we cannot.

In recognizing how far our power extends, in releasing any lingering fantasies of dominion, we can find a new sense of sovereignty within ourselves. This interconnectedness, this vast consciousness of the universe, this acknowledgment of the enigmatic and complex threads that link us to both past and future, is the intricate, compelling significance of the Wheel of Fortune.

· · ·

Change has a peculiar kind of reliability. Even if everything feels completely chaotic, even if we've lost sight of which way is up, we can always count on uncomfortable but necessary cycles of transformation, the certainty of uncertainty. The Wheel of Fortune brings an odd but familiar ease, encouraging us to trust in the process even if we aren't sure where we may end up, to grapple with the forces and movements and shifts and evolutions that are far bigger than we are. There are times when we know that we're the ones spinning the wheel, moving through something larger at our chosen speed and velocity, while understanding that the friction we experience is something we must endure in order to get somewhere better. Other times, we may simply feel ourselves being pulled in a new direction, following the luck, dancing on the shifting winds. Sometimes, all we can do is surrender to gravity, hold on for dear life, and see where we eventually land.

This kind of pandemonium can be frustrating or frightening—but there can also be relief in being released of the responsibility of certain things, in knowing that we are being swept along by something that is beyond our own understanding. The Wheel of Fortune represents inertia, massive shifts of energy and movement, larger patterns of growth and change that push us onto new paths. And after the solitude and reflection of the Hermit, we are reminded with this archetype that our thoughts, feelings, actions, and choices don't exist in isolation. We are all linked together by thin strands of energy and intention, connected in ways that feel too large to grasp, too complex to interrogate fully. It's within the Wheel that we are forced to contend with the scope of who we are, the ways that the ambitions we harbor impact those around us. Sometimes our luck can change in an instant, for better or worse, and this archetype asks us to be aware of what we're doing, of how we're moving, and what it might mean for our own future.

Astrological correspondence: Jupiter

Associated primarily with expansion, Jupiter is also the planet of exploration, philosophy, growth, and fortune. This planet teaches us about abundance, urging us to dream big and bold, empowering us to believe that progress is always possible. In the same way, the Wheel of Fortune is an archetype of karma and cycles, giving us a sense of what is within our control and which larger forces are impacting us that we have no influence over. Think about the difference between inertia and gravity: the first is a force that we ourselves set into motion, while the second is entirely out of our control, a law that we are at the mercy of. When working with Jupiter and the Wheel, we invite in positivity, growth, and celebration, acknowledging all of the ways that joy is possible while simultaneously holding space for mysterious forces, synchronicities, larger energies.

JOURNAL PROMPT: *Where does Jupiter fall in your chart? In which house? In which sign? Consider your relationship with Jupiter, and the areas of your life that feel naturally abundant, joyful, expansive. What do luck and karma mean to you? How do you understand forces of the universe that you cannot control? When do you feel like you're being guided by something larger? Is that a pleasant sensation or an uncomfortable one?*

Numerological correspondence: Ten & One

With an honoring of both independence and community, tens hold endless potential, bursting with promise. There's a feeling of unity and recognition in the number ten, celebrating completion while acknowledging cycles and noting new beginnings around the corner. Ambition and pride are both prevalent in this number, and while we see some of those characteristics in the Wheel of Fortune, there's also an awareness of the unexpected, the knowledge that in spite of expertise and experience, there is so much that is out of our control. One cycle ends as another begins, and just as something starts to find success, another may plummet or fail. Continuation is endless. In numerology we would typically reduce the number ten to one, which points us back to the Magician—but here I want to highlight the number ten specifically, since it also has a place in each of the minor arcana suits.

Ones are powerfully present, motivated, strong-willed, and confident, ready to take on new challenges while staying focused on their bigger goals and dreams. With passion and dominance, the number one is independent and assertive, a pioneer that is ready to push forward and create impactful change. With the

Magician, the number one manifests as vision, awareness, and confidence. When we look at the Wheel of Fortune as ten, we find the number zero reintroducing the element of the unknown and the figure of the Fool. Rather than only trusting in ourselves, we are now putting faith in the forces of the universe, the movements and energies that are far beyond our control. One brings power, potential, and positivity, and with the Wheel, that comes in the form of luck, change, and awareness.

> **JOURNAL PROMPT:** *The number ten blazes trails in many different ways, which becomes clear when we look at the relationship between the Magician and the Wheel. How do these differ? When do you work with each energy, and how can they work together? How do you see energies of both the Fool and the Magician within this archetype?*

In Readings

When the Wheel of Fortune turns, it's a reminder that so many things are beyond our guidance—but we do get to choose how we respond to challenges, how we act in difficult times, how we use our gifts for better or worse. Even when it feels like we're being pulled in multiple directions, we are responsible for ourselves and for what we do when the winds still, when the water calms.

Do you believe in luck, in karma, in fate? Does losing control bring a sense of grief or a wave of relief? How do you find the potential in friction? What does it take for you to open your mind to new possibilities? How do you stay calm in changing circumstances? What does it mean to be in command, and what freedom comes when we lose our grasp on authority?

11. Justice

LIBRA // Harmony, aesthetics, balance, truth, diplomacy

TWO // Healing, choice, intentionality, sensitivity, intuition, psychic wisdom, duality

KEYWORDS // collective crossroads · clarity · purpose · social structures · ideals · examination · ethics · balance · multiple perspectives · seeking truth · fairness · equality · practicality · listening & learning · nuance · decision-making · problem-solving

Our awareness of the influence we hold has expanded, giving us a heightened understanding of purpose. While our personal dream has thus far been a motivating force in our journey, we now begin to identify a broader desire for fairness, equality, and balance. We've gotten a bird's-eye view of the universe and its forces, and now we charge forward, our minds racing, sword in hand, eager to analyze problems and take action to solve them. The ideals and freedoms that we have recognized, the hopes and fears we carry, the vision of the future we have clarified, all offer us ways to move through the world—and we now begin to find opportunities to test out these theories, to see how our ethics and morals play out. There are so many things to care about, so many issues that demand our energy and attention, that it's impossible to devote ourselves to all of them. But as we consider our impact on society, on the future, we also understand our own moral compass more clearly. As we define what we're willing to fight for, we also begin to see that some old ideas are best left in the past.

It's essential to be aware of who is protected and who is not, of how the civilization we envision functions for all kinds of people, and how we ourselves uphold the structures that already exist. In recognizing where we fit and where we can enact change, we find new power and clarity in our purpose. A desire to seek truth, a recognition of how influential and impactful we can really be: this is the clear, perceptive, balanced energy of Justice.

...

Our opinions, our actions, our desires have consequences. As the Wheel of Fortune reminded us, none of us exist in a vacuum. And as we come to Justice, we begin to understand our influence in another way, seeing what our choices lead to, what our work contributes to. It's the moment that we take everything we think we know—the priorities we hold and the dreams we've established and the foundations and beliefs and rituals we've formed—and appreciate how they function or fail. It's a practical application of ideas that until now have been purely theoretical, a chance to observe the ways that our beliefs play out. We admit our biases, recognize our blind spots, and often have our eyes opened into the ways that the world works beyond ideals and theories. In short, we get a taste of real life.

On the surface, the concept of justice seems simple—ensuring that rules are fair, that structures are equitable, that society has laws and limits that keep us safe and protected and honest. Justice could, and should, mean that everyone can thrive, that all are sheltered, that everyone has equal opportunities for success. But in practice, justice is much more complex to execute and tends to reveal peoples' natural prejudices as well as the ways that personal beliefs manifest into discrimination, harm, and violence. And Justice the archetype wants us to be clear-eyed and critical of these systems, to observe the world with an eye for truth instead of avoiding or ignoring information that contradicts our beliefs.

In Justice, we are observing existing friction between the way we dream things could be and the way things actually are. We use the sharpness of our mind, the wisdom of our spirit, and the empathy in our hearts to develop solutions to problems that may feel impossibly big—and through it all, we rely on ourselves, trusting in our own moral compass and ethical analysis. This is community-oriented compassion, a need to operate based on what is right, what is fair, what is truthful. It's an urge to make a difference, to recognize potential and turn it into progress. And while it can sometimes feel like the sharpness of this card demands that we listen only to the rationality of the mind, it's often the opposite—by honoring what we know and observe, we can find more confidence in our instincts, intuition, and emotion, and work to make the world better for everyone rather than for the few.

Astrological correspondence: Libra

 Libra, the sign of cardinal air, welcomes in the autumn and invites us to lighten up, to reach for joy, to celebrate the collaboration and communication that live within all air signs. Libra is often associated with balance, a theme that carries through the card of Justice, but this air sign goes beyond just striving for harmony in all things. It's not just about personal balance, or people-pleasing, but rather about finding harmony between how we think things should function and how they actually work. Justice is an archetype of logic and evaluation, but in the real world this concept is complicated, nuanced, and difficult to achieve.

JOURNAL PROMPT: *Where is Libra in your natal chart? Which element does it live in? Do you have any placements in Libra? Consider what justice as a concept means, and how balance, harmony, and equality do or do not align with your experience of justice. When or how do beauty and truth overlap? How can art help you expand your definition of truth?*

Numerological correspondence: Eleven to Two

Eleven consolidates to two, pointing us back to the High Priestess's thoughtful stillness, deep reflection, and innate trust in self. The number two is all about choice, consideration, and careful reflection. While with the Priestess we see this play out in personal decision-making and a desire for authenticity, with Justice this nurturing, idealism, and wisdom extend outward into society. Caution is paired with hope, with a desire for everyone to feel supported, protected, and empowered. Even if you see the Priestess as a deeply solitary figure, the number two is about partnership, love, and care, themes that are clearly demonstrated within Justice. In fighting for a better world, in standing up for what we believe in, in drawing lines between what is right and what is wrong, we make things better for everyone.

JOURNAL PROMPT: *The number two demonstrates many different methods for connection, helping us see the ways that love, care, and partnership play out in the world. How can the Priestess inform your understanding of Justice? How does spending time in intuitive reflection help you clarify your purpose?*

In Readings

Justice often appears when we need to pull back from purely emotional insights and instead view a decision or situation from a more analytical, logical perspective. In imagining what the Fool's initial desire looks like in practice, in letting it expand out into the world, we see it through a new lens, transforming our vision.

What do we believe in? What are we willing to fight for? Whose viewpoints are we centering? Where have ideals gone astray, been warped over time or with experience? What doesn't work? When we try to play certain theories out in the real world, where are we proved right, and what turns out to need adjustments? What are we learning? How do we grow?

12. The Hanged One

NEPTUNE // Depth, awareness, fantasy, mystery, psychic energy, porousness

THREE // Innovation, creativity, expression, growth, manifestation

KEYWORDS // internal expansion · stillness · reflection · stagnation · halted progress · lack of movement · surrender · sacrifice · perspective · awareness · truth · questions · new viewpoints · waiting for a shift · calm before the storm · patience · discomfort

We've been looking outward, caught up in the complex movements of the collective, imagining the impact that our dream might have on the world. But in the process of putting so much energy toward others, we find ourselves tangled up, slowing down. Perhaps we've lost our way, taken a wrong turn, or changed our mind about where we want to go—or perhaps we're simply exhausted from seeking so many perspectives, from growing and imagining and expanding. Whatever the cause, we find ourselves stagnant, unmoving, twisted up within ourselves, with no way of knowing how long we'll be in this state of surrender. Our limbs lock, mind frozen, heart pounding in our ears. We can feel something struggling within us, feel a release that is slowly building, feel that a change is on the horizon—yet we cannot move out of the way, cannot take action to prevent this shift from finding us. All we can do is breathe through the discomfort of the moment, work to adjust our stance, and prepare to accept whatever is on its way. Like a difficult, inverted yoga pose, we hold our position for as long as we can, knowing that we are stretching unfamiliar muscles, awakening a strained but necessary awareness.

This is a different kind of stillness than we've experienced previously, an inescapable submission that stops us in our tracks. And while this distress is temporary, it also leaves a lasting impression, creating an aching sensitivity that stays with us even after movement is restored. This moment when we are forced to relinquish all control, when we are conscious of our inability to take action, is the unavoidable tenderness and shifting cognizance of the Hanged One.

• • •

Sometimes the world compels us to slow down. With the Hanged One, we come to a place where we must yield, where we are no longer in control. Movement has stalled, progress is halted, and we are powerless to move in any direction. This card is rarely pleasant, but it also invites new ways of thinking, encouraging us to identify all that we cannot manage or structure or organize. When we sit with this archetype, we acknowledge the weight of the world, recognize that there is nothing we can do in this moment. Instead, we wait, observe, and prepare.

This isn't a period of rest and recovery, isn't a soothing break from work or planning or exertion. Yet a lack of visible movement is not the same as a lack of progress. After the inertia of the Wheel and the focused action of Justice, the Hanged One brings a shift that is internal rather than external. We are being pulled toward something against our will with no longer have control over what is being created and what is stagnating. Instead we have to exercise patience, and while we wait, we sit with our unease, process it, try to find meaning in it. Acknowledging our internal difficulties and giving us space to process what is on the horizon, the Hanged One sees us where we are and asks us to stop trying to steamroll past something that is on its own timetable.

Sometimes there is relief in temporary powerlessness: a relaxing of the muscles, a long, slow exhale. There can be intense beauty in submission, incredible joy in releasing the need to control everything and recognizing when we are outmatched. And in these moments of unexpected stillness, a shift in perspective is often both necessary and welcome. Even in discomfort, from our new position we can see our problems or worries or dreams from another angle, perhaps seeing how things may be wrapping up soon or new opportunities could present themselves. While this card comes before Death in the major arcana, the Hanged One does not always herald something miserable and is not always a precursor to sorrow. Instead this energy is one of waiting, of observing, of beginning to see the world through new eyes. It's anticipation from a different perspective.

Astrological correspondence: Neptune

Associated with fantasy, mystery, and psychic energy, Neptune rules the spiritual unknown, giving us space to explore depths and uncertainties with ease. In the same way, the Hanged One asks us to pause physical or intellectual movement and instead sit with our doubts, our fears, our lack of control. Both archetype and planet play with fantasy, inspiring a dreamy quality that can pull us out of our bodies and into the spirit realm. There can be much clarity in questions, in allowing ourselves to stop focusing on what is known and instead indulge in fantasy, wonder, uncertainty. And in being open to unexpected foresight, in letting ourselves drift into uncharted places, we can find new strength when we come back to the physical world.

> JOURNAL PROMPT: *Where does Neptune fall in your chart? In which house? In which sign? Think about how the energy of the Hanged One intersects with the energy of that Neptune placement and with Neptune's energy in general. What does it mean to surrender to fantasy, to explore illusion, to be open to mystery? How does your Neptune placement help you understand this archetype?*

Numerological correspondence: Twelve to Three

Twelve consolidates to three and the Empress, a natural outpouring of creativity, desire, and connection. The Empress is an archetype tied to generosity, abundance, and celebration, of sharing our visions and ambitions, of letting others see us. And in many ways, the Hanged One is the inverse—internalizing new perspectives, the tension between action and stillness, an inability to express what we need or pursue our desires. If we can sink into surrender, there is much to be learned, many ways that we can grow. But if we struggle against that tension, if we refuse to recognize where we are in the cycle, it can cause pain, even damage. The Empress has to push ideas and resources out into the world, but the Hanged One must retain their observations and let their creativity flow inward.

If the Empress is the movement that comes after a decision is made, the Hanged One demonstrates what happens after the intentional work and change brought by Justice. Any time we move in a particular direction, we are sacrificing other possibilities, giving up potential in one area so that we can pursue it in another. The Hanged One shows us what it can look like to wait for movement, to not know what is being unlocked but to trust that this expression is happening anyway.

JOURNAL PROMPT: *The number three is one of creativity, expansion, and external movement—yet the Hanged One is a figure of motionless contemplation, of patient waiting, of stagnant energy. What does it mean to focus Empress expression inwardly? How do observation, stillness, and patience help you nurture yourself? How does it feel to hold your movement back, either willingly or by force? When have you felt this sensation, and what did it offer you?*

In Readings

Just as the Fool was brave enough to leave behind something safe and strike out into the world on an unknown but exciting path, the Hanged One asks us to consider what hasn't been working, what has been crumbling to dust in our hands, what we've been investing our time in, and what we have been neglecting. This is a liminal time, a moment at the crossroads, an opportunity to evaluate what is worth holding on to and what you may need to release.

What are you understanding about yourself? Where are you being called to be patient, with both yourself and your circumstances? How does stopping that forward momentum and letting yourself be still for a while shift the way that you look at your goals, your desires, your experiences?

13. Death

SCORPIO // Privacy, healing, shadow work, power, transformation, the abject

FOUR // Structure, organization, systems, progression, foundations, stability

KEYWORDS // natural order · loss · grief · an inevitable end · permanent shift · transformation · freedom · relief · acknowledgment of change · rebirth · leaving something behind · sorrow · opportunities · movement · releasing a burden · answers

The sensation of being locked in place has eased. Now that the other shoe has dropped, we sit in awareness of a devastating loss, an inevitable goodbye to something that once mattered deeply to us. There's grief, pain, and sorrow, but also a quiet feeling of relief: this burden is something that we no longer have to carry. A dream from long ago, a relationship that has run its course, a situation that is more toxic than treasured is finally out of our grasp—and that release brings a peculiar and perhaps unexpected freedom. Our bodies and hearts may feel heavy, but our minds and souls have a strange lightness: imagining how we will change, who we have the ability to become in the wake of this loss. There is power in letting ourselves feel deeply, in being intensely vulnerable, in honoring what something once was. This is a time for respect and acknowledgment, for recognizing an ending, for making space to grieve. And while this season of mourning may take up all of our focus, energy, and resources for a time, it also helps us to see our remaining wishes, dreams, and ambitions more clearly. In sorrow, we find new purpose, feel richness in the present and hope for the future.

Quiet reflection, aching despair, and authentic bereavement often bring truths into focus, shifting our attention toward the dreams and relationships that matter most. And while not always welcome, endings are often deeply, profoundly necessary, giving us the gift of a fresh start, a rebirth. This sharpness, this truth, this recognition of who we are and what we crave, is the inevitable transformation of Death.

• • •

Death is essential. It makes life sweeter, knowing that we have only a limited amount of time on this earth to experience, connect, build, destroy, evolve. In endings, we give ourselves permission to grieve, celebrate, and move forward, rather than desperately clinging to something that is no longer growing with us, something we may not even want anymore. And by tilling the soil, by removing the weeds and overgrowth as well as the rot, we give ourselves the space and the resources to plant new seeds. Transformation cannot and will not happen before we say goodbye to the old things, the old ways.

The archetype of Death is about uncomfortable change, about closure and acceptance, about surrendering to the inevitable. But this isn't the universe trying to be needlessly cruel, ripping something healthy and positive away from us just for kicks. Instead, this archetype offers an invitation to transform, an opportunity to leave behind something that was once beloved and, in doing so, allow ourselves to grow beyond who we once were. Death as both a concept and an archetype feels so big because it *is* big, and the power and intensity of this shift cannot be overlooked or swept under the rug. It takes time to fully accept this kind of transition, to reckon with the impact that it will have on different facets of our lives.

Endings are not always negative, and sometimes this card is welcomed with open arms. Death can bring freedom as we are able to say goodbye to a demanding burden, something that has been weighing us down or holding us back. Think about what it means to be able to finally release a responsibility, particularly when it's one that we've been carrying for a long time. There's sorrow in this kind of adjustment, of course, but there can also be joy, as we shake our arms out, feel their lightness and their strength, and realize that we can now begin to gather up something else.

Astrological correspondence: Scorpio

 One of the most intense signs of the zodiac, the fixed water of Scorpio is associated with sex, power, and death. Bringing themes of control and intuition, paired with deep insights and obsessive curiosity, Scorpio invites us to cut away bullshit and

reach for all the things we desire. This sign is one of deep transformation, of being willing to release what isn't working and shift into another direction, intention, or purpose. And while the card of Death isn't necessarily a symbol of physical death, it does represent a natural end, an essential and inevitable transition into something completely different. We let go of something that has been quietly fading away, saying goodbye to an old dream or person or situation and instead moving forward toward something that makes more sense for the person we have become.

JOURNAL PROMPT: *Where is Scorpio in your natal chart? Which element does it live in? Do you have any placements in Scorpio? Think about your relationship with endings, transformation, and rebirth. Are you energized by change, or does it scare you? How does the energy of Scorpio help you find the beauty, power, and mystery in the Death archetype?*

Numerological correspondence: Thirteen to Four

Thirteen becomes four, the number of the Emperor and a reminder of stability, purpose, and intentionality. Fours are detail-oriented, systematic, focused, and driven, eager to create structure and patterns that allow them to build and maintain organization. In the same way, Death is a natural boundary, one that cannot be changed, crossed, or avoided. While the four energy of the Emperor's is internal, devoted to personal growth, discipline, and order, Death expands this intention outward, drawing firm lines around what we can and cannot control. And while major transitions or inevitable losses can feel destabilizing, they also help us clarify what matters, what is truly important, and what we want to continue to focus on for our future.

JOURNAL PROMPT: *Four can serve as a critical lens, inviting us to look at something objectively or find truth in practical daily work. How do you see this energy play out differently in the Emperor and Death? How is loss its own kind of boundary, and where can loss bring freedom to create without hesitation, to pursue goals without worry? What relationships do each of these cards have with power? How do you see the Fool's desire for something new in the loss and release of Death?*

In Readings

When we see the Death card it represents something that has slowly been winding down on its own. It can give us permission to begin the process of saying goodbye and letting it go. We have to spend time mourning and processing, coming to terms with what this means for our present and our future—if we push past our discomfort and rush into the next thing, we will not be able to fully immerse ourselves into the next chapter of our story. We owe it to ourselves to take our time.

How do you process goodbyes? What are your rituals around death? What does it mean to give yourself permission to feel relief, even joy, instead of forcing yourself to go through the motions of performative grief? What can you nurture in the wake of this loss?

14. Temperance

SAGITTARIUS // Philosophy, freedom, education, wildness

FIVE // Change, freedom, exploration, tension, growth, adventure, balance, transition

KEYWORDS // Awareness · sacred alchemy · unexpected beauty · coincidence · everyday magic · wonder · moderation · harmony · self-expression · transcendence · balancing tension · contradictions · understanding · clarity · luck & optimism · possibility · integration · discovery

As our grief eases, we rejoin the world's rhythms and rhymes, and a desire for balance and moderation reveals itself. Our passionate fire is soothed by intuitive water, our perceptive air is calmed by steady earth, and we find ourselves weighing our wants and our needs, our extras and our essentials. We discover magic in being deeply, fully present; we feel the kind of offbeat brilliance that emerges when we least expect it. Coincidence? Divinity? Some things cannot be explained and are more powerful for the mystery they contain. Even as our feet are rooted into the earth, even as our body experiences pleasure and peace, we also stretch toward the heavens, reclaiming joy and wonder and curiosity. As we allow the different aspects of ourselves to come together in surprising, inspiring ways, new dreams clarify, new purposes manifest. In the wake of loss, in the freedom we've inherited, the world brims with possibility. And while there may be a sense of hesitancy in moving forward, there's also joy in the potential that has been revealed.

There's a curious longing to move, balanced by an eagerness to understand, that guides our movements with care and consideration. And as joy bubbles up, there's also a need for meaning, a craving for clarity that may feel just out of reach. This desire to analyze and experience, this ability to sit firmly in the present instead of worrying about the future or dwelling on the past, this ability to find the magic in the mundane is the paradoxical charm of Temperance.

• • •

Recognizing incongruities can be a freeing experience. Rather than struggling against sacred mysteries and opposing energies, there are times when we sit in contradictions, allowing ourselves to be comfortable with things that we do not fully understand. Temperance asks us to embrace the disparate elements that shape us: the water of deep emotion and intuitive connection alongside the fire of primal passion and intense desire. In finding our footing, in remembering ourselves, we embrace a period of serenity and observation, and we acknowledge that all is not lost. Temperance is moments of unexplainable magic, breaking free of the mundane, the joy in everyday miracles. It's when we catch glimpses of spiritual work happening in the physical world, observe that life is so much bigger and brighter and more mysterious than we know.

Many things can be true at the same time: we can be eager and also terrified, can be wildly creative and also doubt our own vision, can be restless to move and also desperate for stillness. But Temperance does not ask us to abandon the pieces of ourselves that don't seem to fit. Rather, this card gently and sweetly encourages us to find wonder in our own wanderings, to see how our various desires, fears, and interests overlap and intertwine. This archetype gives us permission to thrive where we have been planted, to find joy and power in our current path. So many new possibilities open up when our fire can burn safely without being smothered, when our air can explore and expand without getting lost, when our water can flow without drowning us, when our earth can stabilize without holding us back. These elements in alignment support our spirit's larger journey, allowing us to tap into the greater flows of the places we inhabit. When we embrace Temperance, we find our rhythm, celebrate a sense of belonging. We understand the ways that our daily spiritual insights contribute to a larger whole.

Astrological correspondence: Sagittarius

 With mutable fire and Sagittarius, we have a sign of rapid movement, joyful exploration, and a deep desire to understand the world. Sagittarius invites us to rediscover our personal magic, to tap into our richest passions and start a new journey forward, expanding and dreaming and learning. Sagittarius is a sign of freedom, a chance to follow our whims and desires, to use magnetic and charismatic energy to discover new purpose in the world. Both Sagittarius and Temperance have a sense of luck, of finding the sublime in everyday occurrences, and they invite us to embrace a spirit of wonder and curiosity in all that we do.

> JOURNAL PROMPT: *Where is Sagittarius in your natal chart? Which element does it live in? Do you have any placements in Sagittarius? Consider the relationships and tensions between exploration, philosophy, and discovery. Do you prioritize adventure, and how does movement help you feel balanced or unbalanced? Does the concept of moderation feel grounding, or stifling? How does the energy of the Fool intersect with this desire to move, discover, understand?*

Numerological correspondence: Fourteen to Five

Fourteen consolidates to five and the Hierophant, another figure of expansion, change, and purpose. Inquisitive, adventurous, and loyal, the number five represents dynamic energy and a desire to understand and explore. Endlessly curious, fives can be a bit restless, conscious of change and eager to see the shifts and growth within and around them. While the Hierophant's curiosity is often explored in an external way—with questions being explored and answered in community—Temperance feels very internal, as we learn to create balance within ourselves. Both the Hierophant and Temperance are eager to explore, to learn, to grow and change and find adventure. And in embracing the natural tension of the number five, each of these archetypes teaches us about the possibilities that are at our fingertips.

> JOURNAL PROMPT: *The number five brings both friction and freedom, urging us to consider rituals, beliefs, and connections. How do you see this energy play out in the Hierophant and Temperance? What do these two archetypes have in common, and how do they differ? How does restriction create new kinds of flow? What does it mean to find comfort within strain, to not fight against internal friction?*

In Readings

Temperance is the kind of magic that is unexpected, that lives outside of cosmic patterns and major forces. These are the coincidences, the sensation of things settling, of being in the right place at exactly the right time. It's asking the perfect question, getting a flash of insight or inspiration, having an opportunity fall into our laps that is just what we've been craving, even if we didn't fully know it yet. We can't always name our desires; sometimes we have to experience different things in order to figure out what feels good and what doesn't. But Temperance is the assurance that in trying and questioning, in understanding and exploring, we can find real truth within ourselves.

How do you trust? What do your experiences mean to you? What mark are you making on the people, places, and things that you encounter and interact with? How do you find pieces of yourself mirrored in loved ones and strangers, in stories? What does it mean to find sacred alchemy within yourself, and to see that kind of particular, unique magic play itself out in tangible ways?

15. The Devil

CAPRICORN // Ambition, infrastructure, development, focus

SIX // Harmony, nurturing, community, caretaking, movement, pride

KEYWORDS // blocked expansion · temptation · vices · destructive behaviors · getting caught up in ambition · power · control · distractions · losing focus · desperation · internal shadows · fears being made manifest · wildness · surrender · captivity · desire · cravings

In our efforts to be attentive to all of our internal aspects, our focus gets a little blurred. Old desires start to take up space in our imagination. Our gaze, once so clearly fixed on a specific destination, wanders toward other paths, longing to retrace our steps and revisit people, places, things, dreams that we walked away from long ago. Patterns that we thought we'd left behind, behaviors we thought we no longer indulged in, creep into our daily routines, pulling our attention away from our biggest ambitions and brightest hopes. Dozens of small decisions build on one another, gradually distracting us from the road we'd chosen into slippery corners and shadowed shortcuts. We try to grasp onto control, but it slips through our fingers—or perhaps we cling to it so tightly that it becomes its own vice, that urge to call every shot, have power over every situation, master every craving. There's a wickedness to being wild, a kind of beauty in letting go and chasing after our most profound, personal desires. But when we no longer have the option of saying *no*, when the ability to deny our impulses becomes impossible, any illusion of control is shattered. And although it can feel like freedom to give in to those seductive yearnings, now we find ourselves in a dark, dangerous place, uncertain of how we got there. The line is so thin between passion and power, and as we dance between sensations, we lose something precious: the skill of discernment.

Sometimes subtle, sometimes shameless, but always alluring—this is a moment defined by an aching need for something that we cannot quite grasp. It's a hunger for something uncertain that can morph into something desperate, something devastating. This fierce temptation, this slipping under the surface, this hankering for more—it's here that we sit with the challenging, seductive lure of the Devil.

We don't always know when we're hiding from the truth. There are times that we deliberately lie to ourselves, cling to our denial, look the other way to avoid confronting the reality of a situation. But other times, we make subtle adjustments, shift our path one way or another, work to avoid fear and inadvertently also avoid showing ourselves compassion, grace, or kindness. With the Devil, we find ourselves tangled in humiliation or regret, telling ourselves very specific stories about why we can't say no to something, why we have no choice but to behave in a particular way. Shame is an ugly thing, one that thrives in shadows, in the unseen, in the secrets we keep. If we can remain open, align ourselves with community that helps us be honest about our needs and motivations, and stay true to ourselves, endless possibilities stretch out before us, and we feel a rich sense of freedom.

When we isolate ourselves, get too fixated on a particular goal, become obsessive or caught up in an old pattern, it can become restraining and lead us into a trap of our own making. The Devil can be insidious, slowly letting us drift toward something that has the potential to ruin us and making us feel like it's our own choice. Whether we are struggling to maintain a tight grip on our control or are unwilling to regain power over ourselves, the Devil lives in those battles, tempting us to indulge our whims and revert to old patterns. Knowing how we respond to stress, how we cope when things get tough, is an important lesson. And with this archetype, we are invited to acknowledge those patterns, to make an effort to change our course. The Devil doesn't have to be catastrophic. It still offers us opportunities to make necessary adjustments, but this card demands that we listen, because ignoring this archetype comes with severe, permanent consequences.

Astrological correspondence: Capricorn

Focused and savvy, Capricorn's cardinal earth is ambitious, driven, hardworking, and high-achieving, welcoming in the season of winter. Determination and motivation are necessary forces, but in always reaching for something, there can be a lack of satisfaction with what we already have. Goal-setting requires imagination, but it can also pull us into temptation, urging us to take dangerous risks or fall into destructive patterns in our desire to win. It's here that we find the connection with the archetype of the Devil. This card asks us to consider the core of our drives, the reasons that we push ourselves, the hidden needs or secret darkness that motivates our impulses. And while Capricorn is steady and focused, rarely giving in to wildness, the obsession that any of us can develop for success or things in the material world is an intense example of the Devil at work.

> JOURNAL PROMPT: *Where is Capricorn in your natal chart? Which element does it live in? Do you have any placements in Capricorn? Think about your relationship with control: the times that it has been useful and powerful for you, and the moments when not enough or too much control has created challenges. How do you understand the Devil's version of control? Where does it differ from your own? And when might releasing a bit of control be a healthy impulse rather than a dangerous one?*

Numerological correspondence: Fifteen to Six

Fifteen consolidates to six and points us to the Lovers, an archetype of alliance and balance, acceptance and joy. Six is a number of nurturing, of identity, of self-discovery. With the Lovers we see this play out in a healthy, joyful, harmonious way; the Devil shows us what can happen when we don't exercise our power in a useful manner, or when we get so caught up in responsibility and the pursuit of freedom that we lose sight of everything else that matters to us. When our connections become toxic, when we abandon those that we care for to pursue our own selfish desires, when we resent our own responsibilities, it can leave us lost and alone, frustrated, or power-hungry.

> JOURNAL PROMPT: *The number six is closely tied to compassion and duty, concepts that are good in moderation but which can spiral out of control if we aren't careful. How do you see these ideas manifest in the Lovers and the Devil? What*

commonalities do you see between these two archetypes? How does the six speak
to challenges of perfectionism or putting a desire for harmony above all else? When
does extending grace, or feeling a strong sense of responsibility, cause problems?

In Readings

For each of us, the Devil may look a bit different. After all, in many ways there's nothing more personal than temptation, than the vices and traps and mental snares that can trip us up, distract us, lure us to stray from the path we set and the destination we've been dreaming of. Ultimately, this card asks us to consider our relationship to control, to the ways that we cling to power, to the times that we insist that we're strong enough to handle our dangerous desires and refuse help. We may see the Fool as a joyful figure of impulse and intuition, but when desire without discernment takes over, things can get messy very quickly.

What is teasing you, calling you, tugging at your imagination? What can't you say no to? Which desires are coming forward, making it impossible for you to see past them? Which addictions are surfacing, or resurfacing? How can dragging those desires into the light help you find clarity rather than staying twisted up in private shame?

16. The Tower

MARS // Strength, action, upheaval, ferocity, pursuit, willpower, motivation

SEVEN // Intelligence, duality, movement, determination, protection, responsibility

KEYWORDS // forced assessment · chaos · destruction · sudden change · transformation · unexpected movement · loss · freedom · permanent & powerful shift · experience · disruption · fear · uncertainty · lack of control · inability to discern · confusion · turbulence

We've lost our way and become distracted by our own contradictory desires. In a flash, everything changes, demanding our focus and attention. A sudden crash of thunder, a bolt of lightning, a violent earthquake knocks us off of our feet, and we find ourselves in free fall, having lost all control of where we are and where we're going. The very foundations that we've been building upon have cracked, and amidst the chaos, we simply fight for survival. Smoke fills the air, our ears ring with pain and confusion, and we choke on our fear, trapped in the destruction that surrounds us. And while in the moment it feels like everything we love is gone, after the ground stills and the fires die down, we are able to assess the damage, able to start picking ourselves up again. This can be a frightening sensation, one that brings anger, sadness, fear, grief, or hysteria as we attempt to figure out which way is up, try to regain our bearings. All we can do in these moments of madness is take it one step at a time, keeping our vision clear and our ears open. We react as best we can, try to ensure our safety, and prepare for whatever we may find when the dust clears.

Destroying something that once seemed impenetrable, tilting our world off of its axis: in this moment we are fully out of control of our own destiny, seemingly at the whims of much greater forces. This sensation of panic, this growing awareness of something breaking down, this massive and sudden upheaval, is the confused frenzy of the Tower.

· · ·

Change can be terrifying. When we've been living with certain assumptions, following a path that feels solid and firm, it's incredibly destabilizing to realize that our world is crumbling underneath our feet. Yet by the time we reach this archetype, we find ourselves in free fall, finally seeing the truth of our circumstances and no longer able to cling to our denial. The Tower is intense, chaotic, jarring; this archetype sucks out the poison, rips the rusted door off of its hinges, separates us from those things that have been holding us back. When breakage happens, sometimes we still cling to what has been harming us, believing that it's been holding us together instead of slowly shredding us to pieces. Yet when the Tower does its magic, it's a call to loosen our grip, to allow ourselves to fly, to see where we land.

Even if we know a change is needed, this card represents a massive disruption to the status quo and can feel impossible to get through when we're in the midst of it. The Tower tears away all the distractions and flaws, forcing us to see things clearly, to recognize where we've found greatness and magic and where we've dropped the ball. This shift is not just in our circumstances—it also impacts us at a core level, making fundamental adjustments that allow for intense transformation and deep, lasting growth.

As tumultuous as this experience is, it's important to remember that the Tower doesn't necessarily mean that everything we've done up to this point is worth throwing out, that our goals were foolish, or that anything we've built is trash. We're not going all the way back to the Fool, taking a leap into a brand new beginning. Rather, we're taking the pieces that work and leaving that cracked foundation behind, eventually using what we know already to build something more solid, more powerful, more authentic. Just like a forest fire that rages in heat and consumes everything in its path, when the embers stop smoldering and the smoke clears, there's space for new growth, and the plants and organisms that could not survive before are now able to thrive. Once our hearts stop pounding and we can breathe normally again, the world will look very different.

Astrological correspondence: Mars

A planet of action, intensity, conquest, and instinct, Mars rules our pursuits, helping us put all of our energy and focus into achieving what we're after. While we may see the Tower's chaos as a complete lack of control, it's undeniable that this violent, destructive force still accomplishes something major. The Tower's upheaval is a motivating energy that forces us to reconsider our movements and put our resources into the things that matter most to us. Mars is about willpower, rapid movement, ferocity, and instinct, and we see that same determination for survival and bracing for impact within the Tower. Both of these energies can be incredibly useful when wielded with intention, but they also bring necessary destruction, a breaking down of something established in order to find emancipation in the new. When we are willing to cut ourselves loose from old ties, when we go into free fall, it can reveal what we are willing to fight for and what we are willing to leave behind.

JOURNAL PROMPT: *Where does Mars fall in your chart? In which house? In which sign? Think about the movement and action-oriented focus of Mars, and the ways that willpower, survival, and instinct manifest in your own life. What does Mars have to teach you about the power of the Tower? Think of the times when you've felt the world crumbling beneath your feet—what did that shift accomplish? How do you see the Fool in this embracing of chaos, and what truths might joy offer in the midst of uncertainty?*

Numerological correspondence: Sixteen to Seven

Sixteen consolidates to seven, pointing us back to the Chariot's energy of drive, observation, and intellect. Seven's association with spirituality, questing, and rapid movement looks very different between the Chariot and the Tower—one is intentional, focused, purposeful, while the other is chaotic, unexpected, and out of control. Both cards bring us to new destinations, but in their own way. Seven can expose friction or discomfort, pushing us to challenge our own boundaries and consider the places where we want to try something new. And with the Tower, we see that manifest in the crumbling of old foundations, the leaving behind of things that are broken, beyond repair, or no longer worth investing in.

> **JOURNAL PROMPT**: *Seven is associated with movement and discovery, bringing us to another place, empowering us to pursue growth or change or healing. How do you see this manifest in the Chariot, and how does that same energy appear with the Tower? When have you experienced each of these energies, and how did it feel? Do you prefer to be in control, or do you find freedom in surrender?*

In Readings

No matter how the Tower finds us, no matter what state it leaves us in, this is an archetype of necessary, essential change. We may not enjoy it in the moment but it's often a shift that we reflect on with appreciation, even satisfaction. When this card comes forward, consider what limiting beliefs are being proven wrong, which old narratives or priorities no longer make sense.

Which fractures or fissures have you been glossing over, trying not to acknowledge? What severed pieces are you clinging to? How might letting them go make space for a healthier, more authentic future?

17. The Star

AQUARIUS // Out-of-the-box thinking, margins, social justice, community

EIGHT // Power, momentum, discipline, assurance, control, practicality

KEYWORDS // internal power · hope · healing · recovery · self-love · compassion · sovereignty · insight · changing perspectives · clarity · reflection · forward thinking · observation · bravery · imagination · inner magic · intuition · kindness · rejoining community · optimism & idealism · steadiness

The sky is clear again, the ground solid under our feet. And while things feel dark, uncertain, a gentle gleam shines far above us, brightening the sky enough that we can see a path stretching out ahead. The starlight we glimpse reminds us of our own internal fire, the dim glow of magic that we reach for, recognize, restore. We feel a powerful internal settling, filling our lungs with crisp, clean air for the first time in a long time—our body is healing, and something deep within us has been replenished. After chaos and destruction, after uncertainty, we let our inner radiance mingle and connect with the brilliant glimmers in the sky, listening once again to our most authentic, truthful self. This isn't about knowing exactly what to do, about seeing our clearest and easiest path forward—instead it's about a return to the self, about respecting that quiet, certain voice within us, about remembering and reclaiming our north star. It's about imagining all that is possible and committing to pursuing it. It's about faith that the future will be better, that we can make it so. It's about believing that we are enough, that our mistakes do not define us, that we learn from every experience.

While there are questions we can't answer, details we can't clarify, we know in our bones that everything is going to work out, that we will eventually pick ourselves up, dust ourselves off, and move forward with more strength, power, and magic than before. We acknowledge the ways that we belong to ourselves, embracing a sense of deep, personal sovereignty that empowers us to move at our own pace, in our own way. This quiet, enigmatic twinkling of distant stardust, offering a mysterious but undeniable sense of healing, restoration, and hope—this is the generous, forward-thinking medicine of the Star.

• • •

Optimism is a skill. It doesn't come without effort, doesn't magically fall into our laps. And especially after times of trauma, crisis, or upheaval, it requires a special kind of courage to be hopeful, to believe that something better is possible. All that we have endured has revealed new kinds of strength, courage, and resilience that we may not have realized we possessed. When the world is chaotic, when foundations are breaking and fires are burning and we don't know which way is up, the Star helps us remember ourselves, gives us a point of focus that reflects our magic back to us. And when we feel fully connected to who we are, we have the space to begin exploring who we could be, who we dream of becoming.

On the heels of the Tower's destruction, it's tempting to see the Star as a return to grace, finding our way back to our chosen path. But the Star isn't about being fully healed, about picking up where we left off—instead this archetype acknowledges the journey of healing that has begun, the powerful transformation that we have started and continue to endure. We open ourselves to the opportunity for joy again, remember what it felt like to be whole, and accept what we have been through as necessary. And although these experiences have fundamentally changed us in ways that cannot be ignored or taken back, we now have the chance to learn about ourselves anew, to choose a path forward that reflects who we are *now* instead of who we once were.

The Star can bring a startling clarity, a sense of personal direction, a different way to navigate. We're making a brand new map for ourselves, seeing our dreams and ambitions through the lens of our recent experiences and insights. But beyond visualizing possible futures, beyond believing that more is possible, we also reclaim our personal agency and magic. This archetype empowers us to move on our own terms, play by our own rules, create a life for ourselves that reflects our values and ambitions and convictions. We see ourselves authentically, genuinely, fully, and feel pride in the clarity of that perspective.

Astrological correspondence: Aquarius

 A sign of fixed air, Aquarius is associated with forward thinking, social consciousness, and revolution. Aquarius is unpredictable and unconventional, making its own path forward with confidence and joy, always expanding ideas and exploring new intellectual paths. And in the same way, with the Star we are learning to see the world through new eyes, to understand the shifting possibilities and opportunities after an intense transition. Aquarius has a hint of rebellion, a desire for uniqueness, and the Star encourages us to move forward, to leave pain and struggles behind and make a bright new future for ourselves.

> JOURNAL PROMPT: *Where is Aquarius in your natal chart? Which element does it live in? Do you have any placements in Aquarius? Are you someone who finds it easy to sink into an analytical mindset, or do you prefer to make decisions based on emotion? Think about the healing of the Star in combination with the community-oriented energy of Aquarius. What does it mean to dream of a better world? How do you find the Fool in this clear, bright-eyed optimism?*

Numerological correspondence: Seventeen to Eight

Seventeen consolidates to eight, a number that is powerful, level-headed, and headstrong. Like Strength, the Star empowers us to observe and take action, to move with balance and assurance, to trust in experience and wisdom. But while Strength is deeply capable of managing their own life and empowering other people, the Star takes that a step further to transform their future, to reimagine and rebuild after the dramatic shift of the Tower. There's a practicality and skill in both archetypes, the knowledge that what we do will succeed and that we are capable of reaching every one of our biggest, wildest dreams.

> JOURNAL PROMPT: *When we think about the number eight, we often first think of power. How do you find authority, control, and mastery within the archetype of*

the Star? What does it mean to look at the world with fresh eyes, and how can Strength show up within the Star's magic? How do themes of opportunity, abundance, and recovery appear in both archetypes?

In Readings

In this journey of evolution, the Star is the moment when we accept all that we've seen and done, everything we've endured, and let ourselves begin the long and essential process of healing. And in that recovery and slow restoration, we find deep, authentic faith in the future and a confidence that we will accomplish everything that our heart yearns for.

What is your most ardent wish? In the wake of dramatic change, in being able to see more clearly than ever, how can you make that dream come true? Which challenges have you passed through, and where are you still struggling? Are you searching for light in the darkness, or have you found a new north star to follow? If you allow yourself to hope, what might change?

18. The Moon

PISCES // Beliefs, dreams, the subconscious, spirituality, collectives

NINE // Observation, personal responsibility, collective growth, expansion, clarity

KEYWORDS // strange wisdom · uncertainty · exploration · internal shadows · confrontation · fantasy & reality · dreams · illusion · embracing inner wildness · cycles · growth & discovery · exploration · introspection · reflection · surrender · instinct · ferocity · freedom from convention · distance

We've rediscovered ourselves, reclaimed our future, and now move forward, eager to pursue those remembered dreams. But as we slip into the shadows, our new-found starlight grows dim. Even if we know where we want to end up, sometimes the path can grow murky, and we can get lost along the way. As the pale light of the moon strips the world of color and twists our grasp on reality, our most fantastical visions and deepest fears reveal themselves in the darkening shadows. We must rely on our intuition, our sense of wisdom and truth, to help us remember who we are, to keep us from getting too caught up in what-ifs. The mind's perceptions become clouded by the heart's fears, and as emotion takes over, we stumble, consider, work overtime to see clearly even as we crave surrender, even as we long to just run free. We have so few opportunities to completely succumb to our wildness, to go feral, to allow instinct to take over—and in giving ourselves permission to explore this untamed part of ourselves, in honoring our impulses and running barefoot through the forest and screaming at the sky, we make fierceness a part of our natural cycle. We acknowledge the need for release, fantasy, illumination. We recognize that tension and friction are not inherently bad things, and that discomfort can help us understand our own needs and desires with sharp new clarity.

This dance between dreams and reality, this odd and otherworldly exploration, this diving into our own subconscious and seeing what kinds of wildness dwell within us, are all part of the peculiar, abstract, cyclical strangeness of the Moon.

· · ·

Fantasy can be an uncomfortable world to inhabit. Sifting through our own fears and cravings, shadows and secrets, unknowns and uncertainties, can be a jarring, off-putting experience. Yet when we allow ourselves to get lost in our own dreams, when we find beauty in the darkness, there can be such wonder to discover. There's essential medicine in exploring our own mysteries, in letting ourselves examine the truths that we are usually unwilling or afraid to acknowledge—and when we work with the Moon, we give in to those hidden impulses, discover where we end up when we surrender any sense of restraint and dive into our own enchanting, intoxicating wildness.

Combining our natural cycles with the many layers of our own subconscious, the Moon is a card of enigmatic awareness, initiating moments when we release expectation and simply move through dreams and fantasies with nothing but our impulses. We see where our mind leads us when we stop controlling it, where our imagination can expand to without any boundaries or restrictions. This can sometimes bring fear or anxiety, a concern that we will get too lost in the shadows to find our way back to reality. And indeed, the Moon can be associated with a feral fierceness, the kind of authenticity that isn't pretty or subdued. But in acknowledging these more hidden parts of ourselves, we can learn to appreciate our shadows, our fears, our darkness, rather than smothering or hiding from them. By moving purely on instinct, by exploring that unrestrained unknown within us, we may find that the shifts and changes that we've endured now push us in new, brilliant directions.

Moving through the emotional and spiritual worlds without restriction or hesitation can take practice; it may feel awkward or unnatural. The Moon serves as our patient guide in this endeavor, illuminating the world with its pale and ghostly light, keeping us company as we howl and run and dance and stretch through the wilds of our own psyche. But we learn so much about ourselves in sifting through our messy essential nature, in interrogating our own eccentricities. Making space for our feelings and our instincts without judgment or ridicule isn't always easy; the world rarely lets us be confused or tangled up for long. Yet there are many layers to all of us, shrouded truths that we may not be able to uncover and delve into without first exposing them. We can't deal with fears or fury that we refuse to acknowledge, with secrets that we keep from ourselves.

Astrological correspondence: Pisces

The last sign of the zodiac and the astrological calendar is Pisces, a sign of mutable water. Spiritual and intuitive, with a vivid imagination and a rich connection to their emotions, Pisces is comfortable exploring the deep waters of their internal selves. It can be challenging to be so immersed in feelings that are often unpredictable or overwhelming—yet Pisces is capable of expansive creativity, rich artistry, deep compassion, and brilliant sensitivity. The Moon is similarly known for cycles and endless shifting phases, an archetype of mystery and madness. Ruler of dreams and secrets, that wild unknown beyond consciousness, the Moon invites us to explore and surrender to our own innate wildness, to recognize the desires and fears we carry, to pay attention to our visions and fantasies.

> JOURNAL PROMPT: *Where is Pisces in your natal chart? Which element does it live in? Do you have any placements in Pisces? Sinking into our subconscious can be an intense experience—do you find this a frightening prospect, or an enjoyable one? What do you learn from your dreams and fantasies, and how often do you deliberately explore your desires? How does the energy of Pisces help you see the Moon archetype in a new light? How does the Fool's dreamy nature find comfort in this archetype and sign?*

Numerological correspondence: Eighteen to Nine

Connected to isolation, individuality, and anticipation, nines are thoughtful and observant, traits we see clearly within the Hermit. But there's also a sense of the unexpected within this figure, a desire for discovery and exploration that is mirrored in the Moon's mystery and illusory wandering. The number nine is also deeply tied to service, philanthropy, and humanitarian efforts, a theme that may feel unusual for the Moon. However, when we consider the fantasies that come forward when we make space for them, when we imagine the world as we desire it rather than as we experience it, those dreams can start to take up space, and we can start to consider possible pathways toward the life we want. Both the Hermit and the Moon are very introspective, but they also go deep within, urging us to pursue authenticity, trust in the self, and generosity.

Nines are the last number in the sequence, inviting us to consider how the Moon can set us up to begin a new cycle. In exploring the self in a wild, fearless way, we make space for blazing new trails, pursuing new goals, opening up new doors.

JOURNAL PROMPT: *The number nine is a complex one, balancing internal explora-tion with external generosity. How do these archetypes empower us to serve? What do we learn about ourselves from engaging with both the Hermit and the Moon? How have you experienced each of these archetypes in your own life, and which one were you more comfortable with? Why?*

In Readings

With the Moon, we take the revelations that we found with the Tower, and the hope that we cultivated with the Star, and put those truths to the test. What we discover within ourselves, hiding in our wildness, can help us begin a new chap-ter, inviting clarity, understanding, and purpose.

What does it mean to believe in yourself, even when fear and uncertainty are present? How does it feel to reckon with your deepest shadows, your most complex anxieties? How do your fantasies and dreams spin out into new terri-tory, pull you into unexpected terrain? What do you dream about when no one is watching? Where do you go in your mind when you need an escape from reality? What do you hesitate to examine or acknowledge, and what holds you back from embracing those shadowy sides of yourself?

FINDING THE FOOL

19. The Sun

SUN // Illumination, clarity, life force, vitality, purpose

ONE // Motivation, confidence, independence, vision, trail blazing

KEYWORDS // multiplying sparks · abundance · clarity · celebration · community · achievement · joy · play · triumph · awareness & openness · self-pride · acceptance · dignity · inspiration · full disclosure · laughter · self-expression · unification

As the darkness of night gives way to gentle dawn, our world begins to reveal itself clearly. Lingering shadows slowly disappear. We're able to see ourselves, our path forward, and everything around us with sharpness, vitality, clarity—and after all that we've endured, all that we've achieved, all that we've discovered, a feeling of pure joy fills us. We dance in the sunshine, laugh and shout and sing, grab those we love, and celebrate the moment in a rich expression of community, opulence, and pleasure. Fear of the unknown no longer dominates us, and instead we understand that we are beings of light and shadow, hope and hesitation, awe and inspiration. We are not one simple thing, on one singular path, with one specific purpose. Instead we contain multitudes, scramble through multiple cycles simultaneously, grow and release and evolve in overlapping, brilliant rhythms. The blood pulsing through our veins, the breath flowing through our lungs, the new ideas that burst into our minds and hearts are all essential pieces of who we are. And in honoring every step of this journey, in recognizing our triumphs and mistakes, in finding joy even in the midst of impossible moments, we experience the delight and satisfaction of rich internal abundance.

Radiance floods our world, sparks are shooting out every which way, and we feel euphoria bubbling up within us, reminding us to take pleasure wherever we can find it. Music and laughter, love and relationships, celebration and bountiful connection: this sensation of being fully present, utterly content, entirely hopeful, is the bright, wondrous warmth of the Sun.

• • •

When we illuminate all of our deepest, darkest corners, truths get exposed. And although this can be an arduous process, it allows us to integrate our wonders and our worries, to stop denying the fullness of who we are and instead feel a sense of restoration, celebration. The Sun teaches us to dance in both the bright sunshine and the flickering firelight, to recognize the ways that the magic in our fantasies and realities comes together. Secrets are no longer something to fear and we release any lingering shame around the dreams and desires that we've hidden for so long. Here, we celebrate just how far we've come and luxuriate in knowing that our goals are within reach.

There's a spirit of revelry in this card, a playful, childlike joy that bubbles up and inspires us to dance, sing, relax. So much of the Fool's journey can feel solitary, but the Sun urges us to connect with our communities, to share our triumphs, to be generous and indulgent with all that we have. We've worked hard, overcome much, allowed ourselves to be changed by the odyssey that we've been on. Rather than dwelling on past hurts or worrying about the next fork in the road, we turn our faces to the light and allow ourselves to be deeply, fully, authentically present. We take delight and pleasure in where we are, feel a sense of personal alchemy, soak up the warmth.

However, after the gentle luminescence of the Star and the Moon, the Sun can be brighter than we're ready for. Left unchecked, that steady, intense blaze can burn delicate skin or blind sensitive eyes. The Sun's indiscriminate glare exposes truths that we had not yet acknowledged, even dragging deeply buried secrets out in a way that is uncomfortable or unsettling. But the gift of this card is in calling us to slowly open ourselves to the brilliance around us, to appreciate this benevolent energy, to find triumph in the process of illumination. And in owning our scars, in acknowledging where we are not perfect, we can access power, magic, even pleasure. We are survivors, victors, fighters. We have endured, and we have achieved. We are brave, perhaps wielding more strength than we ever realized. And in this moment, we celebrate.

Astrological correspondence: Sun

 The center of our solar system and the vitalizing force of all life on earth, the sun is clarity and abundance, light, ego, and courage. And while in our birth charts our sun placement serves as our center of gravity, giving us insights into the ways that we move through the world, in tarot the Sun comes near the end of our journey and serves as a period of joy, celebration, fulfillment. It brings deep satisfaction in where and who we are. There's a clarity to both the planet and the archetype, recognition and acknowledgment, an open examination of the self and a pride in the independence that we have found. But there's also a powerful integration in this card, the alchemy between our light and our darkness, our fears and our hopes, our movement and our rest. The Sun archetype teaches us to stop hiding, to be transparent about our desires and needs, to believe in more. Just like the sun's warmth and life-giving light, we need hope to survive and to thrive.

JOURNAL PROMPT: *Where does the Sun fall in your chart? In which house? In which sign? Sun signs are so often considered the most important of a natal chart, yet this is just one piece of our personal astrological puzzle. How do you relate to your Sun sign, and what might that teach you about your perception of the Sun archetype? Are you comfortable or uncomfortable with this card's meanings of abundance, celebration, and connection? How do you see those manifest in your own life, and what brings you true joy?*

Numerological correspondence: Nineteen to Ten to One

Nineteen consolidates to ten, which brings us back to one and the Magician. Ones are powerfully present, motivated, strong-willed, and confident, ready to take on new challenges while staying focused on their bigger goals and dreams. With passion and dominance, the number one is independent and assertive, a pioneer that is ready to push forward and create impactful change. And with the Sun, that clarity of purpose and powerful sense of self is magnified, boosted in a way that everyone around us can also see and feel. When we step into full alignment with ourselves, when we allow our desires and accomplishments to take up as much space as necessary, it gives us new courage, deeper threads of magic. One as a number is deeply tied to individual authenticity, and with the Sun, we see the ways that being our true self allows others to find us, support us, and cheer us on.

JOURNAL PROMPT: *The Sun encapsulates themes of both individual achievement and community celebration—how do you see each of these ideas manifesting within the number one? Do you see the Fool in this card? What ties do you find between the Magician, the Wheel, and the Sun? How does working with the Magician help to expand your perspective on all of the one archetypes?*

In Readings

This isn't the end of the road, isn't the culmination of all of our efforts—but we're getting close. We can taste it, that shift on the horizon. The Sun reveals our path, helps us see our way clearly, reminds us of our strength and our purpose. With this archetype we acknowledge our radiance, our brilliance, our abundance.

What do you love about the life you're living? Where do you feel triumph and comfort, happiness, strength? Which connections have grown, which dreams have flourished, which aspirations have revealed themselves? How does understanding your shadows and fears give you courage to face them head-on?

20. Judgment

PLUTO // Transformation, power, destruction, change, release, regeneration

TWO // Sensitivity, intuition, psychic wisdom, choice, awareness, duality

KEYWORDS // a necessary internal crossroads · forgiveness · awareness · self-acceptance · compassion · a final choice · release · clarity · generosity · moving forward · stepping out of a cycle · consequences · evaluation · confidence · transformation · belief in the self · taking a chance

With fresh revelations behind us and our destination now within reach, we find ourselves hesitating. Everything we have been dreaming of, everything we have been striving for, is a heartbeat away—yet we know that we have one final, essential choice to make. There is something heavy that we've been clinging to since the very beginning, something that we have carried through every step on this journey, something that we have integrated so deeply into who we are that it feels like it's always been there. And whether it's guilt, fear, anger, sorrow, loneliness, frustration, or something else, that tender piece is weighing us down, holding us back. When we first began the journey, this piece of our history may have spurred us on, given us courage, helped us remember what we were working toward. But the sharp memory of who we were no longer benefits us; instead it prevents us from completely evolving, from reaching the fullness of everything we crave. The only way that we can cross that threshold, enter this new stage, is by setting down this burden and forgiving ourselves for who we no longer are. In acknowledging our struggles, in showing ourselves compassion and grace, we are able to fully move forward. We have all that we need to fully realize our biggest, wildest, most beautiful dreams; we just need to be brave enough to release the old and grasp the new with trembling hands.

Even this last step is one into the unknown—but it's one that we choose, one that we own. This final period of awareness, this desire to forgive ourselves, this ability to see ourselves clearly and accept the person that we have become: this is the certain, generous, compassionate energy of Judgment.

• • •

There comes a point when we are the only ones holding the keys to our own cage. Every barrier has been removed, every obstacle has been overcome, and the only things standing in our way are our own hesitations, our own fears, our own baggage. Judgment asks us to sit with that truth, to examine where we are, and to forgive ourselves for the person that we once were, the people that we haven't been able to be. We consider the path that we've taken, the choices and twists and turns, the many ways that we've grown and changed along the way. And we look at the pieces of ourselves that we haven't yet been able to release, the bits that still feel scared or scarred, that we're afraid to let go of. We might not know who we are without our anger, our jealousy, our fears. We may have gotten so used to certain kinds of pain that the idea of living without it leaves us breathless and paralyzed, unsure of who we'd be otherwise. But Judgment makes space for all of that confusion and asks us to try anyway, to trust ourselves enough to keep growing. With Judgment we acknowledge what we are, and what we are not.

As the last step in the Fool's journey, Judgment sets the stage for one final integration. In recognizing the things that we've been afraid to release, in validating any old identities that we've been unable to leave behind, we can break through all of those old limits, and find authentic freedom within ourselves. When an emotion, experience, or belief feels like an essential part of us, it can be hard to see past—hard to imagine ourselves without that trauma, without those scars, without our most deeply held fears. Judgment doesn't ask us to forget that person, doesn't demand that we abandon our past or our memories or our failures. But it does ask that we forgive ourselves, that we make space for new possibilities, that we embrace all that we are and all that we are becoming. Judgment encourages us to look at ourselves clearly, rather than clinging to memories of who we used to be, who we dreamed of becoming. This is a mirror, not a photograph.

In challenging the beliefs that we hold about ourselves, in questioning our personal narratives, we simultaneously open ourselves up to new truths. It's not easy to see ourselves through a new lens, to call ourselves out on our own bullshit. But with Judgment we set ourselves free, which can bring both unease and deep, intense relief. It's an awakening, an emerging, a moment when we accept our own power and magic, and finally believe the full truth about ourselves. We recognize our purpose and acknowledge that we are truly strong enough to fulfill it.

Astrological correspondence: Pluto

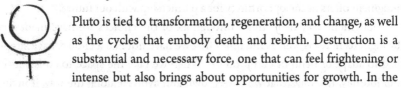

Pluto is tied to transformation, regeneration, and change, as well as the cycles that embody death and rebirth. Destruction is a substantial and necessary force, one that can feel frightening or intense but also brings about opportunities for growth. In the major arcana, Judgment comes right before the end of the cycle, giving us one last push toward full evolution—and as part of that journey, we have to release some aspect of self, some old wound or fear or doubt that has been preventing us from full change. In forgiveness, we find freedom, and that can be a very empowering shift, enabling us to truly move on from old patterns, beliefs, fears, or desires in a purposeful and healing way. Pluto and Judgment both bring revelation, helping us embrace clarity, truth, and purpose. We learn things about ourselves that we may have never acknowledged before.

> JOURNAL PROMPT: *Where does Pluto fall in your chart? In which house? In which sign? Where have you experienced major transformations in your life, and how did it impact your own sense of growth, agency, and power? Consider what you know about Pluto and the relationship that you have with forgiveness. How might your Pluto placement create new layers of meaning for the ways that this archetype appears in your life?*

Numerological correspondence: Twenty to Two

Twenty consolidates to two, a digit associated with choice, consideration, and careful reflection, brimming with a deep desire to understand and be aware of all of the layers involved in a situation before making a decision. Both the High Priestess and Judgment are about making a decision that will set a new series of things into motion, allowing our deepest desires and needs to guide our path. And while the High Priestess appears very early in the Fool's journey, helping us clarify our purpose before the outward expression of the Empress, Judgment is the second to last card in the major arcana, the final transformative effort before the completion of the World. If the Priestess is a partnership with the self and Justice is a partnership with society, Judgment offers us the opportunity for a partnership with our future.

Judgment asks us to think through all of the choices we have made that brought us here, as well as the times that we have not had a choice, have simply had to adapt or bend or compromise. When we take the space to consider the full journey, the ways that we have grown and evolved along the way, it invites deeper compassion and empowers us to forgive past versions of ourselves for any mistakes, regrets, or uncertainties. Only by nurturing our spirit can we fully let the past go and step into our future with clear, determined eyes.

JOURNAL PROMPT: *In thinking about Judgment, we make space for introspection, awareness, and new discoveries. What does it mean to be fully authentic? How do you understand the two's major arcana archetypes of the High Priestess, Justice, and Judgment? What story do these three archetypes tell together? How do they each serve as a crossroads? And where does the energy of the Fool come into this archetype?*

In Readings

When working with Judgment, it's essential to balance grace with truth, to recognize where expectations about potential have manifested and where they've left us longing for more. The stories that we tell ourselves are rarely the full and complete truth, and in leaving self-limiting beliefs behind, the whole world opens up before us. There is always room to grow—yet we can define success for ourselves, can empower ourselves to set down old burdens that have been holding us back.

How deeply do you believe in yourself? Which personal convictions have you never challenged? Why have you been afraid to evolve? How has your world view expanded, and where do you fit into this new vision of the future and yourself?

21. The World

SATURN // Mastery, discipline, boundaries, responsibility, structure

THREE // Innovation, creativity, expression, growth, manifestation

KEYWORDS // expansion of self · completion · full circle · stability · clarity · joy · personal power · serenity · calm · rest & recovery · abundance · satisfaction · completed cycle · knowing something is finished · overflowing magic · tranquility · strength · personal fulfillment

Everything is still, calm, stable. Our feet are firmly on the ground, our hearts are full, our minds are clear, our souls are satisfied. Air fills our lungs slowly, purposefully, and we release each breath with joy, satisfaction, and power. We feel held, supported, encouraged, inspired, content, secure, joyful. Our goals have been reached and surpassed, our dreams have come true beyond measure, our magic has expanded beyond our wildest expectations. We have all that we need, perhaps even enough to share with those we love, with those who have less. It's almost too good to be true, the joy that overflows and surrounds us, the confidence that sustains us, the optimism that calms us. We feel like the best possible version of ourselves and can hardly remember what it felt like to be the person that we were at the beginning of our journey. Yet in spite of the happiness and satisfaction that we feel, in spite of the ways that we have grown and evolved and connected, we know that this sensation will not last forever. Eventually a new dream will start to curl around the edges of our consciousness, will capture our fancy, will demand that we begin the cycle of growth and creation anew. But for now, all is still, peaceful, utterly right.

This tension between joyful serenity and curious anticipation, this understanding that all is well at the present paired with the knowledge that movement is inevitable, is the magical fulfillment and tranquil ease of the World.

• • •

Dreams come true. After all the magic and wisdom and creation and chaos, the discoveries and shifts and reflections, the periods of struggle and the times of deep healing, we've completed a cycle, evolved into something new. That elusive dream that began with the Fool, the power and insight and structure and focus that we found through the course of the major arcana, has now been fully realized, and we are forever changed by the journey we've taken. The World is an important ending: one that invites a new beginning.

This energy can be a lot to grapple with. For many of us, it can be impossible to acknowledge our work as finished, to see our longings as fully realized, to feel true fulfillment and pleasure in our present. But as hard as it can be to honor these moments of real satisfaction, it's so important to take time to appreciate progress, to mark times of triumph. Rather than seeing this card as representative of perfection or completion, it may be easier to consider this a leveling up of sorts: an opportunity to rest and commemorate the moment, to take pride and delight in how far we've come. With the World, we look at the person we've become, the vision that's now a reality, and we are filled with joy and strength. We can look at the work we've done, the intention we set and fulfilled, and be proud of the thing we achieved. But bigger than that, we can reflect on the evolutions we ourselves have undergone, the ways that our wisdom has expanded, our intuition has deepened, our patience has grown, and rejoice in this new person that overflows with magic, with courage, with brilliance.

It's with the World that we find ourselves both forgiven and reborn, ready to begin the cycle anew. This card is not the end of everything, but it does signify a major milestone, a powerful evolution, an important celebration. While it may be tempting to immediately rush to the next ambition, the World urges us to take some time to celebrate, relax, enjoy the fruits of our labors. This is the stillness that comes with satisfaction, a deep exhale, a powerful triumph. In recognizing our completed transformation, we can feel real joy, dignity, pride, even, with the quiet knowledge that eventually we will find ourselves reaching for another star in the sky, asking more questions.

Astrological correspondence: Saturn

Ruling structures, limits, boundaries, and discipline, Saturn teaches us about responsibility, saying no, and keeping track of our time. This may seem like a strange pairing for the World, an archetype of completion, satisfaction, and evolution—but Saturn also speaks to mastery, reaching our full potential, and having the focus to achieve our goals. The World is not simply about finished projects or complete perfection, about having accomplished every single thing we ever wanted to do. But it does help us recognize good work, the ways that we protect ourselves as we progress, and gives us the space to be proud of our achievements. With Saturn and the World, we honor our own discipline and take satisfaction in how far we have come.

JOURNAL PROMPT: *Where does Saturn fall in your chart? In which house? In which sign? Does Saturn feel empowering to you, or does it make you uncomfortable to imagine saying no, drawing boundaries, or creating limits? What is your relationship to rules, time, and responsibility? And how might your Saturn placement impact your understanding of what it means to complete something?*

Numerological correspondence: Twenty-one to Three

Twenty-one consolidates to three, pointing us back to the Empress. This archetype is innovative, creative, brimming with joy and positivity, demonstrating the number three's powerful expression and brilliant promise. While the World is a definitive ending through one lens, an idea or expression or change taken as far as it can go, it also sets up our next beginning. The World is not about perfection, but about evolution, about the constant cycles of birth, growth, death, and rebirth that we are endlessly moving through.

Even within the structure and finality of the World, there's still that sense of possibility that we find within the number three. There's an opportunity for new expansion, without the worry around exactly what it will look like yet, or which form it may take. Our growth may be tangible, expressed in a way that others can see and celebrate—but we are not finished, are never finished. This ending is paving the way for our next beginning, helping us see ourselves through a new lens that we will carry forward into another adventure.

JOURNAL PROMPT: *How could the World be expressive, authentic, connective? Which similarities do you see between the Empress, the Hanged One, and the World? How do they each explore various facets of the number three? What does it mean to have the cycle of the major arcana end on a three, and how does that diversify your understanding of this number?*

In Readings

When the World comes forward, it's confirmation that we are worthy, that we are enough, that we are already whole. Even if this archetype emerges in the midst of a cycle, it still calls us to believe in ourselves, to appreciate progress, to celebrate our present. Instead of struggling against this kind of steady, contented fulfillment, this card asks us to embrace it, to find joy in all that we have been through.

Who have you become in pursuing this particular dream? How has your original objective grown and changed along with you? And in embracing this ending, how do you anticipate the Fool's energy beginning to build once again, or manifesting in a new way?

THE MINOR ARCANA

Every day is not a major arcana day, and every event is not a major arcana event. Throughout our time on earth, we face constant choices, obstacles, joys, and challenges as we tackle work, play, connection, solitude, rest, creation, celebration, loss, and gradual shifts. The minor arcana includes fifty-six cards separated into four suits of fourteen cards each and explores the ways that we grow physically, emotionally, spiritually, and creatively in our daily lives. Each suit moves from ace through ten and also features four court cards, who offer different approaches to harnessing their particular brand of magic.

The four minor arcana suits are each associated with both an element and an aspect of self:

Wands // Fire explore our driving force, the sparks that live within our souls and propel us to creation, motivation, creativity, development, and personal passions.

Swords // Air analyze our personal intellect, the ways that we use knowledge, logic, communication, ambition, and understanding to seek truth and clarify our experiences.

Cups // Water flow through our heart center and give us insights into emotions, relationships, connections, empathy, and intuition, showing us how we relate to and engage with other people and with our deepest, most personal selves.

Pentacles // Earth ground us in the physical world, including themes of health, wealth, family, legacy, career, and sensation, giving us anchors to tactile sensations and embodiment.

The numbered cards of ace through ten are typically referred to as pips, and we can find similarities across the four elements and suits:

Aces (Ones) begin the journey and reveal the full potential and power of the suit, inciting a spark of inspiration, insight, clarity, or energy that pushes us to start something new.

Twos bring us to a moment of choice, as we consider options, make a plan, and decide how we want to achieve our new goal in a way that also creates balance.

Threes indicate our first tangible steps, as we tap into authentic expression, make visible and expansive progress, and grant others access to our work.

Fours explore boundaries and foundations, as we use rationality and limits to protect ourselves and move at a steady, deliberate pace.

Fives reveal a critical point of change and uncertainty as we experience friction, clarify our purpose, and move through obstacles.

Sixes find us making a transition, experiencing harmony and freedom, leaving old habits behind, and establishing new relationships.

Sevens are for assessment and seeking, recognizing what we've accomplished and taking wise, thoughtful, meaningful action toward our clarified objective.

Eights depict personal power and new kinds of stress, as we press on with bold intention and begin to feel the momentum of our journey shifting.

Nines make space for individual achievement and incoming change, emphasizing how close we are to the end of the journey.

Tens clarify what happens when we push the energy of the suit to the limit, giving us opportunities for celebration and reflection, and defining the ending of a cycle—which in turn sets the stage for the next one to begin.

Each of the forty numbered pip cards is a combination of an element and a number, giving them their own unique flavor, dignity, and purpose. The sixteen court cards depict each of the four elements through the lens of individual people and can be used in various ways. Some readers use these cards as signifiers, choosing one to represent themselves or the person they're reading for. Others view these cards as specific people in their lives who may hold the particular combination of energy and authority represented by the figure depicted. You may also read court cards as aspects of the self, urging you to embrace a particular quality, power, or intention.

However you interpret court cards, their structure offers various ways to understand and utilize these energetic combinations:

Pages are students, philosophers, seekers, novices: motivated people that are questioning and expanding their own natural abilities. Curious, eager, and unafraid to break the rules, these students explore and experiment, trying whatever intrigues them. Pages are the eleventh card of the suit.

Knights are adventurers, explorers, apprentices, travelers: competitive figures that are eager to prove themselves with a quest or a challenge, that have gained knowledge and now want to put their ideas to the test through experiences. Knights are the twelfth card of the suit.

Queens are compassionate, self-assured leaders, and bring insight, observation, boundaries, creativity, and precision to their work: they teach and transform, guiding others with gentle wisdom and encouraging everyone around them to be the best possible version of themselves. Queens are the thirteenth card of the suit.

Kings are discerning, attentive leaders, and provide clarity, authority, shape, vision, and organization to their realm: they advise and challenge, helping others make actionable and lasting change through individual and community efforts. Kings are the fourteenth card of the suit.

• • •

As you work with the minor arcana, take care not to dismiss these cards just because they aren't as flashy or dramatic as the major arcana. These cards are depictions of familiar daily experiences: building, changing, observing, growing, celebrating, fighting, retreating, learning, moving, resting, being. Take these cards seriously, treat them with respect, and you will uncover many layers of meaning and power within your readings.

When it comes to the interpretations that I share in these pages, take what resonates, and leave anything that doesn't behind. These descriptions are in no way definitive and are meant to offer you a place to start, with plenty of room to grow. Record your discoveries in your journal, ask questions, and remember the energy of the Fool and the magic of discovery.

You are writing your own language: let your intuition be your guide.

THE SUIT OF WANDS

FIRE

Passion, inspiration, creativity, drive, purpose, instinct, associated with the soul

Fire is the fastest-moving element in the tarot, and the suit of wands explores our motivating force: the sparks that live deep within and drive us to invention, spirituality, and personal passions. These are the dynamic, influential desires that give our lives shape, that establish our place in the world, that provide insights into who we are—foundational, lifelong cycles of pursuit and transformation that help us understand what we love, what we crave, what we hunger for.

As an element, fire is bewitching, intoxicating, compelling in its temptation and inspiration. It burns hot and bright, demands our attention, captures our fancy with its flickering light and beautiful, complex movements. Fire is tied to the primal self, our natural sense of instinct, adventure, passion, and motivation, our celebration of the erotic. Through this concept of soul fire, we can explore the interests and ideals that animate us, inspire us, drive us, keep us captivated and engaged. The flames and embers reflect our impulses toward both creation and destruction, the ways that bright ambitions or risky ventures can build a blaze of glory or leave us smoldering in a pile of ash. What do we lust for? What can't we stay away from? What connects our various passions and pleasures, offers joy and rejuvenation, captures our imagination?

In the same way, the suit of wands ignites our most progressive, enthusiastic aspirations, the burning ache within us that pushes us to try new things, take new chances, pursue new goals. Within these cards we find themes of adventure, risk, passion, promise, ingenuity, awe, willpower, collaboration, trail blazing, and attraction—in other words, the suit of wands tells the story of inspiration and reflects the ways that we utilize that inspiration for better or worse. With the suit of fire we acknowledge the fantasies and ambitions that matter to us on a fundamental level, the hungers that we cannot possibly deny. Wands help us realize our potential, urge us to be brave and authentic, empower us to chase our dreams and never give up.

Of course, the faster we burn, the faster we burn out. The stakes are high. There's inherent unpredictability in this level of pursuit. In devoting ourselves to something that matters deeply to us, that feels tied to our happiness, confidence, and sense of self, we take chances, try new things, may even put ourselves in danger. While the suit of wands has much joy to offer, these cards also show the darker side of the fire element: the potential for restlessness, impatience, distraction, destruction. As excited and inspired as we may be by our latest creative vision, fire can devour and scorch, blazing through our reserves and leaving us exhausted or directionless. With so much light and heat, it can be a challenge to stay focused or commit to seeing something through to the end, and this suit acknowledges the struggles we may face in bringing our creative vision to life.

• • •

As you get to know the suit of wands and the element of fire, consider instinct, purpose, motivation. What lights you up, sets you ablaze, pushes you to reach and strive and dream? What never fails to excite you, energize you, electrify you? When do you feel like you're doing exactly what you're meant to be doing? And how do fiery cycles of creation and destruction contribute to your own personal pursuits of transformation?

Ace of Wands

ONE // Motivation, confidence, independence, vision, trail blazing

FIRE // Passion, inspiration, creativity, drive, purpose, instinct, associated with the soul

KEYWORDS // innovation · catalyst · creative spark · a new idea · high energy · excitement

Out of nowhere, inspiration strikes. Like a match igniting, light and heat instantly fill us up, capturing our attention and feeding our creativity. We're entranced by the dancing flame; we scramble to absorb every last detail, overwhelmed by the excitement and passion and pure delight that flow through us. That instantaneous spark, that explosion of vitality, that magical gift from the muse—that is the crackling brilliance of the Ace of Wands.

• • •

An original idea can start a fire in our belly, put flames in our eyes, give us the itch to use those flashes at our fingertips to generate something wild, new, inspiring. The Ace of Wands is an invitation to innovation, a spirit of adventure, a joyful expression of possibility and potential. In this beginning we find optimism, wonder, and opportunity: the magic that comes when the sky is the limit, when anything and everything feels attainable.

Aces and ones are the mark of a fresh start, a powerful beginning, a desire to make change. In the suit of wands, we embark on a creative quest, an imaginative and deeply personal initiative. This is a time for dreaming, for visions, for passion—everything within us is brimming with abstract concepts and far-off theories. We don't know yet what we'll be able to accomplish, what might actually come true, but that isn't the point just yet. This is raw energy, fervent desire, intense and unrestrained enthusiasm.

This card invites optimism, even idealism, urging us to let our fantasies build and our impulse to create run wild. There are no silly ideas, no small dreams, no ridiculous notions. This ace says *yes* to everything, urging us to begin something fresh and different, to see where our artistry can lead us when we embrace freedom and resources. And beyond serving as a catalyst for change and transformation, this card also represents something deep within us being able to break free, demanding to be seen. There's an authenticity to the Ace of Wands that urges us to be our true selves, to seize freedom and pursue what we really crave. When our desires are empowered to take up space, when we take our own longings seriously, change becomes imminent.

In Readings

This card is usually an indication that things are about to start moving quickly, that ideas will rush forward, and our imaginations will run wild. It's an incredible feeling, getting excited about something new, trying to get everything down on paper before it slips away—and it's absolutely one to be celebrated. But this is also a fleeting, temporal kind of energy, one that we need to utilize rather than analyze. Starting something important and lasting will take more than a shiny and captivating vision, and this ace is only the beginning. As the fastest moving suit in the minor arcana, wands hold a powerful lesson, reminding us to maintain balance and control, to not get so swept away by the blaze that we lose sight of our ultimate goal.

> **JOURNAL PROMPT:** *What fires you up, turns you on, feeds your magic? What raw potential is revealing itself? How can you use this momentum to propel yourself toward something that you've been dreaming of?*

Two of Wands

TWO // Sensitivity, intuition, psychic wisdom, choice, awareness, duality

FIRE // Passion, inspiration, creativity, drive, purpose, instinct, associated with the soul

KEYWORDS // planning & organizing · slowing down · clarifying intentions · finding purpose · anticipation

The fire is still burning brightly but we have a decision to make: how to sustain the flame? What to feed it, how to support it, where to shelter it? Our eagerness to move forward and begin the process of creation may feel overwhelming, yet in this moment we know that we have to make critical decisions about our next steps, to clarify and understand our full vision. This sitting with our thoughts, reflecting on what we really want, is the considerate pause and essential awareness of the Two of Wands.

• • •

Honoring our desires isn't all about action; it also requires patience with the self, taking the space to clarify and sharpen our vision. The Two of Wands sits in the restless tension of an idea that demands our attention and a longing to make sure those ambitions succeed. Rather than burning out before we can even get started, the Two of Wands makes space for consideration and focus, asking us if we have what it takes to get this project off the ground.

This isn't about dousing brilliant flames with cold water, isn't meant to discourage or dissuade us. Fire is quick and agile, able to burn brightly as soon as we strike the match—but here we're asked to remember the partnership and duality of the number two, to let the embers smolder, to give ourselves time to think. What will it take to accomplish this dream? How can we build what we want in the most authentic way possible? Are we ready and willing to devote ourselves to this cause, or is this something that we might need to shelve for a while? Just because we have a great idea doesn't mean that we have to execute it right now. Would it be better to pursue this objective down the road, to let it simmer and stew for a bit?

In the process of assessing our current bandwidth, the Two of Wands creates space for out-of-the-box thinking, for bold ideas and unique strategies, for authentic reflection. This is a crossroads of manifestation, an opportunity to do something different: we don't have to pursue our vision the same way that everyone else does, use the same old road map or resources or tools. Instead, this is a chance to dream big, to truly blaze our own trail, to think about what makes the most sense for us and our skills. Whether we decide to do the damn thing right now or promise ourselves that we'll follow through at a later date, the Two of Wands wants us to be true to ourselves and to honor the ways that this particular project will let us express something deeply and profoundly important.

In Readings

This card demands that we move with patience and purpose, that we go forward only if we know that we can commit. In taking the time to assess our needs, gather fuel, and put together a plan for feeding those flames, we can make sure that our fire endures, that our vision persists. In making choices about what we really want to accomplish, we can ensure that our dreams will come true, that our work will not fall short.

JOURNAL PROMPT: *What does the final version of this project actually look like? How do you envision your ideal, and how might you achieve it? What necessary steps will you have to take to reach your goals? What might this dream require, and are you up to the task? And what might you need to organize or delegate or postpone in order to make it happen?*

Three of Wands

THREE // Innovation, creativity, expression, growth, manifestation

FIRE // Passion, inspiration, creativity, drive, purpose, instinct, associated with the soul

KEYWORDS // making dreams reality · manifestation · looking ahead · collaboration ·
taking action

Once clarity has been found, once we have a distinctive idea of what we hope to achieve with our work, our plans are refined and we get to work. Our creation starts to manifest in the world, our original vision coming to life before our eyes. Yet so much of what we are doing in the present is represented by our dreams for the future, and as we look ahead, we innovate and imagine, celebrate and generate. In this moment of growth, in seeing hope of that final fantasy in our current work, we embody the momentum and ambition of the Three of Wands.

· · ·

Our energy has been building, and now that we've captured and clarified the spark of an idea, have committed to feeding and sustaining it, we *act*. The Three of Wands is the moment in a new project when things start to come together, when we take tangible, actionable steps toward our vision. We've started doing the work and are eagerly awaiting results, feeling an intoxicating sense of anticipation, wonder, expansion. As we run toward our destiny, as we feel our magic building and changing, our ideas find purchase, and we burn with awe, wonder, and pride.

The Three of Wands represents individual growth and expansion, but it also speaks to community, collective energy, and the gathering of external resources. It isn't just us anymore, alone with our sparks and hope, dreaming of turning a little crackle of heat into a rolling flame—now others are beginning to see the potential in our work, getting caught up in our energy and ambition. Remember three's energy of connection and amplification: in putting our creativity and expression out into the world, we attract attention and eagerly share our plans with those we trust, inviting them to come along for the ride.

There's an awareness of both present and future in this card, the overlapping knowledge that what we're doing right now will directly contribute to the vision we are holding in our minds and hearts. After all of our planning and dreaming, after envisioning what we hope to achieve, every action feels tethered to our desires. It's satisfying to create, it's pleasurable knowing that others can see our accomplishments, it's exciting to be charting a course toward a distant horizon—yet we also feel a bit restless in our eagerness, impatient for things to come together as quickly as possible. We are simultaneously working hard and waiting with bated breath, focusing on everything that's building while actively dreaming of more, sitting in this creation of activation and wondering what may happen next.

In Readings

This card serves as assurance, offering positive reminders of where we are and where we're going. There's magic here, crackling energy, wondrous joy in creation. The Three of Wands wants us to feel good about what we're doing. It wants us to keep going, finding delight and curiosity and exhilaration in this explosive, powerful movement.

JOURNAL PROMPT: *What is guiding you, motivating you, encouraging you? How is your confidence growing? What does inspiration look like for you? How are you replenishing yourself? What visions of the future are pulling you forward?*

Four of Wands

FOUR // Structure, organization, systems, progression, foundations, stability

FIRE // Passion, inspiration, creativity, drive, purpose, instinct, associated with the soul

KEYWORDS // steady growth · exuberance & excitement · supported efforts · celebration · creative structures

Abundance is everywhere. Our foundation is firm, crackling with power and bolstering that brilliant vision. Others are lending us their strength and their ideas, we are supported in multiple ways, and our work feels both solid and inspiring. Our plan is coming together in a way that we can't help but be excited about, pulling us into the joyful triumph and vigorous drive of the Four of Wands.

• • •

Fire can't blaze endlessly without consistent fuel. No matter how brilliant the spark, no matter how inventive the kindling, even the strongest flames will burn themselves out if we don't take the time to gather logs, protect the embers, and establish a plan to tend consistently and regularly to all we have begun. Passion and potential have gotten us this far, but with the Four of Wands we take pride in where we are while doubling down on our aims for the future. Our belief in ourselves and our purpose continues to build, and we keep going, putting everything we have into our continued success.

Budgets and spreadsheets and plans of action may not sound like the sexiest things, may even feel at odds with the explosive creative flow that we've been embracing with this suit. Yet the number four is all about deliberately establishing spaces for further generative work, recognizing our limits, and clarifying goals. These actions turn raw potential into something that won't slow down or fade away; they help us establish creative discipline. This kind of focused energy creates opportunities for continued adjustment, allowing us to dream even bigger, to build upon what we already have, to set ourselves up for success. Instead of throwing caution to the wind and hoping that our dreams come true, this card invites us to do the work, to design the world we want, to get organized about our achievements.

But the Four of Wands is about more than just planning and executing—there's also a confident, authentic joy in this card, a sense of alignment and power that inspires us to keep pushing, to celebrate every step. Within the Four of Wands there is a deep knowledge that we are doing something important, something necessary, something unique. We've managed to turn a fantasy, that glimmering spark of mystery and magic, into something real and are on track to build it into something incredible, something lasting. As ideas align with expertise, as we continue to generate innovations and inspirations, we are called to celebrate, to take both control and pleasure in the process.

In Readings

This card speaks of confidence and courage, deliberately empowering ourselves to think through our next stages of progress without fear. The Four of Wands wants us to find joy in control, to take ownership of our work and our future, to recognize what we've already accomplished and consider what will give us the edge. By taking the time to clarify our purpose and establish limits for ourselves, we ensure that what we are creating will thrive.

> JOURNAL PROMPT: *How are you protecting the work you love, the vision you carry, the wonder and potential that you feel? Where does control allow you new kinds of freedom, expression, creation? What are you doing to expand and experiment, rather than clinging to what is safe or expected?*

Five of Wands

FIVE // Change, freedom, exploration, tension, growth, adventure, balance, transition

FIRE // Passion, inspiration, creativity, drive, purpose, instinct, associated with the soul

KEYWORDS // distraction · friction · lack of direction · frustration · indecisiveness · restless movement

We've been working so hard, yet our projects have multiplied and we find our attention drifting in multiple directions. The focus that once felt so clear is completely scattered and it's harder to make decisions, harder to keep building at the same pace. Creation hasn't stopped but it does feel more difficult, as any attempts at movement chafe and shred. This sense of confusion and irritation, this uncertainty about where we're heading and what we're really doing, is the distracted, impulsive energy of the Five of Wands.

• • •

Friction isn't always a bad thing—but it can be vexing, whether it comes in the form of internal chaos or through external means: others getting in our way, distracting us from our goals, challenging our authority or abilities. We may have already navigated similar obstacles with ease and grace. But when we sit in the energy of the Five of Wands, we often surrender to our irritation, we get caught up in petty bullshit and let our natural fire rage until it threatens to engulf everything. This can manifest as picking fights, lashing out, sloppy work, needless conflict: wanting to burn it all down and start again, even if the work itself is good, even if our desire to create is still present.

Getting frustrated is natural, and there are plenty of reasons that we might find ourselves in a Five of Wands state. Whether we're trying to do too much too quickly, refusing help, or ignoring the plans we so carefully laid in favor of something more immediately satisfying, our ability to focus has scattered in the wind. Sometimes this card indicates a struggle with desire, our attention getting caught up in a new ambition that's distracting us, or a feeling of dissatisfaction. Have we lost pride in our work? Do we need a break? Are we just bored? These are all solvable problems but, by ignoring our struggles, we inevitably make them worse.

The Five of Wands isn't always negative, isn't necessarily destructive. Sometimes a change of direction is exactly what we need. Five invites us to consider where tension is coming from, to pay attention to where we are craving freedom. If we're able to cool down and recognize what the problem is, we can make the necessary adjustments, blow off some steam, accept offers of support or try new ideas or just do something else for a little while. Using this friction to propel ourselves forward can result in imaginative, fantastical ideas, and may be the kick in the ass that we need to find the joy in our work again.

In Readings

The Five of Wands reminds us that this challenge is not the end of the story—far from it. But it is an important and often unavoidable turning point, a moment when we have to make big decisions about what we want to pursue and be realistic about what it may cost us. This card asks us to slow down and regroup, shifting the emphasis from forward momentum to focused movement. What is driving our choices? Do we want to do everything, or nothing? Is there a larger problem at stake, or are we just pissed off and in need of an outlet, a break, a shift in direction?

JOURNAL PROMPT: *Where have you been scattered, irritated, distracted? What are you really fighting for? How can you burn off some steam rather than destroying everything you've been working toward? And where might some careful delegation help you make progress?*

Six of Wands

SIX // Harmony, nurturing, community, caretaking, movement, pride

FIRE // Passion, inspiration, creativity, drive, purpose, instinct, associated with the soul

KEYWORDS // moving forward · pride in our work · healthy ego · joy · vision for the future · pursuit of dreams

After shaking off our annoyance and getting our eyes back on the prize, we find our speed picking up again. We reach a major milestone, and a sense of triumph fills us. We're proud of our achievements, confident that everything we're working toward will succeed, and feel excitement and passion stirring within us again. Our efforts are not finished, yet victory, joy, and enthusiasm fill us. That desire to keep rushing forward with renewed vigor, that need to keep pushing toward our goals, is the courage and intentionality of the Six of Wands.

• • •

Sometimes we can feel ourselves leveling up, learning and growing and making change, becoming a leader in our field. Bigger than just hitting our stride, with the Six of Wands we feel a powerful sense of confidence and accomplishment, knowing that we're making waves, that others are impressed, that what we're doing is going to succeed. And while we've loved our work and believed in the potential of this project since the very beginning, with this card we reach a new level of joy, courage, strength. This is the shift from seeing potential to making progress.

At its heart, the Six of Wands is often a creative breakthrough, an expansion of ego. After the chaotic, restless frustration of the Five of Wands, with the six we step into our power, embrace our brilliance, run forward with passion and purpose. Any excuses or hesitations fall by the wayside and we find new sparks of inspiration, renewed focus for all that we are working toward. Beyond just hoping that we get where we want to go, we now absolutely believe that if we keep our eyes on the prize, we can't possibly lose.

But in making a name for ourselves and gaining recognition for our efforts, it's important that we don't get so puffed up in hubris, so awestruck by our own genius, that we blow off our team or forget how hard we worked to get here. Fire may reflect our soul's passions and drives but it is also a deeply collaborative energy, an element bursting with charisma, energy, enthusiasm, passion, and sparkle. And sixes crave harmony, seek to nurture not only the self but also communities, relationships, chosen families. No matter how much of a trailblazer and innovator we may be, isolating ourselves is a certain path to burnout, and nobody wants to work with someone who is insufferably arrogant. The Six of Wands wants us to continue letting others stoke our fire, share our heat, shelter our embers, and burn alongside us. Artistic alliances and joint efforts can create incredible magic, and in the give and take of energy, we thrive as a team and as a community.

In Readings

The Six of Wands is an invitation to keep moving forward, a chance to celebrate our efforts and then double down on our work. Remember the friction you may have recently moved through, the frustration that led to new clarity, and don't be afraid to take some bold new chances. The best creative work balances belief in the self with a willingness to keep learning, to keep listening, to keep growing.

> JOURNAL PROMPT: *What and who are inspiring you? How do you sustain your natural confidence, joy, pleasure in creation? Where are you finding new freedom, and how does that impact your personal goals?*

Seven of Wands

SEVEN // Intelligence, duality, movement, determination, protection, responsibility

FIRE // Passion, inspiration, creativity, drive, purpose, instinct, associated with the soul

KEYWORDS // independence · defending our ideas · belief in the self · courage · protecting our work

In continuing to press on, we find ourselves standing alone, burning brightly, attracting attention. Not everyone has the same clarity of vision that we do—not everyone is convinced by what we are building or understands our goals, believes that we will accomplish everything that we've set out to do. In this moment, we have to defend our work, show courage and passion, and protect our truth. As we let our fire stretch out into the darkness, and trust that our goal is worth the effort it will take to achieve it, we fully step into the daring independence of the Seven of Wands.

• • •

With renewed confidence, we come up against another obstacle. Rather than a sense of restless friction, the Seven of Wands represents a need to stand tall, to believe in our work, to prove why our efforts are important. We might be the only one who fully understands the plan—yet in the process of courageously pressing on, we turn any lingering fears into power, overcoming challenges to achieve everything that we want. The Seven of Wands is sparks of light in the darkness, burning brightly even if we must burn alone. It's protecting our work, inspiring others, channeling our strength.

This is a card of independence and fire, a moment when we embrace the sparks and flames we've been building and find the courage to hold that blaze proudly, to stand behind our vision, to double down on our future. Sometimes this can look like defensiveness, and indeed, the seven does ask us to answer the questions that are thrown our way, to ensure that our perspective and desires are aligned with what we are actually creating. This card urges us to believe in ourselves, to trust in our instincts and abilities, to advocate for our work. Inspiration can be hard to come by, and this is no time to give up.

Rather than reckless obsession, clinging to an idea or ideal at all costs, the Seven of Wands wants us to take responsibility for what we are creating and to continue moving forward even if there are things to navigate along the way. Adaptation is not the same as surrender, and compromise doesn't have to be a dirty word. After the lessons of the Five and Six of Wands, the Seven of Wands wants us to flex as we grow, to continue building confidence, to make this a quest for independence and refinement. Seven seeks wisdom, spirituality, a sense of something bigger. And by continuing to chase our own unique objectives, we also motivate and encourage those around us, reminding our communities that good work requires effort, and that great plans take time and dedication to execute.

In Readings

The Seven of Wands can serve as a reminder to trust your instincts, to honor your intentions, to respect the ideas that are bubbling forth. It's a moment to believe in ourselves and our ideas, and to continue reaching for that brass ring. We have what we need to succeed, and a risk may prove necessary to keep moving forward.

> JOURNAL PROMPT: *How are you adapting to changing circumstances, and where are you unwilling to compromise on your vision? How is your work distinctive, and how does that give you courage and confidence to keep moving forward? Are there places that you can collaborate, or are you determined to go it alone at any cost?*

Eight of Wands

EIGHT // Power, momentum, discipline, assurance, control, practicality

FIRE // Passion, inspiration, creativity, drive, purpose, instinct, associated with the soul

KEYWORDS // rapid movement · joyful energy · clearing of obstacles · accomplishment · breakthroughs

Our fire is catching, our spirit is energized, our magic is emboldened. We're moving at rapid speed, blazing ahead, with no obstacles in sight. We've overcome so much, and now our momentum continues to build, as everything falls into place just as we've always believed that it would. This streaking forward, this unencumbered progress, is the dazzling and fleeting rush of the Eight of Wands.

• • •

Think about the burst of energy that runners get when they see the final mile marker of a race: unfettered optimism, movement without pause, throwing every last bit of energy and optimism into a goal. It's seeing an open roadway and slamming on the accelerator, with a full tank of gas and no obstacles in sight, knowing that there's nothing that could possibly slow us down. The Eight of Wands is that exhilarating moment when we know that everything is flowing freely, when we have the resources and energy and talent to accomplish our goals, along with a plan to get to the finish line. There's pure joy here, reckless abandon, the sensation of pathways opening up before us and momentum building with no need to pump the brakes. Every barrier falls away, every challenge strengthens us, and we feel completely, utterly unstoppable.

Sometimes this looks like taking a big creative risk that's immediately paying off, while other times it's being absolutely in sync with our desires, knowing just what we want to do and how to do it. But regardless of the actual shape that this card takes in our lives, eights represent powerful, confident manifestations paired with absolute pleasure and satisfaction in what we are creating. With the suit of wands this results in trusting the foundation that we have created, being able to put every last shred of energy and brilliance into our work, having power over our own doubts. It's the joy of knowing that we are in exactly the right place, at exactly the right time, doing exactly the right thing.

This energy is fleeting by nature. No one can go at full speed for too long, give everything they have without eventually needing to slow down, refuel, assess their position. But for as long as it lasts, the Eight of Wands is pure magic.

In Readings

This card urges you to take chances, believe in yourself, and not get bogged down by doubts, fears, or uncertainties. The energy of the Eight of Wands is trusting in both your instincts and the plans that you have made, knowing that your work is brilliant, that your skills are up to the task at hand, that you have purposefully and knowingly surrounded yourself with the people and resources needed to make massive strides forward. If you've been hesitating, afraid of vulnerability or failure or dreaming too big, the Eight of Wands tells you to knock those doubts to the side and keep moving. This is the moment to put mind, heart, and soul into your ambitions and to see what happens when you create with absolute confidence.

JOURNAL PROMPT: *How often do you let yourself rush forward with joy instead of holding back out of fear? Which new skills, dreams, desires are you discovering within yourself, and how can you give them space to breathe and grow? What are you ready to reach for?*

Nine of Wands

NINE // Observation, personal responsibility, collective growth, expansion, clarity

FIRE // Passion, inspiration, creativity, drive, purpose, instinct, associated with the soul

KEYWORDS // diminished energy · perseverance · overcoming obstacles · asking for help · pressing forward

We've been going hard for so long, and we find ourselves slowing down, gasping for breath, nurturing our inner flames as best we can. One final challenge lies before us, a last difficult task to complete before we can cross the finish line. And in spite of our fatigue, in spite of our doubts, we press on. Perseverance is at war with weariness, and in knowing that we must tread carefully, in trying to manage our energetic resources, we experience the exhaustion and exhilaration of the Nine of Wands.

• • •

We're so close. That big goal, that massive accomplishment, is just within reach— and yet our work is not yet done, our objective has not yet been reached. With the Nine of Wands, we start to come up against the limitations of who we are and discover unexpected boundaries around creativity, inspiration, and energy. Stamina is a powerful force, and perseverance can be a valuable asset. We've already accomplished so much and feel a certain amount of satisfaction in how far we've come. Yet in this moment, we are forced to slow down, to consider how we will overcome one final, massive obstacle. We have to make a decision about how hard to push ourselves and examine how badly we want to reach our goal.

There's a push-pull that lives within this card, a desire to finish strong at war with a sense of self-preservation, a need for wisdom in pacing. Nines always speak to the end of the cycle, to a change that is inevitable. Are we so focused on completing our task that we're willing to risk it all? Finding the right balance of drive and protection can be complicated, and if we're too dedicated to our original path, too fixated on a particular plan, we may miss opportunities to receive help, to make adjustments, to rest and heal before pressing on. Are we ready to be finished? Or are we so caught up in movement that the thought of completion feels unappealing?

Within the Nine of Wands, we grapple with the natural tension between different versions of success. Is it more important to stand by our original vision, or to care for our physical and emotional well-being? How much are we willing to sacrifice in order to finish our work? None of us are invincible, can survive without rest or support or encouragement, are capable of burning endlessly without consuming all of our resources. If we can recognize where something solid has slipped out of place, can interrogate and identify our own needs, are willing to make adjustments that will allow us to keep moving forward without breaking into pieces, we can still reach those big goals with enough energy to enjoy them.

In Readings

This card gives us a choice, helping us look at our current position through a new lens. We may be able to push forward at any cost, to endure painful consequences for the sake of success—but we also have the option of showing ourselves grace and flexibility, adjusting our expectations, accepting help, or changing our path.

> **JOURNAL PROMPT:** *What does success really mean? How much are you willing to give in order to make your dreams come true? Do you have what it takes to accomplish your goals? And if not, can you find a way to show yourself care instead of burning yourself out on principle?*

Ten of Wands

TEN & ONE // Unity, vision, pride, independence & community together, trail blazing, confidence

FIRE // Passion, inspiration, creativity, drive, purpose, instinct, associated with the soul

KEYWORDS // exhaustion · responsibility · overwhelm · burnout · depletion · acknowledgment

The flames are gone, the heat is lost, the rush is over. We've given it all that we could but in pushing past our own limits, in taking on so much alone, in ignoring offers for help, we've completely burned out. We may have achieved what we'd hoped but it's cost us dearly, and now we sit in the ashes, wondering where it all went wrong. This sense of depletion, this need for rest and recovery, is the drained and debilitated energy of the Ten of Wands.

• • •

We've disregarded the warnings, taken on far more than we can handle, and now find ourselves struggling beneath an immense burden. The Ten of Wands is a card of overwhelming responsibility, a sensation of creative and emotional burnout. All that we have has gone into our work, we've taken on the crushing responsibilities for everything and everyone around us—and now our internal fire is dim, even extinguished. We have nothing more to give. And even though we've reached the goal we set for ourselves, accomplished everything we dreamed of, and feel a sense of pride in all that we've built and done, we may not have the energy, attention, or awareness left to actually enjoy it.

It's wonderful to be the strong, creative one—to be the person everyone turns to for advice or comfort, inspiration, or assistance. For many of us, being able to accomplish so much is a big part of who we are, something we identify fully with. And it's a powerful thing to be able to say that we're independent and strong, that our creative fire will always burn brightly no matter how much we're taking on. Yet no matter how strong we are, how much passion and purpose we feel, there's always a breaking point—and the Ten of Wands captures that devastating, gut-wrenching moment.

There's a certain satisfaction to knowing that we've done everything we can. Tens are endings, for better or worse, pointing us back to the number one's sparks of hope and movement, reminding us of where we started. This card is free of pressure and obligation, with no more tasks to check off or goals to meet. And even if we've completely burned ourselves out in the process of getting here, there's still an element of rest to this card, a feeling of release, a sigh of relief. While the Ten of Wands can be exhausting in its scope, we also have no choice but to spend time in recovery, resting and reflecting on what our future now holds in the wake of this success.

In Readings

The Ten of Wands urges us to set boundaries for ourselves, to be thoughtful and intentional about how much we give and how quickly we offer it. Creativity and inspiration are valuable resources and rather than treating them as endlessly renewable, this card encourages us to pace ourselves, to delegate, to know when to say no. Even if every single thing on our to-do list is exciting to us, we don't have to do everything right away, and we certainly don't have to do it all alone. Rather than crumbling under the weight of our desires, or getting lost in a dizzying array of ambitions, the Ten of Wands asks us to balance passion with patience.

JOURNAL PROMPT: *Where is your sense of urgency coming from, and how can you be more realistic about the timelines or pressure you're operating under? How might you let others help you reach that finish line instead of insisting that you take care of every duty and responsibility yourself? What would it mean to incorporate rest and self-care into your routines?*

Page of Wands

ELEVEN & TWO // Healing, choice, intentionality, sensitivity, intuition, psychic wisdom, duality

FIRE // Passion, inspiration, creativity, drive, purpose, instinct, associated with the soul

KEYWORDS // experimentation · confidence · passion · desire to move · playfulness · creative questioning

New ideas come fast and hot, setting us buzzing with energy, brimming with possibility. We may have a sense of the rules but refuse to be impeded by them. Instead, we are ready to blaze our own trails, make our own mistakes, change the world with our brilliance and our joy. When it feels like our very blood is humming with energy, when the idea of capturing our visions in different mediums fills us with power and excitement, when absolutely anything feels possible, that is when we exemplify the joy and optimism of the Page of Wands.

• • •

Crackling with artistic fire, the Page of Wands is an outpouring, someone who is overflowing with ideas, energy, and heat. There's an intoxicating rush that comes with inspiration, an authentic and intense flow that lets us return to ourselves even as we expand outward—and when we start a new journey with an open mind and a curious heart, magic quickly takes hold. Pages in the tarot may lack experience and discipline, may be unfamiliar with conventional rules. But this fresh perspective doesn't make them clueless, bumbling children; rather, it generates wild, brilliant creativity, raw enthusiasm, incredible and authentic purpose. And the Page of Wands in particular refuses to be restricted by stuffy rules or restrictive conventions.

This sense of courage and confidence empowers the Page of Wands to take risks without doubting themselves and gives this figure a sense of endless, generative strength. The page may not have a clear vision for what they want to create just yet, but there are so many mediums to experiment with, so many methods to try out, so many people to meet and learn from and collaborate with. Given fuel and oxygen, fire can catch so quickly, burn so brightly, spread so contagiously—and in the same way, sharing inspiration and bringing other people into our work or play can invigorate. Pages love this sense of connection, and with the suit of wands, we see a real intentionality in this kind of drive, a lively enthusiasm that builds and builds.

Remember the numerology of pages, the eleventh cards of their suits. This is the balance and clarity of Justice (11) alongside the intuitive awareness and quiet observation of the High Priestess (2). Creativity doesn't always look like paint on a canvas or movement on a stage. Sometimes creativity is problem-solving, thinking outside the box, finding a solution that no one else has suggested or considered— and sometimes that creativity comes from rest, observation, awareness, introspection. Being able to think and dream outside of restrictions is a gift, and this page fully exemplifies free thinking, unrestricted imagination, and art as a healing method. This isn't just a kid playing with matches: it's a student learning how to build a campfire, gather kindling, shield the flames, and ultimately provide the heat for cooking or warmth or protection or artistic experimentation. The Page of Wands embodies the joy in new beginnings, the wonder in open movement, the contagious excitement in undefined exploration and developing new skills and challenging themselves to grow. And when we allow ourselves to play, when we aren't making decisions based on fear, sparks can fly in unexpected directions, lighting fires and building momentum in ways that we may have never discovered otherwise.

In Readings

The Page of Wands urges us to dream big, to try new things, to ask creative questions. There can be a lot to discover in adventure, a lot of pleasure in chasing after our purpose. A new opportunity may present itself in a fortuitous way, and by being open-minded and willing to try something different, we can move forward driven by passion rather than a sense of obligation or pressure.

> JOURNAL PROMPT: *What is brewing within you? What lights your fire, makes you burn, fills you with anticipation and passion and desire? Where can you ask more questions, try more methods, chase more adventures? How are you being held back by convention, and what happens if you trust your instincts instead?*

Knight of Wands

TWELVE & THREE // Expansion, manifestation, growth, abundance, creativity, experimentation

FIRE // Passion, inspiration, creativity, drive, purpose, instinct, associated with the soul

KEYWORDS // charisma · restless seeking · building community · inspirational · visionary ·
creative exploration

After considering different projects and methods, we gain confidence in our vision. We're eager to prove that our way of moving through the world is not only valid but expansive, important, even necessary. We set our eyes on a big, ambitious prize, bring other people into our energy, captivate and collaborate with those who see the same vision that we do—and as more people find inspiration from us, we may get a little distracted by all of this energy and attention. These efforts at leadership and building, this desire to connect and share, this struggle to balance all of the fire that burns within us are the potent excitement of the Knight of Wands.

• • •

Potential can be intoxicating. Brimming with wild energy and exhilarating magic, the Knight of Wands holds the power of fire's creative and destructive capabilities in trembling hands, eager to channel it into their latest vision of brilliance. This is a figure of ideas, of desire, of running headfirst into whatever new idea or project or ambition is filling them with joy and need. Think of a young, inexperienced firefighter: brave and bold, proving their strength and rushing into dangerous situations, making quick decisions with grit and courage. The Knight of Wands inspires with everything they do, motivating everyone nearby, and is eager to demonstrate their talent and value with every mission and scheme.

This is someone everyone flocks to and watches, who is juggling a wide variety of interests and multiple sets of collaborators. They're brilliant in so many ways but aren't always able to focus on one thing long enough to actually finish it; they may feel constantly pulled in many directions, lighting fires, and letting others burn out. This energy can be incredibly useful but is also hard to manage, difficult to harness in a productive way. Yet there's a vitality to this explorer, a sense of adventure and desire that energizes, stimulates, rouses. It's impossible not to be joyful around this person, impossible not to get caught up in their passion.

From a numerological perspective, knights—the twelfth card of each suit— balance the energy of the Hanged One (12) and the Empress (3). This can be a complex and dynamic push-pull, tangled between abundance and stagnation, between manifestation and relinquishing control—and with the Knight of Wands, we see this in a desire to start projects but an uncertainty of how to finish them, an eagerness to collaborate but a sensation of blockage once too many people get involved. The Empress reflects the power, brilliance, and generative effort the Knight of Wands can provide, while the Hanged One honors self-doubt, a desire to prove the self, a struggle to stay focused or keep moving forward. These two arche-types together build additional layers into the Knight of Wands, giving us context. This figure wants to prove their skills but doesn't always know how, wants to share their abundance but may do so in a way that's rough and unrefined.

Above all, this is someone who wants to create opportunities: brainstorming, collaborating, fantasizing. There can be a restlessness to this energy, a desire to take action and get things moving without committing too fully to one particular path— and while at the end of a project this might be frustrating, at the beginning of some-thing new this is often an energy we want to embrace. Creativity can really thrive without boundaries but knowing when to leave freethinking behind and actually make a plan that we can execute takes experience, awareness, and consideration.

In Readings

The Knight of Wands reminds us of how much fire we have at our fingertips and urges us to be conscious of how we are utilizing it. New possibilities can be dazzling, intoxicating, but if all we pursue is beginnings, those ideas may never become tangible realities.

> JOURNAL PROMPT: *How are you putting energy and focus into your fantasies? What does it mean to fully devote yourself to something instead of letting your desire scatter across multiple projects?*

Queen of Wands

THIRTEEN & FOUR // Focus, pragmatism, independence, determination, organization, expression

FIRE // Passion, inspiration, creativity, drive, purpose, instinct, associated with the soul

KEYWORDS // ambition · loyalty · inspiration · courage · magnetism · bold choices · creative boundaries

Experimentation, adventure, and education lead us to a place of poise, courage, and conviction. We have learned how to artistically and confidently wield our fire, know the magical power that the flames can hold, understand how to motivate both ourselves and others with our talent and skill. Creativity flows with joy and intention, inspiration crackles at our fingertips, and we bring others into our orbit, connecting and generating with everything we do. We defend those that we teach, build a collaborative community of artists, push the limits of what is possible while still enforcing necessary boundaries of protection. This effortless brilliance, this ability to energize and encourage with equal measure, is the intoxicating charm of the Queen of Wands.

• • •

The page and the knight of the suit of wands both hold a lot of restlessness, curiosity, and passion. But the queen stands apart as a ruler, a master of the element of fire, someone who understands how to care for and nourish that natural spark of creativity, inspiration, and instinct. This is magic forged in flame, infectious ambition and abundance mingling with loyalty to a specific vision. The Queen of Wands is a fire dancer, an artist and leader who understands how to let flames burn and sizzle, who knows that the heat of this specifically brilliant element can bring about evolution, necessary change, and dynamic personal power.

Just as with the younger court cards, there's still a rich sense of adventure and curiosity here, a desire to learn, grow, change, experiment, play, and be dazzled by the world we live in. But the Queen of Wands doesn't get distracted, isn't intimidated, refuses to settle. This ruler finds inspiration in everything and always seems to know exactly what to do with it, relying on their instincts and their community to weave shape, purpose, joy, and excitement into everything they do. The Queen of Wands is brave, bold, courageous, and confident. They trust in the foundations that they have established and are able to balance big risks with thoughtful expression.

The thirteenth card of the suit, queens are a numerological combination of the inevitable release of Death (13) and the powerful, protective boundaries of the Emperor (4). Together, these archetypes speak to a figure who understands how to balance change and limits, who puts rules in place that create space for creativity and wonder, who isn't afraid to let something old go. The Queen of Wands in particular finds a lot of wisdom in this blend of energies, understanding fire's inherently transformative properties and putting them to good use. By establishing rules and limits, this queen can decide when to protect their creative energy and when to color outside of the lines. And when we trust in our own talent and know that we have put systems in place that will protect us from outside influences, it frees us up to take even bigger chances, to be as authentic as we can possibly be.

In Readings

The Queen of Wands asks us to be brave, to be fearless, to not let outside influences change our vision for ourselves. There's no shame in standing out, and big risks can invite big rewards—but we need to act with intention rather than restlessness, need to recognize which chances are worth taking. Consider your cycles of initiation, growth, dismantling, and recovery, and give equal weight to each phase, recognizing the power and importance of every step in the process.

> JOURNAL PROMPT: *What sustains your creativity? How do you build systems for long-term care and inspiration? Where do wisdom and excitement intersect, and how do you balance these two energies? What makes you feel brave, encourages you to take risks, allows you to pursue bold actions?*

King of Wands

FOURTEEN & FIVE // Personal freedom, change, leadership, curiosity, knowledge, observation

FIRE // Passion, inspiration, creativity, drive, purpose, instinct, associated with the soul

KEYWORDS // transformative ideas · originality · drive · vision · brilliance · creative expansion

We understand how to use our fire to inspire, encourage, challenge, motivate, recreate. And as our community increases and diversifies, as more and more people come to us for counsel, stimulation, and collaboration, we step into a new kind of leadership role: one that empowers others, that establishes new avenues for change and growth. Our vision expands, encapsulating different corners of the world, and we become the architect for artistic visions, for evolutionary projects and community efforts. This outward encouragement, this sense of ownership and desire for lasting, essential transformation, is the power and wisdom of the King of Wands.

• • •

If the Queen of Wands helps us establish creative boundaries that empower us to play, release, and grow, the King of Wands fully embraces the power of evolution, gaining strength from the cycles of revolution, exchange, and reconstruction. Burning away the excess and clarifying purpose, this king is driven by a need to transmute energy, to rise to challenges, to leave a lasting impact. With boundless energy and an impressive vision for the future, the King of Wands juggles multiple projects with ease while simultaneously helping others with their own work. Think about a controlled-burn manager, someone who plans and sets wildfires in specific, intentional ways to destroy, generate, and rebuild. In taking big risks, the King of Wands invites in epic, generational rewards.

The King of Wands is impossible to ignore. They light up every room, enliven every conversation, invigorate every planning session, and encourage every person they come into contact with. Natural leaders with quick minds and brilliant instincts, this king accepts their calling with enthusiasm and joy, believing that they can change the world, and that it's their duty to do so. But this is more than just individual shifts—this is powerful, systemic transformation. The King of Wands creates frameworks for others to work within and isn't afraid to lean on their past efforts while also trying new things, listening to feedback, and making ongoing adjustments. There's a necessary mutability to this figure, a willingness to be flexible and learn that is empowered by education and experience.

Kings are architects, paying attention to the big picture, holding space for past, present, and future all at once. They see where things are going because they understand where they have been. As the fourteenth card of this suit, the King of Wands holds the energy of Temperance (14) and the Hierophant (5). This is a figure that encourages both tension and shifts, creating collective opportunities to examine, discard, and start anew. Fire as an element is uniquely suited to this kind of movement, and the King of Wands instinctively knows how to wield it, using its brilliant light and consuming flame to enact permanent, powerful modifications. Unafraid of what may lie ahead, the king sees broken systems and flawed rules, and is willing to do the hard work to tear things down and build them back up. By bringing others into their efforts, by joining voices and letting ideas flow freely, this king establishes something brilliant, bold, and beautiful.

In Readings

The King of Wands encourages us to own our fire and to not fear authority. If our instincts are tugging us in a particular direction, if we want to build something from the ground up, if we have a clear vision for what we hope to accomplish, this card urges us to listen. Powerful shifts don't happen overnight—by committing to something specific, bringing others into the work, and making a plan for how we will enact change, anything is possible.

JOURNAL PROMPT: *How do you combine your sense of purpose with your learned skills? What does it mean to let your dreams take up space in a way that transforms and refines? What kind of leader are you, and where could you let your fire shine more brightly?*

THE SUIT OF SWORDS

AIR

Logic, pragmatism, information, communication, knowledge, associated with the mind

Moving with speed and awareness, the airy suit of swords analyzes our personal intellect—the questions we pose, the viewpoints we take, the methods that we use to gather and process information, and our ever-evolving relationship with truth. Within the suit of swords we find themes of authenticity, ambition, pragmatism, logic, wisdom, strategy, boundaries, discernment, rationality, understanding, and problem-solving. With a sharpened blade and a perceptive outlook, this suit shows us all that our minds can do.

As an element, air is transparent, not always easy to perceive, sometimes still and quiet while other times swirling, agitated, mighty in its invisible force. We so often see it tangled with other elements since air can impact everything else with its keen authority and ability to disrupt. Air can be sharp, pointed, helping us move to a precise location—but it can also bluster, confuse, or disorient, depending on how clear and calm it is. The element of air is tied to our intellectual self, our sense of truth and perspective, our communication style, our boundaries. This is the way we process and analyze the world, the methods that we use to decide what to let in and where to protect ourselves. Air gives us the rationality we rely on to understand, consider, and make decisions. Just like our minds, air interrogates ideas of truth and justice, intellect and analysis, but can easily drift into secrecy, harshness, or a lack of sensitivity.

Mirroring many of these concepts, the suit of swords explores the decisions and choices that follow a flash of insight and understanding as we choose a path, confront internal and external truths, set boundaries, move forward with purpose, gain confidence in our strength, and experience isolation or doubts. Swords help us recognize how strong we can be, the things that we are able to conquer and overcome, the ways that the rational mind balances problem-solving, perception, and interrogation. This suit contextualizes our experiences, empowering us to analyze our decisions, to recognize what stimulates and activates us, and to consider the consequences of our decisions, actions, and ideas. At its core, this suit tells the story of understanding the self, the narratives that shape our identity, and the ways that we make choices.

Just like a storm can leave destruction in its wake, the suit of swords brings up a lot of challenging questions, emotions, and triggers. These cards tackle intensely personal issues like mental illness, nightmares, harmful words, and destructive beliefs, forcing us to confront the ways that fear, anxiety, frustration, and isolation influence our perspectives on ourselves, our ambitions, and our communities. Negative thought patterns can be absolutely devastating, and it takes a lot of strength, courage, and support to confront them. While it's not always easy to be truly honest with ourselves, this suit encourages us to be authentic about what we want and what we are capable of, to balance any harsh truths with compassion, kindness, gentleness. We are all products of our environments and our experiences, learning as we go, doing the best we can with the information that we have at any given time. The suit of swords may explore difficult topics, but it also reminds us to celebrate curiosity, understanding, and the ways that learning and growing can connect us to bigger, brighter concepts.

• • •

As you investigate the suit of swords and the element of air, consider perspective, awareness, inquisitiveness. What stories do you tell yourself, and how often do those stories change? How do your perceptions shape your choices, and how might they limit them? Who do you believe yourself to be, and where did those ideas come from? How are boundaries useful, and when are they harmful?

Ace of Swords

ONE // Motivation, confidence, independence, vision, trail blazing

AIR // Logic, pragmatism, information, communication, knowledge, associated with the mind

KEYWORDS // sharp truth · sudden insight · clarity · awareness · recognition · a new idea or vision

In the process of examination, sometimes we make exciting discoveries. We're looking at something that we've studied in depth but suddenly our perspective shifts, an unexpected truth piercing through our awareness in a way that we cannot ignore or deny. Our newfound clarity has a ripple effect, inspiring a hunger to reexamine everything, to ponder what we know and what we don't know, to question and pursue and scrutinize. This powerful desire to understand, this recognition of fresh knowledge and shifting viewpoints, is the sharp magic of the Ace of Swords.

• • •

Sometimes we get a glimpse of truth so dramatic, a rush of insight so intense, that we cannot possibly ignore what we've learned. An important fact clicks into place, our perspective shifts just enough to reveal an elusive answer, an offhand comment causes our minds to reassemble information in a new way. In these moments, we are channeling the power of the Ace of Swords. It may be a theory or notion that changes our trajectory, alters our reality, or pushes us to adjust and move forward with a new sense of determination and ambition. In this crackle of lightning, everything changes.

The Ace of Swords challenges our assumptions, which at times are sharp and energizing and in other moments feel heavy, awkward, even overwhelming. Sometimes we may struggle to process this realization, may even wish that we could forget or ignore what we have discovered. It's not always clear where this path will lead, but in spite of our uncertainties, this ace prompts a desire for new revelations, pushing us to ask difficult questions, examine things with fresh eyes, initiate hard conversations. Aces and ones always begin new journeys, and with the suit of swords we are challenging assumptions, pushing our intellectual self past our natural limits, and identifying an issue or obstacle that we hope to conquer.

Where other aces may feel inspiring, exciting, or generative, the Ace of Swords can be intimidating. It represents a mentally rigorous task, a demanding energy, a test of our strength and courage. The Ace of Swords is rarely playful but instead requires scrutiny, assessment, careful evaluation—yet we may also find a curious desire stirring within us, a kind of invigoration that we can't deny. Our eyes have been opened, a new path extends before us, and in following this line of questioning, the possibilities of all that we may discover feel endless, infinite.

In Readings

The Ace of Swords asks us to really grapple with the truth of what we have learned and to consider what may come next. When a new idea strikes, when our viewpoints shift, it's a chance for us to interrogate our experiences, to imagine something different than we have always known. Growth is happening, change is occurring, whether we like it or not. And as we adjust our grip on this unfamiliar blade, we need to remember that this sword is both a tool and a weapon.

JOURNAL PROMPT: *What opportunities are emerging that may push you to question and reconsider old assumptions? How do you handle a paradigm shift? What are you curious about, and what do you feel pulling you into a full investigation?*

Two of Swords

TWO // Sensitivity, intuition, psychic wisdom, choice, awareness, duality

AIR // Logic, pragmatism, information, communication, knowledge, associated with the mind

KEYWORDS // balance · blockage · a difficult decision · uncertainty · examination · contemplation

We've picked up this dangerous new blade but are immediately faced with a choice. How to wield it? Where to aim it? There are several paths forward, and while any of them could serve to bring us to our ultimate goal, each will also bring challenges, transformations, knowledge. As we examine our options, we may feel stuck, trapped, uncertain of where our sword will be the most useful. Yet not choosing is also a choice, and we cannot stay in this place of contemplation forever. This sensation of struggle, this unexpected obstruction, is the energy of the Two of Swords.

• • •

New information can call everything into question. After the shocking clarity of the Ace of Swords, the two finds us lost in fog, bringing us into a tense period of indecision, uncertainty, and perhaps even fear. We have discovered a clashing truth, an insight that may have shaken us to our core and forced us to reevaluate that which felt steady and certain—and now, faced with multiple paths forward, we aren't sure what to do next, aren't sure that we trust ourselves. It may feel like every option is bad, like anything we do with this new information or insight is dangerous. Yet by not acting, by refusing to decide, we are still making a very specific kind of choice.

When anxieties creep around the edge of our consciousness, they can leave us second-guessing every possibility, worried about making the wrong move. Internal blockages are often incredibly stressful, and can leave us feeling inadequte or ill-equipped to move forward. And as a card in the suit of the mind, the Two of Swords emphasizes that this is an intellectual struggle, a need to pursue a particular truth. Remember that twos work to find balance and harmony, craving authenticity, partnership, and duality. How has what we've learned with the ace impacted our sense of self, our understanding of the world, our capacity for exploration? How does overcoming an intellectual stalemate help us clarify what we want to achieve?

It can be tempting to brush past this card when we draw it, or to feel uncomfortable with what it represents. After all, no one likes to believe that they could be wrong, or that they are choosing something that could hurt them down the line, and a crossroads of discovery can feel overwhelming. But by taking the time to grapple with what this new truth means and moving forward with clarity and intention, we can go in a direction that is best for us, that acknowledges everything we know up to this point. This is a card for processing, for being brutally honest with the self, for recognizing what we fear and being willing to confront it anyway. Just because we can't predict the future doesn't mean that we are unable make a well-informed decision about what to pursue in our present.

In Readings

The Two of Swords gives us space to air out our anxieties while also firmly reminding us that we need to move forward. There's only so long that we can sit around panicking, indulging our fears and worries—the choice is not going to change simply because we refuse to make it.

JOURNAL PROMPT: *Where are your doubts coming from, and how can you evaluate your options with clarity and purpose rather than fear? How do you balance patience with drive? What is holding you back from movement? What are you really afraid of?*

FINDING THE FOOL

Three of Swords

THREE // Innovation, creativity, expression, growth, manifestation

AIR // Logic, pragmatism, information, communication, knowledge, associated with the mind

KEYWORDS // unexpected truth · heartbreak · painful revelations · turmoil · necessary acknowledgment

A path forward was chosen and we pursued it with focus and determination. Yet in the process of following our truth, in investigating and examining with new knowledge in tow, a harsh reality comes crashing in. Something comes to light that we did not anticipate, and we experience feelings of hurt, betrayal, even anger. This divulgence is painful but also deeply necessary, reminding us of our strength, wisdom, and courage in questioning and enduring things that others may avoid. This powerful disclosure, this sense of revelation, is the bitter medicine of the Three of Swords.

• • •

Perhaps we took a chance that didn't pay off or acted on an assumption that was quickly proven false—but no matter what's happened, we're scrambling to adjust and grappling with the pain of the unexpected. The Three of Swords can feel like a small slight or a massive betrayal, but in spite of our hurt and frustration, this is something we must contend with, something we cannot overlook. Sometimes this is self-sabotage, a pain that we have inflicted on ourselves, while other times it's a wound given to us by someone we trust, love, or value. But regardless of the circumstance, we find ourselves struggling, suffering, caught off guard, and uncertain of how we will get through it.

This card hurts. It's a painful blade of truth sliding into an unsuspecting heart, a harsh and surprising revelation that knocks us off of our feet. But the positive thing about the Three of Swords is that this is genuine awareness, an acknowledgment of something that is really going on. Threes offer genuine and truthful expression: there are no lies here, only revelations. And as painful and challenging and frustrating as this can be, as much as we may feel like we've been let down by someone or tricked or manipulated, we can now start the process of accepting the way that things truly are. Truth is not always kind, but it does create freedom.

While this card can be difficult, we learn so much about who we are and what we are capable of through this struggle. It's here that we find our resilience, our magic, learn what inspires us and keeps us motivated and allows us to move forward. The Three of Swords may initially feel like something that could destroy us, but it's important to acknowledge that this card is not the Tower, or the Devil, isn't some catastrophe that reshapes everything. It's a wound, one that will become a scar, and it helps us recognize and eventually reclaim our power.

In Readings

This card often gives us the space to acknowledge our pain, our anger, our sadness. It gently encourages us to consider where we may be nurturing that pain, clinging to that sorrow, or ripping open old wounds again and again to prevent healing. Heartbreak can sometimes feel like protection, indulgence even, but in giving ourselves permission to recover, we often find that we are stronger than we realized. This card has a lesson to offer, but we can discover its truth only by actually dealing with our pain.

> JOURNAL PROMPT: *What are you clinging to, indulging in, and where might you be able to grant yourself freedom? How does your strength manifest, and what do you need in order to heal? What are you learning about your own habits, and how can you look forward instead of backward?*

Four of Swords

FOUR // Structure, organization, systems, progression, foundations, stability

AIR // Logic, pragmatism, information, communication, knowledge, associated with the mind

KEYWORDS // mental rest · recovery · stepping back from movement · establishing boundaries · healing

On the heels of a tender truth, we crave retreat. Our minds need time to rest and recover. Rather than pressing on, we step back from movement, creating boundaries of protection and healing. We set down our sword, tend to our internal selves, leave those unexplored roads for another day. And in choosing self-care and self-compassion, in recognizing our limits and not judging ourselves for them, we embrace the necessary retreat of the Four of Swords.

• • •

There are times when sanctuary is necessary. After a struggle, challenge, or major obstacle, our minds often need intellectual discipline: quiet opportunities for reflection and self-assessment. And while the Four of Swords may not be something we choose deliberately, it's almost always something that we desperately require in order to truly heal from all that we have been through. Here, we sit in the eye of the storm and allow ourselves to wait, to settle, to ponder. We set down that heavy blade and offer ourselves a much-needed respite.

Taking control of healing is not just about being productive when we start working again; it isn't just giving ourselves a break so that we can come back fresh with new ideas and additional energy. Instead, the Four of Swords is about taking space for insight and protecting our perceptions of all that has happened. When we push past our own hurt or exhaustion and force ourselves to endure for the sake of pride, it can cause real harm, prohibiting us from processing our experiences fully and learning from our mistakes. No one can see clearly through exhaustion, can make wise decisions when in excruciating pain. Instead, this card wants us to take the time to evaluate where we are, setting new boundaries so that we can adequately prepare for the next challenge.

But rest is hard, and this card can often be a difficult one to see, particularly if you're someone who struggles to turn off your problem-solving mind or delegate to even the most trusted companions. The Four of Swords isn't telling us that we aren't needed, that we don't matter—but it is acknowledging that anything we do right now will not be particularly useful. Fours establish and protect stability, and in this card, we see that manifesting as a need for mental and intellectual recovery. This is a chance to set some new boundaries for ourselves, to put protections in place that will help us eventually move forward with new clarity.

In Readings

The Four of Swords demands that we pause without expectation. This isn't a break that we need to "make up for later," and isn't time off that we will have to pay back. Instead this is proper recovery, shoring up defenses, refusing to get caught up in falsehoods or deceptions. With this card, we lay down our swords and consider the world outside of whatever battle we're fighting, reflecting on our path and our priorities. In other words, put the cards down and take a fucking break.

> JOURNAL PROMPT: *How can you protect yourself from intrusive thoughts, create boundaries for your mind and heart? What do you need in order to actually, truly, find rest? What helps you heal?*

Five of Swords

FIVE // Change, freedom, exploration, tension, growth, adventure, balance, transition

AIR // Logic, pragmatism, information, communication, knowledge, associated with the mind

KEYWORDS // disastrous movement · ambition · determination · inflexibility · conflict · conquering at a cost

Having completed our rest, we now grab our sword and eagerly charge ahead, ready to get back on our chosen path. But our energy is erratic, our determination distracting, and we rush headlong into conflict, determined to win at any cost. That intense desire to prove ourselves becomes destructive, and we find ourselves frustrated, even if we come out on top. This kind of fruitless friction, this craving to fight, is the restless clamor of the Five of Swords.

• • •

Intellectual adjustments can feel complicated. After the heartbreak of the Three of Swords and the deliberate retreat of the Four of Swords, the five comes charging in with tenacity and grit, desperate to win something, *anything*. This is sharp edges and harsh words, clashing blades and throwing our hands up, a sense of frustration and irritation that isn't soothed by being declared the victor. If you know anything about the Santa Ana winds, this may seem familiar: it's swirling, infuriating chaos. Our efforts lack conviction because they don't move us forward in any way—instead we are full of hot air, getting in our own way rather than clearing a path toward something real. And while all of this pointless conflict might burn off some steam, it also brings out the worst in us, resulting in hostility, intimidation, or even bullying. The Five of Swords is not a good look.

It can be tempting to think, when we're in this space, that we took too much time to rest and heal, that we've gone soft somehow. We want to come back in with our sword sharpened and flashing, bringing a fresh idea that wins everyone over and lets us prove our value. Fives want to change things up, want to challenge restrictions and find freedom and push through uncertainty. But winning at any cost can be the same as losing, and when we're willing to sacrifice anything to gain a hollow victory, it's usually more damaging than useful.

The Five of Swords can also manifest as an inability to compromise. We're all susceptible to stubbornness in different ways, and intellectual obstinacy can lead us to cling to certain ideas, dismiss alternative perspectives, even go to war over a difference of opinion. By refusing to learn or grow, by doubling down on even the worst plans simply because they're ours, we can get ourselves into all kinds of sticky situations, alienating ourselves and pushing even our most trusted advisors out of the way. With the Five of Swords, we're so eager to make progress that we ignore new information or the experiences of other people, sharpening our sword for a battle that may not really matter. Yet intellectual adjustments and shifts in perspective are possible, and by looking at our work through a new lens, we can reframe our struggles, even find new ways forward that don't cause lasting damage.

In Readings

The Five of Swords demands that we stand down, back off, chill out. We're a hot mess: not actually accomplishing anything, and almost certainly making things worse instead of gaining progress. This is an opportunity to consider what is truly driving us, to think about what we're saying instead of just reciting old beliefs or stirring up trouble.

JOURNAL PROMPT: *What are you fighting for? Where are you being harsh, destructive, obnoxious? Are you trying to prove something to other people, or to yourself? What would feel even better than winning?*

Six of Swords

SIX // Harmony, nurturing, community, caretaking, movement, pride

AIR // Logic, pragmatism, information, communication, knowledge, associated with the mind

KEYWORDS // travel · moving away from harm · a fresh start · clarity · purpose · decisive action · change

We've managed to extricate ourselves from conflicts and confrontations, and have recognized the need for a new path. Although it's hard to leave old patterns behind, we take our sword in a different direction, vow to pursue truth in a way that does less harm to us. And while there is still uncertainty ahead, we know that this is the best, healthiest, smartest move for us right now. This strength of purpose, this willingness to start again, is the power and magic of the Six of Swords.

• • •

Breaking personal patterns of thought, action, and emotion can be incredibly difficult, and with the Six of Swords, we make an important mental shift away from a particular pathway, belief, or expectation. In liberating ourselves, we experience true movement and growth, and often this intellectual expansion is accompanied by literal travel or physical relocation. We prioritize clarity, find a new sense of purpose, and create distance between old methods and new ambitions. And by processing all that we have learned so far, we are able to understand the lessons we've been offered and put our energy into new, necessary growth.

Essentially, this card is about getting out of our own way. After the conflict and frustration of the Five of Swords, the six gives us the gift of a fresh start—but it requires work on our end, flexibility and humility and a willingness to try another solution to existing challenges. Sixes always seek harmony, and in leaving something old behind, we nurture the self, making a new path toward whatever we hope to achieve. There's a clarity to this card, an ability to suddenly see things through a new lens, that's reminiscent of the ace: a flash of insight, an awareness of where we've been fucking up, a fresh determination to see our ideas through. We shake off the cobwebs, make an important, boundaried choice, and take decisive action toward our future.

There can sometimes be bitterness or regret with this moment. We're in the calm after the storm and in spite of the clear skies ahead, the lucidity about our experiences, we are also able to now see our mistakes in stark simplicity—which can be an intensely painful experience. Yet in admitting where we've gone wrong, in understanding where and how we went off course, we can create opportunities for adjustment, growth, and forgiveness. In spite of our stubbornness, we are not alone, and not without options. We simply have to be willing to admit our faults and regroup.

In Readings

This card gently but firmly holds space for our more difficult experiences. It often acknowledges any hurt that we may be feeling, any tenderness or uncertainty or fear that is accompanying our movement. The Six of Swords knows that what we are doing is not easy, not simple, not without effort—and also recognizes that we may be tempted to turn back, to return to the familiar in spite of the pain that we have escaped. But this card is cheering us on, reminding us that we are doing something hard but necessary, that we are prioritizing our own needs in a way that is not selfish but compassionate. We are allowed to choose ourselves.

JOURNAL PROMPT: *What stories have you been telling yourself about your choices and circumstances? How are you making real change, and what narratives are you releasing? How are you learning to use truth as a tool instead of as a weapon?*

Seven of Swords

SEVEN // Intelligence, duality, movement, determination, protection, responsibility

AIR // Logic, pragmatism, information, communication, knowledge, associated with the mind

KEYWORDS // secrecy · hesitation · lack of trust · holding back · assumptions · doubt · insecurity · strategy

After removing ourselves from a challenging situation and starting down a new path, we find ourselves cautious, uncertain, untrusting. Our willingness to share and receive information has changed, and we crave secrecy, hesitating to act or collaborate. There's a deliberation to our movements, a kind of vigilance that we haven't yet expressed. And in this self-protective mode, this fear of acting too quickly or being deceived again, we embody the wavering prudence of the Seven of Swords.

• • •

Truth is a sticky thing. Even in times of real clarity, we can struggle to see what is right in front of us, avoiding looking directly at something ugly, something uncomfortable, something unfair. We find all kinds of ways to change the subject, rationalize, or reprioritize, hoping that if we wait for new information it will somehow offer us the reality that we really want to see. The Seven of Swords sits in this tension between wanting to know the truth and being afraid of what it may reveal. This is a card of reluctance, assessment, trying to control or hide from information—and in working with the Seven of Swords, it often calls us out, indicating that we are putting ourselves first without knowing the consequences of that choice.

Even if we are completely aware of our own doubts and indecision, the Seven of Swords does not necessarily indicate a vicious or deliberately harmful choice. Sometimes denial is a form of self-preservation, a way to keep the peace or maintain the status quo—and other times we are simply too exhausted, too overwhelmed, to deal with another difficult truth, or to take an action that may potentially blow up in our faces. This card holds a lot of complexity, as we attempt to appraise timing, adjust expectations, and seek truth.

The Seven of Swords can speak to a lack of trust, a worry that we are missing crucial information or that someone else is trying to do us harm. Information is powerful and those that hold it or hide it can end up wielding control over those around them. But truth can also be paralyzing, causing us to doubt our own actions and choices, leaving us stuck in a stagnant cycle of worry and doubt. When we aren't sure whom we can talk to, whom we can share information or realizations with, it can make any decision feel loaded—and when we don't even trust ourselves to act rationally or think through all the angles of a problem, it may feel easier to hide.

Yet this card demands that we take the time to consider what we are doing. Sevens want to understand what lies underneath, want to appreciate the spiritual and personal motivations for actions. Depending on your identity and the amount of privilege you enjoy, it can be easy to ignore ugly realities, difficult truths, painful events. Particularly in our current political climate, it can be simpler, more comfortable, to pretend that certain things are not happening, to ignore the storm brewing on the horizon and hope that if we ignore something for long enough, it will simply disappear. And while giving ourselves rest during traumatic times is important, while it takes more than one person to enact wide systemic change, ignoring major issues for too long inevitably causes real harm to everyone—ourselves included.

In Readings

The Seven of Swords asks us to be honest with ourselves about our circumstances, our actions, and our intentions. If you've been staying out of the path of conflict, consistently choosing the options that keep you comfortable or allow you to disengage, this can be a wake-up call to acknowledge realities and to expand your perspective. Rather than avoiding truth or rationalizing your strategies, consider the secrets you're keeping, the ways that you may be isolating yourself.

> JOURNAL PROMPT: *Which facts have you been denying or evading, and how does clinging to one particular perspective make you feel safe? How is hiding serving you, and is it harming anyone else? Whom do you trust, and how can you rely on additional outlooks?*

Eight of Swords

EIGHT // Power, momentum, discipline, assurance, control, practicality

AIR // Logic, pragmatism, information, communication, knowledge, associated with the mind

KEYWORDS // feeling trapped · uncertainty · powerlessness · limited perspective · pessimism · fear of failure

That desire to be careful about whom we share with has continued to grow, and we find ourselves stuck, unwilling to move in any direction. Everything feels corrupted, traitorous, and we don't know where to go, aren't sure whom or what we can rely on. We may hear advice from people we once trusted, may recognize that others are trying to help us—but our fear is too overwhelming. That paralyzing worry, that trap of our own making, is the frustration of the Eight of Swords.

• • •

Fear has a way of choking everything else out. When we don't take the advice offered by the Seven of Swords, instead doubling down on our doubts and avoidance and hesitation, we can find ourselves in a dark and confusing place. The Eight of Swords explores what happens when we deliberately ignore the storm that's been brewing, in spite of the clouds and the hail and the strong, destructive winds. This sometimes manifests as dismissing help, not wanting to burden anyone else or believing that we aren't worthy of assistance. And when we are caught in this kind of intellectual trap, when we don't know how to access support, it can feel that we're completely out of options.

The shitty thing about this card is that it depends on a warped or overly harsh personal narrative and rarely reflects our actual circumstances. What we think we know is not the truth. Remember that eights are about power—but when we feel that we have none, it can stop us dead in our tracks. With the Eight of Swords, we believe that we have no options, that failure is imminent, that solutions are impossible. We're so caught up in the potential dangers that we can't take strides to avoid them, are so paralyzed by the sound of tornado alarms that we can't make ourselves run to the cellar. It feels safer, easier, to just cover our eyes and ears and hope that the storm will pass—yet this level of denial and avoidance accomplishes nothing,

The solution to the Eight of Swords often lies in addressing our inaccurate beliefs and reclaiming our power over vulnerability, something that is much easier said than done. A different perspective can make everything much more explicit, but it may require us being honest about our fears and perceptions with someone we trust, and believing them when they offer compassionate, honest advice. This card captures the disconnect between what we want to do and what we need to do, but if we can recognize the trap we're caught in, we can also find the key that will grant us freedom.

In Readings

The Eight of Swords is a reminder that we have far more options available than we think, but that change will not happen without effort. When we look critically at our personal narrative, we must analyze what we know for certain and acknowledge where we are making assumptions. If there are options we have dismissed, solutions we haven't considered, this is a chance to test limits out, to see what happens. At this point, any movement is better than staying where we are.

JOURNAL PROMPT: *Where are harsh thoughts taking over, doubts limiting your creativity? How are you giving up before you've even started? Who can you lean on, turn to, ask for a fresh perspective? What would it take for you to recognize that you are worthy of support, that your safety and comfort are worth fighting for?*

Nine of Swords

NINE // Observation, personal responsibility, collective growth, expansion, clarity

AIR // Logic, pragmatism, information, communication, knowledge, associated with the mind

KEYWORDS // nightmares · being paralyzed by fear · isolation · lack of trust · darkness · spiraling · anxiety

We've thoroughly isolated ourselves from everything and everyone, and now are plagued by nightmares as our deepest fears and worries overwhelm our minds. It feels like nothing is safe, like there is nowhere we can go and no one we can trust, and we retreat even further into ourselves. And in surrendering entirely to anxiety and terror, in feeling our sanity beginning to fray, we are forgotten in the twisting chaos of the Nine of Swords.

• • •

There are moments when we can feel ourselves breaking apart. When our thoughts keep spiraling, when we can't separate fear from truth, when wretchedness is eroding the edges of our most rational self, the Nine of Swords has a hold of us. This is desperation warring with defeat, drowning in hopelessness, feeling lost within our own darkness. We're convinced of our own failure, cannot hear advice or insights, and are deeply, wildly isolated in our terror. Even if the path to freedom is right in front of us, we have abandoned all concept of movement or deliverance—instead, we believe that there is no possible way forward and cannot conceive of living in any other state.

If the Eight of Swords is ignoring the sirens and warnings, the nine is getting swept up in the terrifying storm, lost in the swirling winds, with no idea which way is up or how to survive. This is a grim, frightening sensation of powerlessness, reflecting the darkness that our minds are capable of creating. It's a miserable place to be and can speak to trauma, PTSD, anxiety, depression, and the kind of paralysis that accompanies our most primal fears, our most deep-seated terrors. When nightmares tint our realities and we cannot untangle dreadful fantasy from true fact, it can feel utterly impossible to find our way back to the real world. Yet in making space for this intensity of emotion and confusion within the tarot, we honor this experience, recognize its validity as well as its challenges. There are times when seeing ourselves reflected in the cards is incredibly comforting, and when this card emerges, it can serve as acknowledgment and make us feel seen.

Letting fear take over is another means of giving up—it gives us an excuse to stay trapped, to surrender responsibility, to sink into our sorrow instead of looking for a way out. Nines can be solitary but in removing ourselves completely from reality, we remain stuck, haunted, longing for change but doing nothing to create it. Sometimes there's a kind of comfort in this sensation, a relief in refusing to make progress, permission or even encouragement to wallow in our own misery. Yet the longer we stay in this Nine of Swords place, the harder it can be to get out. We must take active steps to show ourselves love and compassion, must be intentional about dealing with the severity of the situation, must use wisdom to assess our convictions and find truth rather than scrambling for lost control.

In Readings

This card indicates a real need to ask for help from those we trust: friends, chosen family, and medical professionals. Nines are often about service, but with the Nine of Swords, we need to let others serve us. These people can help us remember how to access our power, reminding us of our strength, our brilliance, our magic. And by reconnecting with the loving community that knows and cherishes us, we can find our way back to ourselves, can begin to recover and even heal from all that we have endured.

> JOURNAL PROMPT: *How have you isolated yourself, and how might that be contributing to any feelings of hopelessness, loneliness, or pessimism? Where are your doubts taking over, and what would help you find your way back to reality? Which repetitive thoughts are you clinging to, and why? Where is fear shaping your perceptions?*

Ten of Swords

TEN & ONE // Unity, vision, pride, independence & community together, trail blazing, confidence

AIR // Logic, pragmatism, information, communication, knowledge, associated with the mind

KEYWORDS // defeat · unwillingness to act · rock bottom · victim mindset ·
darkest before the dawn

Our fear and lack of trust in the world have left us crying out in agony, and we shriek out our story to anyone that will listen—the ways that we've suffered, been betrayed, lost any hope. It's a little overdramatic, bordering on ridiculous, but we have lost all sense of perspective and are completely caught up in a personal, twisted narrative of our victimhood. This sensation of hitting rock bottom, this inability to see truth, is the grandiose misery of the Ten of Swords.

• • •

When we ignore the red flags of the Seven of Swords, get tangled in the mental traps of the Eight of Swords, and refuse to ask for help in the Nine of Swords, we find ourselves in a place of complete ruin. This is utter defeat, a sense of bitterness and exhaustion that leaves us gasping for air, insisting that anyone who has the audacity to look our way acknowledge the grief and tragedy that we have endured. The storm may have passed, we may have made it through this dark night of the soul, yet we are still lost to the winds, ignoring the dawning light that has broken through the clouds. In other words, the Ten of Swords has gone beyond any real obstacles we've faced and is now fully entrenched in a victim mindset, insisting that there is no possible solution to our problems, no feasible path to healing, power, or joy. There's a passivity here, a contentment with melodrama that can be impossible to understand from the outside. Rather than trying to escape our circumstances, the Ten of Swords finds a kind of pleasure in the pain, relishes avoiding any actions that might shift our outlook or alter our situation.

With the Ten of Swords, we may be clinging to a particular narrative, demanding that our perspective be validated, wallowing at the end of this particular cycle. Yet in spite of the despondency here, tens also hold space for a new beginning, setting us up for a desperately needed Ace of Swords moment, a new flash of insight and awareness and curiosity. The only thing that can cut through all of this self-pity may be truth, and although we're at our lowest point, the only way to go is up.

It's important to note that this card doesn't pretend that nothing bad has happened; it isn't ignoring the real struggles and heartbreak that have occurred. It's not mocking us or gaslighting us, isn't just telling us to love and light our way out of these struggles. But the Ten of Swords does serve as a reality check, calling us out on our bullshit, serving as a swift kick in the ass that begs us to take ownership of our current condition instead of simply bemoaning it. If we're only seeking pity, we may be disappointed. But if we're willing to be critical of our own choices, if we're able to own up to the choices we've made and the denial we've clung to that landed us here, there's potential for escape, healing, and even new discoveries.

In Readings

The Ten of Swords asks us to acknowledge the ways that we have been intensely focused in our thinking. This is an opportunity to challenge our current version of truth, to unpack where our opinions have come from, to interrogate our desire to stay in our pain instead of looking for ways that we might heal.

JOURNAL PROMPT: *Where is your sorrow really coming from? Which outlooks are you ready to release? How can you recognize what you have been through while also making space for future healing?*

Page of Swords

ELEVEN & TWO // Healing, choice, intentionality, sensitivity, intuition, psychic wisdom, duality

AIR // Logic, pragmatism, information, communication, knowledge, associated with the mind

KEYWORDS // endless ideas · curiosity · unique insights · fresh perspective · brainstorming · logical questioning

We may have a lot to learn but we also have a million questions. This fresh perspective on the world, this desire to investigate and question and examine, gives us an edge over those that are less curious. We love our intellect, rely on our ability to perceive and interrogate, and are eager to find and share information, to make sure everyone is as well-informed as we are. In starting down a new path of discovery, in being open to whatever we find, we embrace the inquisitive presence of the Page of Swords.

• • •

A beginner's mind is a gift. In being free of rules and assumptions, in being able to look at ideas and concepts and theories and fantasies and realities through fresh eyes, we can see things clearly, the way that they truly are. With the Page of Swords, we find a figure with a spirit of interrogation, a curious and active wit, someone clever and intellectually flexible. Rather than trying to bend facts to fit a certain mold or concept, the Page of Wands honors every idea and insight, seeks truth above all, is eager to ask every question and test every hypothesis. A whirlwind of energy, this student of air can seem hectic, unusual, even peculiar. Yet their desire to understand every facet of their reality can open so many doors, exposing flaws and obstacles, revealing opportunities that merit further investigation.

Think of this as a zealous research assistant, an eager new intern, an enthusiastic and inquisitive child—someone who wants to understand exactly how something works, why it came to be that way, and what we could do to improve or enhance it. There is an energy of problem-solving here, a desire for scientific analysis and discovery paired with a need to logically explain something's origin and purpose, to prove its value as a specific component, to recognize its connection to a larger whole. This student appreciates systems, wanting to scrutinize them for what they are as well as to brainstorm different possibilities for new growth.

The numerology of pages, as the eleventh card of their suits, combines the balance and clarity of Justice (11) with the intuitive awareness and quiet observation of the High Priestess (2)—and with the suit of swords, this gives us curiosity and perception, a desire for idealism that is tempered by an ability to perceive reality. There are times when this energy may hit us like a freight train, and other times when we deliberately step into this kind of mentality, recognizing how this open, inquisitive approach can be the most useful path forward. The Page of Swords offers an opportunity to consider new perceptions, curiosities, and beginnings, to put all of our energy and brainpower into something that we don't fully understand yet. But they can also rush to make assumptions; they are so eager to understand that they don't always double-check their facts—remember two energy, always seeking balance. It's here that we indulge our fascination around a particular subject, goal, or idea that we let the things that intrigue us take up space rather than feigning disinterest.

In Readings

The Page of Swords urges us to let our minds wander freely, to indulge our curiosities rather than trying to corral our imagination toward a specific purpose. Even if a question seems random, even if it feels like a stray thought leads you down a bizarre or trivial rabbit hole, give yourself permission to chase intellectual satisfaction. This is a time for experimentation, not final drafts.

> JOURNAL PROMPT: *How are you being intellectually stimulated? What are you curious about, fixated on, eager to examine more closely? Where might more information help clarify your sense of purpose and joy? What do you know, and what are you learning?*

Knight of Swords

TWELVE & THREE // Expansion, manifestation, growth, abundance, creativity, experimentation

AIR // Logic, pragmatism, information, communication, knowledge, associated with the mind

KEYWORDS // intense focus · rapid pursuit of success · intellectual purity · trail blazing · logical exploration

Our many investigations and new discoveries have given us a powerful confidence. We're eager to charge into the world, focused on a goal that we will do anything to achieve. All of the information we've found feels empowering, exciting, and we feel certain that everyone will agree with us if they'll only take the time to listen. Yet sometimes difficult truths can pierce us with impossible precision, leaving us gasping for breath, trying to defend ourselves against something we cannot fight. This desire to expand and explore, this need to prove ourselves, this effort to balance truth with perspective is the decisive striving of the Knight of Swords.

· · ·

The sensation of things falling into place, of one logical conclusion leading to the next, can be incredibly energizing, even intoxicating. We discover something important, and it reveals other truths, allows us to rearrange what we know, helps us understand how to accomplish something in a pivotal way. The Knight of Swords is incredibly determined but they're also deeply realistic, understanding the importance of limits and recognizing the power of functionality, utility, and common sense. This isn't a pie-in-the-sky dreamer but rather someone who wants to accomplish, organize, systematize, all while proving their brilliance, courage, and problem-solving capabilities. Think about a storm chaser, someone who knows that in spite of the danger, their work provides vital data and contributes to collective knowledge in an intensely valuable way. These knights want to have practical applications for their ideas, want to see things go from imagination to reality as quickly and efficiently as possible.

There's an intensity with this figure, a desire for clarity and precision at any cost, that can make this energy both effective and overwhelming. Knowing what we believe, feeling that we have facts and logic on our side, can be empowering—and we can find so much joy and confidence in rapid movement, in putting everything that we have into a specific ambition. But being stubborn to all other perspectives can limit our ability to grow. And sometimes, knights are so eager to move forward, so anxious to prove their worth and individuality, that they can get caught up in visible progress and risk missing the forest for the trees.

What does an intellectual quest look like? Sometimes it's fact-finding, exploring every mental pathway, reading experiments and papers and studies and research, looking at something as objectively as possible. But at other times, it's being certain that we're right about something and looking only at the evidence that supports our argument. It might be correct, our perspective—we might be onto something important, even revolutionary. In spite of our eagerness, if we listen only to information that corroborates our opinions, we won't have the full picture and may come to conclusions that aren't nearly as logical as we believe. Knights, as card twelve in their suits, balance the energy of the Hanged One (12) and the Empress (3), and in the figure of the Knight of Swords we see an eagerness to prove intelligence at war with a potential lack of flexibility. They possess a desire to dominate, an inability to control how and when we move in exactly the way we might want.

In Readings

The Knight of Swords offers a challenge: to keep our minds clear, pay attention to everything, and be receptive to learning and losing instead of obsessing over a desperate need to prove ourselves the smartest person in the room. This card wants us to enjoy our sense of confidence while still making room to interrogate our assumptions, to challenge our assessments, to slow down and remember that logic is not the only tool we have in our toolbox. Intense focus and concentration are powerful gifts, and we need to use these gifts with intention rather than getting swept up in a craving for success.

JOURNAL PROMPTS: *How do you know your idea is the best idea? How do you know when you're right? Where are you operating from a place of authenticity and where are you craving validation? What truths are you willing to accept and where might you be denying something because it's inconvenient?*

Queen of Swords

THIRTEEN & FOUR // Focus, pragmatism, independence, determination, organization, expression

AIR // Logic, pragmatism, information, communication, knowledge, associated with the mind

KEYWORDS // sharp questions · honesty · authenticity · intelligence · perception · logical boundaries

Our studies and experiments have paid off. We have grown, changed, and learned more about ourselves and our world. This keenly developed insight has given us an ability to set boundaries and see through bullshit, and we become known for our wisdom, our advice, our intelligence. We don't act with haste but instead seek to understand multiple perspectives, and many come to us for counsel, appreciating our honesty and pragmatism. In stepping into an advisory role, in teaching others how to move through the world with both caution and courage, we embody the shrewdness and discretion of the Queen of Swords.

• • •

Words, ideas, and information hold an incredible amount of power. And when we understand how sharp these tools can be, when we know how to wield them with intention and clarity, we're able to see through bullshit, to pierce through deception. Rather than struggling to honor impressions or perceptions, the Queen of Swords recognizes the value of their own experiences and trusts in their innate capacity to move independently. Like a brilliant meteorologist, this is someone who can read patterns and understand anomalies, who studies with patience and shares information that helps everyone around them make intelligent, informed decisions. The Queen of Swords isn't afraid to create structures of safety, putting a high value on their own viewpoints without dismissing the experiences and knowledge of other people.

Truth can be sometimes painful to hear and process, yet this astute queen doesn't let that serve as an excuse for hiding important information. There's a way to be honest while still being kind, and the artist of air is able to dance that line with grace and compassion, giving people what they need to make an informed decision without belittling them. Queens know how to divide and conquer, respecting the flow of the world around them and establishing a safe, secure place for themselves and those they trust—and the Queen of Swords recognizes the necessity of discernment, knowing what to share and what to keep private, understanding how powerful it can be to wait for the right moment instead of pushing to make things happen as quickly as possible.

There's a deep sense of responsibility in this figure, a balance of justice and compassions, a desire to prioritize authentic movement. As the thirteenth cards of the suit, queens are a numerological combination of the inevitable release of Death (13) and the powerful, protective boundaries of the Emperor (4)—and in the suit of swords, this translates to logical building blocks, an ability to see what needs to be done and create a system that accomplishes it. The Queen of Swords is a visionary, someone who thrives within structure, who is able to understand how the known and the unknown each hold weight while simultaneously creating safe constructs for others to theorize within. Our questions and curiosities can reveal so much about who we are and offer deep insights into the people that we are becoming. In embracing intellectual uncertainty, in making space for facts as well as fiction, the Queen of Swords teaches us about being brave enough to be honest, about confronting challenges head on instead of deceiving the self.

In Readings

The Queen of Swords asks us to temper control and discipline with compassion, gentleness, and love for the self, honoring multiple perspectives while still trusting our own discernment. Kindness and boundaries are not opposites, and saying no can help us define our values, our needs, and our desires in a necessary and intimate way.

JOURNAL PROMPT: *How are you organizing your thoughts, or creating structures around intellectual pursuits? What helps you integrate accumulated knowledge with lived experience? How do you decide when to act and when to observe or gather new insights?*

King of Swords

FOURTEEN & FIVE // Personal freedom, change, leadership, curiosity, knowledge, observation

AIR // Logic, pragmatism, information, communication, knowledge, associated with the mind

KEYWORDS // mediation · seeking truth · balance · focus & concentration · discernment · logical expansion

Our ability to lead by example has thrust us into a more public-facing role, and we find ourselves serving as an arbiter of truth for others, solving complex problems and using our most rational, practical minds to navigate issues and see the bigger picture. While we can sometimes come across as cold or unfeeling, we have learned how to balance the head and the heart, and recognize when the mind is our best possible tool. This certainty and confidence, this ability to distinguish and mediate, this power of perception and observation, is the assertive, responsible integrity of the King of Swords.

· · ·

Intelligence is not just about the recitation of facts, the ability to memorize information or gather proof for a particular argument. It's also about capacity and wit, knowing when we have been bested, understanding which questions are worth engaging with and which ones we can leave for another day. The King of Swords values shrewdness, and while they are fully capable of solving problems, this ruler also knows that their position requires them to delegate. Leadership is so often about putting the right person into the right position and then trusting them to handle whatever comes their way, empowering them to make decisions and judgment calls without interfering or hovering. Think of this king as a climate change scientist, logically tracing patterns between the past and the future, someone who can predict outcomes and works to research, educate, and drive necessary change.

Dedicated to both protection and restructuring, the King of Swords gives us opportunities to analyze and criticize, to trust our convictions but balance them out with observations. When we direct focus and know what matters, we are able to devote consistent concentration and attention to our most valuable efforts rather than getting caught up in negative thought patterns or spiraling emotions. Kings are leaders, visionaries, architects: these are people that understand how much strength they hold, how distinctive and valuable their magic is. In trusting our sense of logic, wisdom, and reason, we can use a combination of good sense and risk assessment to make major moves forward, adjusting and shifting in ways that expand our mindset and change the conversation around difficult topics. This king has the power to guide others through deductions, to challenge the status quo, to expand perspectives. And when we look at a problem through a new lens, all kinds of solutions begin to emerge.

Both the King and Queen of Swords have valuable insights and imaginative visions, clear ideas about what they intend to accomplish. But while the queen thrives by setting limits and empowering others to work within or around them, the king works beyond these boundaries, knowing when to break them and how to build new ones, carving out space for powerful change. Navigating the energy of Temperance (14) and the Hierophant (5) as the fourteenth card of the suit, the king of air is like a brilliant teacher who utilizes the Socratic method in conversations, constantly challenging and conversing, asking endless questions without trying to force someone into a particular perspective. They may have opinions, even know certain things as fact, yet they encourage and interrogate, bringing everyone into the conversation and making space for endless solutions, adventures, and changes. This leader knows how to dig for the truth in ways that invite multiple perspectives and understands how to listen without flinching.

In Readings

The King of Swords asks us to utilize our intellect, insights, and observational skills to think beyond existing limits. Tradition and convention have their place, but when it comes to facts, experiences, and truths, it's necessary to challenge and question, to interrogate, to constantly reconsider what we know and what we are simply assuming.

JOURNAL PROMPT: *What does integrity mean to you? How do you uncover and understand truth? What do you never question, and where would debate expand perspectives for an entire community? How do you lead with your mind, and how do you balance controversy with conservative ideas? How do you decide what is true, and what do you do with that kind of certainty?*

THE SUIT OF CUPS

WATER

Emotions, connections, love, intimacy, community intuition, associated with the heart

Water is a slower and more methodical element, and the suit of cups traverses our inner depths—our feelings, relationships, connections, intuition, dreams, empathy, faith, and community. Cups explore our personal emotions, the ways that our passions impact and influence us, the vulnerabilities that we share or hide, the spiritual beliefs that we hold about ourselves. In knowing what dwells within us, in recognizing our own ebbs and flows, we also allow our hearts to mingle with others, building relationships, partnerships, and communities. Intimacy is a vulnerable, sensitive thing and can have a major impact on how we show ourselves love, compassion, and kindness.

As an element, water is sweeping and surging, powerful, with endless depths that can rage or trickle depending on its environment. We can't always see what's under the water's surface, don't always understand what is simmering, aren't always certain which currents may be impacting movement. Water explores the emotional self, holding space for mystery, intensity, uncertainty, desire, jealousy, anger, joy, pleasure, and so many other sensations—some of which grow from within us, and others that result from our interactions with individuals and communities. We may not be able to control our emotions themselves but we do have power over how we express (or hide) them, over the ways that they influence our responses, decisions, and actions.

Similarly, the suit of cups flows through vulnerability and sensitivity, connections and loneliness, support and loss, as we work to identify our personal and relational needs. Sometimes we let ourselves be seen by those we trust, and other times we crave secrecy and protection. We put boundaries around our hearts in the hopes that we won't be hurt. The story of the suit of cups is one of compassion. From the cups we learn to be open and to name our desires. By identifying our longings and asking for what we need, by allowing ourselves to receive support and empathy, we learn to love ourselves. And by getting in touch with those deep emotions, this suit also makes space for intuition, wisdom, and personal magic, teaching us to perceive more than meets the eye and to rely on senses beyond logic.

The challenge of this suit is vulnerability. No matter how authentic and open we work to be, our hearts are tender things, and no one wants to be hurt. Allowing others access to our wildest dreams and most powerful longings can leave us open to harm—and the suit of cups holds space for experiences of loneliness, betrayal, heartache, grief, and a lack of trust. If we struggle to show ourselves the kind of generosity and compassion that we offer to others, it can lead to resentment, anger, or depression—difficult circumstances to be sure but ones that we must acknowledge and navigate rather than bottling up. Within these cards, we find encouragement and support as well as advice on navigating difficult relationships and knowing when to leave something toxic behind.

• • •

As you dive into the suit of cups and the element of water, consider tenderness, attraction, understanding. What does it mean to allow yourself to be seen, noticed, held, appreciated? How does getting to know other people help you get to know yourself? When does intuition come into play, and how often do you trust your gut feelings? What do emotions teach you?

Ace of Cups

ONE // Motivation, confidence, independence, vision, trail blazing

WATER // Emotions, connections, love, intimacy, community intuition, associated with the heart

KEYWORDS // wellspring · open heart · joy of connection · faith · big dreams · vulnerability · seeking love

There are moments when we can feel our hearts expanding, when new emotions flood us and new connections inspire us. The world is beautiful, and sometimes we feel a door opening, a pathway extending out before us, a community welcoming us in a way that unlocks inspiration and magic. As feelings spill over, as optimism and possibility flood us, we embrace the enchanting wonder of the Ace of Cups.

• • •

Vulnerability is beautiful and necessary—but it also takes intention, focus, and a willingness to be seen. When we are conscious of having the choice to open ourselves up or stay closed, and when we opt to take the risk of letting others see us, it initiates a brand new adventure, launches a beautiful emergence. It's in the Ace of Cups that we see the deep, fathomless potential of relationships, that we discover our own needs and longings, that we honor our truest beliefs and personal sense of faith. This is a flash of heart, a desire to nurture, a rush of attraction. Within the Ace of Cups we get a glimpse of all that is possible when we find the strength to lay our hearts bare, own our intensity, and trust our intuition.

This kind of unveiling does not happen in a vacuum; it is not as simple as flipping a switch or opening a door. We need to feel safe enough to let our feelings and desires overflow, to allow ourselves to soften, to undo the many locks and chains that we may have layered over our tender hearts. The Ace of Cups is only the beginning of this journey—the first gasp of emotional anticipation—when we recognize the magic that is growing within and around us. This is the moment when we decide to view the world through a lens of hope, to be ready for the full spectrum of love and emotion.

We may have recognized a craving for connection, love, intimacy within ourselves before now; we may have grappled with loneliness or dissatisfaction at various points in the past. But in addition to the longing we feel, the Ace of Cups also signifies a shift in belief, an awareness that we are capable of receiving all that we desire, an assurance that we deserve to share our wishes and dreams, to build community, to enjoy intimacy. Aces and ones represent the spark of anticipation, the desire for fulfillment, the discovery of something new within ourselves. When we allow that optimism to grow, when we acknowledge that we are receptive to the care and affection of others, we have fully stepped into the magic of the Ace of Cups.

In Readings

This card indicates that a new possibility is at our fingertips. There are opportunities ahead for us to trust ourselves, to give and receive, to connect in deeper and more profound ways than we previously have enjoyed. When we share our hearts with others or do some soul-searching on our own, we risk so much—but we also find the potential for endless, beautiful rewards. The Ace of Cups indicates a hopeful future, reminding us that when we're vulnerable, we have so many more chances for genuine, powerful connection.

> JOURNAL PROMPT: *What kind of access do you extend to others, and how do you practice accessibility within yourself? How deep are you willing to go to understand your wishes and hopes and fears? Are you consistently making space for your intuition to speak, or do you need to be more deliberate about listening to your gut, about letting your heart call the shots?*

Two of Cups

TWO // Sensitivity, intuition, psychic wisdom, choice, awareness, duality

WATER // Emotions, connections, love, intimacy, community intuition, associated with the heart

KEYWORDS // soulmate connection · being seen · intimacy · falling in love · taking a chance · desire · attraction

We move into the world with heart in hand and seek another soul whose energy matches ours—someone who is cut from the same cloth, who makes us feel both safe and wild, who inspires and encourages and delights us. The potential for this kind of deep recognition, this profound desire to know someone better and to be known in the same beautiful way, is the awe and reciprocal pleasure of the Two of Cups.

• • •

Opening our hearts is a choice. We may have recognized a desire for authentic connection with the Ace of Cups, we may have even celebrated our willingness to be vulnerable in the pursuit of relationships. But now that wish becomes a real possibility as we are given an opportunity to establish the kind of intimacy that we've been craving. We meet someone whom we want to know, whom we long to understand, and we feel a passionate desire to be known in return. This is the Two of Cups: a taste of the sweetness and joy of being truly valued by another person, the giddiness and wonder that happen when we have an intense or personal experience with someone else.

No matter what kind of love this card explores—whether friendship, romance, partnership, or community—the Two of Cups feels keenly optimistic. It brings the potential for deep pleasure and rich satisfaction, offering us something more than we currently have. Twos urge us to consider our options. This is a crossroads of connection, an opportunity to build a strong and solid relationship, to let another person or group see us for all that we are. And while there may still be some hesitance in this moment, an awareness of just how big a chance we are preparing to take, we also are allowing ourselves the joy of hope.

Knowing ourselves can be a challenging thing. It is often the work of a lifetime. Although it's important and healthy for us to understand self-sufficiency, to be able to rely on ourselves and identify our needs, we also have the human desire to lean on others, to be cared for, to be loved. No matter how much of a loner we believe ourselves to be, there's magic in finding synergy with another person or group of people. Powerful bonds can be transformative. When we find a new connection that really suits us it can feel effortless, intoxicating, so vibrant that everything else pales in comparison. But we alone control how much time, energy, and vulnerability that we invest into another individual or a community. We alone have to decide if we are simply going to dip our toes in the water of companionship, or if we're brave enough to dive all the way in.

In Readings

The Two of Cups invites us to take the kind of chances that make intimacy possible. This is a choice of the heart, a dizzying rush of attraction or interest that requires us to determine whether or not we want to fully commit to the process. It can be easy to get carried away when it comes to romance or sentimentality, so this is a reminder to be deliberate in our actions, to be thoughtful about how vulnerable we want to be.

> JOURNAL PROMPT: *Where can you feel potential, and what might it take to feed that connection in a way that feels sustainable? How does love help you to be strong, capable, authentic? What do you really desire, and what are you willing to risk in order to find it?*

Three of Cups

THREE // Innovation, creativity, expression, growth, manifestation

WATER // Emotions, connections, love, intimacy, community intuition, associated with the heart

KEYWORDS // community · expanding connections · support & encouragement · chosen family · warmth

Our rich connections keep growing, and we find ourselves with a community of chosen family: people that see us, know us, love us; people that we trust with our hearts and souls. A deep joy flows through our collective as we share dreams, wishes, fears, the things that inspire us, the ambitions that drive us. Knowing that we have this kind of support, that we have people we can lean on and share our magic with, is the communal power and acceptance of the Three of Cups.

• • •

In choosing to be vulnerable, in deliberately sharing our hearts with those we love and trust, new joys emerge. There are many different kinds of connection and affection, many ways to feel and express those sensations. With the Three of Cups, we enjoy the kind of authentic, enduring relationships that support us in our present and empower our future, that consistently remind us of our strength while simultaneously pushing us to grow. This is chosen family, collective magic, transformative friendship, and joyful bonds. It is a feeling of wondrous and awe-inspiring celebration. The Three of Cups is one possible reward for diving into warm, soothing waters, for allowing ourselves the pleasure of intimacy, affection, and vulnerability.

When we let ourselves be seen, and when our intuition guides us to people that genuinely care for us, growth can feel boundless and endless. Remember that three is tied to expression and expansion, and with the suit of the heart, we see this manifest in a genuine, celebratory way. This is the creation of community: when energy and love pool and overflow, when multiple people combine awareness and intuition and emotion together, letting one cup spill into another, ensuring that no one is ever empty. We become more than the sum of our parts, more than our individual vessels, more than a single person moving independently—now we can take renewed pride in what is working, show up for one another in both triumphs and stumbles.

Taking emotional risks can be terrifying. But real, lasting friendships, connections, partnerships endure only when we continue to take those risks, when we choose over and over to be vulnerable. The Three of Cups is a reminder that we are not alone. It represents our commitment to relationships and communities, making space for our most intimate and powerful connections to shine.

In Readings

This card in the suit of cups urges us to celebrate what we have built and to take pride and pleasure in the ways that we experience intimacy. The Three of Cups reminds us of how dearly we are already loved and supported; it can also encourage us to continue taking chances in our relationships, to let ourselves be seen in new ways, to not hide from emotional growth. If we are still in the process of building community, this card can give us a sense of hope that we're on the right track. And if we have started to take for granted the important people in our lives, the Three of Cups can encourage us to express gratitude and joy for their presence.

JOURNAL PROMPT: *How do you build and maintain community? How often do you take risks in friendships, in love, in partnership? If a current pattern or habit isn't working, how might shaking things up help establish new layers of intimacy?*

Four of Cups

FOUR // Structure, organization, systems, progression, foundations, stability

WATER // Emotions, connections, love, intimacy, community intuition, associated with the heart

KEYWORDS // retreat · boredom · isolation · emotional walls · selfishness ·
disappointment · introspection

We may have found strong community and powerful ties—yet the bloom has gone off the rose somewhat, and we find ourselves bored, withdrawn, closed off. Everything exhausts us, annoys us. But rather than investing more deeply in the people we've found, we feel resentful of them, wishing they would make more of an effort yet being frustrated when they do. This internal tension, this desire to isolate, is the disappointed, unsatisfied energy of the Four of Cups.

• • •

Boundaries are not a bad thing. There are times when we must protect ourselves, when we feel the need for limits or rules around how much of our hearts other people have access to. This is particularly true if we are someone who has endured abuse or trauma: putting walls up around our emotions can feel necessary for emotional security and safety. Four is the number of protection, safeguarding, stability, and sturdy, reliable foundations, and with the suit of cups we often find this manifest as relational discipline. If we muddy the waters and distance ourselves to the extreme, if we refuse to engage with our communities and emotions in an authentic way, it can lead to isolation, frustration, or dissatisfaction. The Four of Cups lives in this stifling, awkward place and speaks of a lack of trust or a feeling of boredom with our relationships.

When we don't want to be exposed to hurt but still want to reap the benefits of vulnerability, we can feel incredibly frustrated, even trapped. Intimacy costs something, and while at one point we may have been willing to pay that price, the Four of Cups often represents a moment when the risk no longer feels worth the potential reward. As much as we might like to be able to control our emotions completely or force other people to feel a certain way about us, the reality of the world we live in is that these things are simply not possible. We can be responsible only for ourselves, and sometimes, controlling or understanding our emotions is beyond our capabilities.

One strategy for coping with this lack of control is avoidance and denial of any hurt feelings or anger, while another strategy is keeping relationships at surface level, refusing to let others get past a certain threshold of intimacy. Either way, we're not getting what we actually need. Yet if we can be brave enough to share those burdens, to acknowledge our mistakes, to hold space for those we love and allow them to return the favor, relationships can make this sensation of loneliness easier to bear.

In Readings

The Four of Cups invites us to consider what is really bothering us, to recognize our feelings and be willing to engage with them in a genuine way. There may be layers of hurt buried within us, and it will likely take effort to get through our own emotional barriers. Periods of introspection and contemplation will help us find the truth within. Messy realizations and conversations are simply a reality of being human, but ignoring our difficult emotions rarely helps us heal and may make the issue worse.

JOURNAL PROMPT: *Where are you feeling unsatisfied in your relationships or communities? What do you wish you had, and why are you so sure that it isn't already in your hands? How can you get back in touch with any difficult emotions, and what caused you to bury them in the first place? Are you being selfish in your relationships, and how can you engage in a generous and meaningful way?*

Five of Cups

FIVE // Change, freedom, exploration, tension, growth, adventure, balance, transition

WATER // Emotions, connections, love, intimacy, community intuition, associated with the heart

KEYWORDS // grief · loss · loneliness · heartache · internal scrutiny · guilt · emotional adjustments

We have come through a period of drawing back and contemplation, but now a relationship has fractured, and we find ourselves drowning in grief, overwhelmed by sorrow and sadness. This pain is real and must be recognized as such, with a truthful acknowledgment of what we have endured. Yet we still have people around us that care, that want to extend love and support to us, that will be ready to pick us up when the time comes. This sensation of loss mingling with love is the intense heaviness of the Five of Cups.

· · ·

When real sorrow comes, it must be attended to. With the Five of Cups, we receive an invitation to honor our grief and to grapple with regret, heartbreak, or isolation in an authentic way. Waters that we thought were safe and clear actually caused us harm, a relationship that we leaned on constantly is no longer there, and it feels like we have to rebuild our world without its cornerstone. This is sharp anguish, a mourning for something lost. It can consume us for a time, leaving us gasping for breath and uncertain of what to do next.

Getting to this place required risk, vulnerability, and opening ourselves to the possibility of pain. To this end, the Five of Cups can sometimes indicate remorse: we wonder if we've given too much of ourselves; we worry that we should've made different choices. Fives explore change and tension, a desire for freedom and disruption that can force us to grapple with uncertainty. Rather than seeing this card as an admission of fault, look at the Five of Cups as a reminder that this suffering is temporary. It honors our restricted capacity for hope, the change in devotion that we are experiencing. We may want to reach out to others, may feel desperate for forgiveness or understanding, but all we can do is recognize our pain, surrender to our misery. Hope feels completely out of reach and it may be hard to remember how beautiful intimacy, support, and love can be.

However, this card also makes space for true reflection, asking us to attend to any destructive emotional habits or tendencies to cling to flawed perspectives. When we are able to identify any painful or harmful choices, we can make space for hidden needs and begin to explore the parts of ourselves that haven't felt attended to. The cups may all be spilled but the five reminds us that all is not lost, that the personal progress we've made around vulnerability, relationships, and intuition will not simply disappear as a result of this setback.

In Readings

The Five of Cups honors our pain and recognizes feelings of loss and loneliness. Don't feel guilt or sink into this sorrow—the five asks us to listen to our hearts' needs and gently reminds us that this is not a permanent state of being. Eventually we will turn our gaze from the broken cups at our feet to the whole, filled cups that we've been overlooking. We will heal from this loss but it will take time, and this is an opportunity to show ourselves grace and compassion.

JOURNAL PROMPT: *How do you grieve? Where might you need time, space, or support in processing your hurt, and how can you allow others to assist you during this difficult time? What could interrogating the source of your pain offer you, and how can you be truthful with yourself about where this suffering is coming from?*

Six of Cups

SIX // Harmony, nurturing, community, caretaking, movement, pride

WATER // Emotions, connections, love, intimacy, community intuition, associated with the heart

KEYWORDS // nostalgia · optimism · happy memories · inner child work · joy & hope · celebration · comparison

After a period of grief and recovery, we find ourselves remembering joys past and dreaming of a more hopeful future. Our community has rallied around us and our sense of hope expands, helping us to deepen existing connections and discover new ones. Nostalgia mingles with wonder as we reflect on how far we have come. This beauty and pleasure, this deep sense of comfort in all that we have, is the magic and safety of the Six of Cups.

• • •

Part of overcoming sorrow is finding a new awareness that blessings, connections, and love have never left us. And in the wake of the Five of Cups, the six offers us a chance for a fresh start, new opportunities for beauty and pleasure, alongside remembrances of where we have been. The Six of Cups is a card of roots and nostalgic choices. When we look back on our own history and growth, we can trace the patterns of our development and remember the important relationships and experiences that shaped us. In reflecting on the cool, gentle waters that have soothed us in the past, we can appreciate the flows of the present and begin to embrace essential connections once again.

It takes skill, effort, and intention to view things as they really are instead of making them more complicated than they need to be. Intuition is something that we all possess but must learn to utilize—sometimes it's easier to drown in hurt or avoid something entirely than it is to engage with a challenge, unpack our biases or fears, or acknowledge what it is we truly desire. By remembering beauty, by seeking relationships, by prioritizing pleasure and giving ourselves permission to be authentic, we can establish rituals of joy, integrating love into our daily lives.

We can expand our understanding of self-love. And in making space for everything that we have endured, we can get to know and appreciate ourselves better, remember our strength and courage and power.

Sixes crave harmony, and the Six of Cups is a card often associated with nostalgia, family, or simpler times. This can empower us to consider the foundations that we are building upon, as well as to honor the ones we no longer need. Safe spaces are important, particularly for marginalized or traumatized communities, and this card can make space for the times that we have felt nurtured and comforted, as well as the times that we have needed protection.

In Readings

This card encourages us to consider the gifts that we give to ourselves, the ways that we show ourselves grace, kindness, love, and sweetness. No matter what you have endured, no matter how many times you've had to start over, you are strong, magical, resilient. Rather than comparing our lives or talents or relationships with the ones we see around us, the Six of Cups wants us to celebrate what we have and to continue fostering the dreams that we carry.

JOURNAL PROMPT: *When old feelings or memories come forward, how do you engage with them? What does nostalgia offer you, and how can recognizing former patterns help you be more deliberate about your present choices? How can you be gentle with yourself? What kind of future are you dreaming about, and how has your past helped to shape those dreams?*

Seven of Cups

SEVEN // Intelligence, duality, movement, determination, protection, responsibility

WATER // Emotions, connections, love, intimacy, community intuition, associated with the heart

KEYWORDS // fantasy · illusions · daydreams · indecision · lack of perspective · emotional confusion

In all of this rich expansion, new possibilities stretch out before us. We dream of potential futures, let our imaginations run wild, find ourselves lost in fantasy and wonder and magic. As beautiful as it can be to wander through new worlds, illusions can be deceiving. It's essential that we find a way to balance idealism with realism, to recognize what is possible and what is a pipe dream. This sifting through ideas, this examining of options, is the romantic reverie of the Seven of Cups.

• • •

Sometimes through relationships we find the courage to dive deeper into our own imaginations, learning about hopes and wishes and fears that we didn't know dwelled within us. Yet in traversing the more hidden chambers of our hearts, we find endless possibilities, may even get a bit lost in the idyllic dreams we discover. In the same way, the Seven of Cups has a soft, blurred quality to it, reflecting the many fantasies and possibilities that we can pursue. Family, friendship, romance, partnerships, communities—what is most important to us? What kind of future feels the most authentic, could bring us the most happiness?

There are beauty and magic and wonder in imagining where we might go, in carving out space to trace different pathways forward and consider where they may lead us. And sevens love depth, seeking, questing. They want to understand the *why* of our choices. Yet when we refuse to choose, when we can't or won't identify our most powerful longings, we can be left frustrated, uncertain, and lost. The Seven of Cups can serve as an emotional assessment, an opportunity for intuitive discovery. Saying yes to one path often means saying no to a number of others, and when we struggle to do that, it can feel like we don't know ourselves at all. The challenge of this card is in making a choice rather than getting caught up in fantasies, in knowing our hearts' real desires instead of chasing after something simply because it dazzles us in the moment.

While there is not necessarily a wrong answer here, sometimes things are not exactly what they seem—and if we drift too far away from reality we may start to see things through a distorted lens. The longer we let ourselves sit in this place of rich imagination, tracing the lines of connection and emotion that tether us to our pasts and our futures, often the harder it can become to commit to one choice with real decisiveness. The Seven of Cups carries a gentle warning, advice to make a firm choice and not back down. We cannot necessarily afford to view these decisions through rose-colored glasses, or to indulge in too much dreaming about what could be—instead this card asks us to be realistic about the possibilities.

In Readings

The Seven of Cups helps to clarify which fantasies are tripping us up and urges us to make a decision instead of getting lost in the swirling currents of our interior. Give yourself the space and time to think through each possibility that's before you, but once you identify what you want, make a choice, and move forward. It's essential that you listen to your intuition instead of letting other voices or impulses drown out the whispers of your heart.

JOURNAL PROMPT: *How do you tell the difference between an idea that's fun to indulge and a deep-seated desire? What helps you identify real longings, and how do you prioritize the things that you crave? If you really could have anything you wanted, what would you pursue first? What does your imagination keep leading you back to, and how can you translate that fantasy into a reality?*

Eight of Cups

EIGHT // Power, momentum, discipline, assurance, control, practicality

WATER // Emotions, connections, love, intimacy, community intuition, associated with the heart

KEYWORDS // a necessary rift · walking away · choosing the self · boundaries · a new path · detachment

Choosing one path sometimes means leaving others behind. By opening ourselves up to a new possibility, we find clarity in toxic patterns and relationships, and we acknowledge where our unique magic has been taken advantage of. We become aware of all we have truly done to salvage the situation and now must walk away from something or someone who is causing us harm. In choosing ourselves, in believing that a better way is possible, we find the quiet optimism of the Eight of Cups.

• • •

It's not always obvious when a relationship, situation, or dream is unsatisfying. For so many of us, it's hard to claim what we want—and it feels impossibly selfish or even potentially dangerous to prioritize our needs over the needs of others. Yet the Eight of Cups affirms that sometimes the best thing we can do for ourselves, and for everyone around us, is to recognize when we are being harmed, taken advantage of, or treated as disposable. This is a card of choosing the self, of being brave enough to dream about another kind of friendship, romantic partnership, or community.

The Eight of Cups does not indicate that a new connection has hit its first bump in the road; it doesn't speak of a relationship that's going through a small but undeniable rough patch. Rather, the Eight of Cups provides a moment of internal clarity, a reckoning with toxic, destructive patterns. Eights are about power, and with this card, we recognize where we may have surrendered our personal power and make an effort to reclaim it. Instead of suffering in silence, or tolerating harm, the Eight of Cups asks us to be brave enough to take up space, to take the necessary steps that will allow us to thrive rather than be silenced. This is courage, acknowledging that we believe that we deserve more, choosing to exercise power over old ties.

Don't misunderstand me—I am not advocating that you blow up your life every time something goes wrong. Don't give up your willingness to help other people, or abandon community any time you're overlooked or harmed. But sometimes we keep trying to fix a cup that is shattered beyond repair, putting time and effort and vulnerability into someone who is doing active, consistent, intentional harm. The Eight of Cups is urging us to be honest about the relationships that we are investing in and to consider if the bonds that we are clinging to are hurting us. Is a situation emotionally or physically abusive? Are you constantly expected to put the desires of others before yourself, with no care or awareness of your own needs? Is someone always challenging or ignoring your boundaries, making you feel unsafe?

In Readings

This card asks us to examine the people who have access to our hearts and to consider making adjustments. Sometimes this means a hard conversation or two, while other times it requires a full shift in the structure of a relationship. And while the Eight of Cups can be a painful realization, potentially bringing up feelings of anxiety, fear, or unworthiness, this card is an essential invitation to authentic, compassionate self-care.

> JOURNAL PROMPT: *How often do you choose yourself, and what does it feel like when you do? Where are you tolerating harm, and why? Even if you've worked very hard to reach a certain point in a relationship or community, does it feel as satisfying and valuable as you had hoped? Are you clinging to something that once worked and no longer does, simply because you're too afraid to make a change?*

Nine of Cups

NINE // Observation, personal responsibility, collective growth, expansion, clarity

WATER // Emotions, connections, love, intimacy, community intuition, associated with the heart

KEYWORDS // contentment · pride in the self · wishes · fulfillment · self-respect ·
curiosity · dreaming

We've created so many beautiful things, experienced wonder and love and pleasure, and find ourselves in a state of personal contentment. So much about our life is satisfying. We feel real pride in the communities we have built, the relationships we have cultivated and sustained. And while we still have some hopes and wishes tugging at our hearts, we believe that even more magic is possible. This state of joy, comfort, and fulfillment is the beauty of the Nine of Cups.

• • •

Learning to accept and navigate our emotions, balancing strength and vulnerability, and showing ourselves compassion are incredibly complex skills. There is a power in openness that is often dismissed and minimized by people in power. Yet the Nine of Cups reflects someone who has done the work, has kept their heart soft, has made the time and space for essential relationships while still valuing their own joy. This is a card of loving ourselves and having others love us in return; a sensation of achievement, luxury, contentment, and celebration; a recognition of our wishes coming true. With the Nine of Cups, we have found so much of what we were looking for, have achieved the desires that we have named, and it feels incredible.

The Nine of Cups often also holds something deeper: a glimmer of other, quieter dreams, a small but significant hope for more. Nines speak to expansion and change, setting us up for a new beginning, challenging us to consider what is truly fulfilling. It is possible to feel whole and secure, to be deeply satisfied, and still have space for more wishes, more longings, more expansion. This isn't a lack of gratitude; rather, it is an urging to dig deeper, to consider the wants we haven't fully recognized, the longings we still carry. As we continue to show ourselves love and grace, as we keep trusting our intuition, new ambitions or dreams often reveal themselves. And this isn't a bad thing—it's a beautiful one. Having new desires signifies that we truly understand that wanting things is not inherently selfish. We are learning how to listen to our hearts, to honor those deeply personal dreams, to find the wisdom in vulnerability. In allowing our wants to carry weight, to take up space, we also learn how to validate the longings of other people. We learn how to process desire without shame.

Self-care is a consistent, daily practice, one that is much bigger and broader than a bubble bath or a face mask or an hour at the gym. We all deserve to love ourselves, to shower ourselves with affection, to give ourselves the same grace and kindness and devotion that we show to others. And a major part of this practice is in listening to ourselves, in honoring the cravings we feel, in taking the time to interrogate those desires and understand where they're coming from, how we might achieve them. The Nine of Cups illustrates someone who recognizes the importance of this, someone able to be content in their present moment while also appreciating any new longings that emerge.

In Readings

The Nine of Cups offers comfort and compassion, and reminds us that we are living out a dream, doing something that may have once felt out of reach. We have something now that was once only a fantasy, and that is worth celebrating, worth enjoying. Love is essential and takes many forms. Learning to love ourselves is a gift that keeps on giving, a joy that never fades. Show yourself grace and kindness by toasting to your present and by continuing to dream of an even bigger, brighter future.

JOURNAL PROMPT: *How can you see your accomplishments and achievements in a new light, one that gives you credit for all that you've done? How is your heart soft, open, vulnerable, and how do you maintain that level of gentleness with yourself? What are you learning about yourself from your desires, and how have the things you've achieved created space for new growth? What are you still reaching for?*

Ten of Cups

TEN & ONE // Unity, vision, pride, independence & community together, trail blazing, confidence

WATER // Emotions, connections, love, intimacy, community intuition, associated with the heart

KEYWORDS // reciprocal energy · satisfaction · rich community · flow · deep love ·
collective healing · pleasure

The lingering dreams that we've had are all coming true, and we are living a life of rich harmony, deep joy, powerful connection. Energy flows among us and our loved ones with the ease and gentleness of water, and we are inspired, supported, encouraged, and challenged in all of the best ways. Hope fills our hearts and we feel intensely satisfied in the lives that we have, the love that overflows. This feeling of euphoria, this luxurious and powerful contentment, is the magic of the Ten of Cups.

· · ·

What started as a sense of rich potential—the awareness that an emotional journey was just beginning—has blossomed into a powerful sense of community, an endless outpouring of love, support, encouragement, joy, and warmth. We have built relationships that feel essential, have found people that we trust with our secrets and whose histories and vulnerabilities and desires we want to hold, and have created a chosen family that shares energy equally and openly. We have learned to love ourselves deeply, to celebrate our triumphs and grieve our sorrows, to share our experiences with those we love and to hold treasured memories close. The Ten of Cups is a card of open emotion, a satisfying and ongoing exchange of energy between ourselves and those we love.

While the Nine of Cups is contentment within the self, an expression of compassion and grace in the face of our constant emotional growth, the Ten of Cups expands to encompass the collective, our chosen family, and beyond. This is true happiness: an experience of sharing every part of ourselves, even those parts we fear or avoid or don't completely understand. Those raw, unfinished pieces can sometimes be the most authentic, and within the Ten of Cups is the opportunity to appreciate those aspects of self, to value them and even celebrate them. When energy flows among people evenly and openly, it makes space for so many kinds of magic.

The Ten of Cups is a card of fellowship. It's the small, daily joys; the sweet intimacies between partners and families and friends; the rich pleasure of knowing our place in the world. It's feeling connected to those around us, knowing that we have value, recognizing how loved and appreciated we are. Sometimes we can give more, other times we need to receive. Sometimes we require care, other times we're in a position to provide it. But no matter what is happening, no matter our circumstances, kindness continues to be extended, vulnerabilities continue to be shared, hopes and dreams continue to be achieved. This love and energy are truly reciprocal, a deep flow that unites the collective, a rich and ongoing effort toward healing. When we feel supported in our desire and joy, and we recognize the ways that we feel complete, then Ten of Cups has done its work: it sets the stage for a new beginning, a new longing, to safely emerge.

In Readings

The Ten of Cups urges us to tap into our communities and chosen families and to acknowledge and celebrate the ways that we are supported. The message of this card is not to obsess over perfection but to honor the fact that we are in relationship with people who are willing to try, to learn, to keep growing and transforming and repairing harm. In making space for the full spectrum of emotion, in tackling problems with empathy and sensitivity, we ensure that all of us can thrive.

> JOURNAL PROMPT: *How authentic are you with yourself and with those you love? What does it feel like to be completely open and vulnerable, with no fear of rejection? Where might you be ready to reach out to someone in a new way, and how might that offer real, necessary healing to both of you?*

Page of Cups

ELEVEN & TWO // Healing, choice, intentionality, sensitivity, intuition, psychic wisdom, duality

WATER // Emotions, connections, love, intimacy, community intuition, associated with the heart

KEYWORDS // artistry · empathy · intuition · drifting between worlds · imagination ·
compassionate questioning

Everything that we can see and feel is lovely, inspiring, wonderful. There's so much joy and magic overflowing. All we want to do is revel in it, find new methods of connection and expression so that we can share it with everyone around us. We're lost in our imaginations, moving through the world like it's an awe-inspiring dream. And while we still have plenty to learn, we trust ourselves implicitly, and know that we are capable of wielding our magic with brilliance and beauty. This sense of joy, this rich intuition and artistic ability, this desire to experience everything that the world has to offer is the sparkling spirit of the Page of Cups.

• • •

When we dive deep into fantasy, when we follow our hearts, when our emotions are something that we celebrate rather than suppress, we tap into the power and wonder of the Page of Cups. There's a sense of awe in this figure, a delight in every experience, a desire to connect and believe. This is not some silly, vapid child but an idealist expressing a deep need to belong, a student writing stories and songs about the worlds they imagine in tide pools, an artist finding inspiration and mystery in every ripple of water.

The world can be a harsh place, one that paints vulnerability as weakness, needs as cowardly, and emotions as foolish. But this page refuses to buy into that narrative, ignores rules or expectations that urge us to shield our hearts, and instead lets their emotions flow and breathe, take up space. They don't hide their delight in the world, in beauty and magic and coincidence—instead they laugh and cry openly, exclaim about new discoveries, invite others to see the world through their optimistic, joyful eyes. And when we're not afraid of expression, of deep feelings, it makes it so much easier to connect and build community, to find others that are brave enough to live the same way.

Pages are always driven by a sense of curiosity and exploration. With the Page of Cups—the child of water—we see this expressed in natural intuitive abilities and in deep, meaningful connections. Like all pages and elevens, we see both the balance and clarity of Justice (11) alongside the inherent awareness and quiet observation of the High Priestess (2), creating a powerful sensitivity, an awareness of emotions and desires, an urge to help others achieve the dreams they're longing for. Even though every page is a bit naïve, inexperienced, and unsure of just how much they can achieve, they also aren't afraid to rebel, don't feel beholden to the rules or traditons that are often clung to. This student of the heart doesn't feel shame at their intensity or dreaminess, doesn't deny what they feel. Instead they celebrate the wisdom of their intuition, allowing emotions to sweep through them with urgency and authenticity. They remain deeply present and connected to their deepest, truest self.

In Readings

The Page of Cups validates our sensitivity, urging us to trust in the value of difficult or complex feelings. Rather than fearing or avoiding our depths, this is an opportunity to fling wide the creative floodgates, to welcome our intuition with open arms, to explore our hearts with curiosity and wonder. When we let our hearts wander rather than forcing ourselves into a particular relationship, community, spiritual journey, or artistic endeavor, we learn so much more about who we are and what we are capable of.

> JOURNAL PROMPT: *What does it mean to wander through your own dreams and fantasies, to make as much space as you desire for longings? What leaves you awe-struck, breathless, overwhelmed with beauty? How do you find joy in potential? What is your subconscious urging you to explore more deeply?*

Knight of Cups

TWELVE & THREE // Expansion, manifestation, growth, abundance, creativity, experimentation

WATER // Emotions, connections, love, intimacy, community intuition, associated with the heart

KEYWORDS // romance · idealism · dreaming · jealousy · sensitivity · desire · compassionate exploration

Our experiments with artistry and intuition have given us a new craving for exploration, and we find ourselves wandering through the world with our heart in our hands, sharing our dreams and desires with anyone that will listen. We covet new connections, long to care for others and to be cared for in return, expand our creative aspirations. And while we find beauty and magic and artistry, we also discover new sensitivities, letting ourselves be vulnerable in ways that may not always pay off. This hunger to love and be loved, to live in a state of deep wonder and expression, paired with a need to balance the water and emotion that flow within us, is the romantic idealism of the Knight of Cups.

• • •

Artistic vision is a powerful thing. When we realize what we want to create, when we figure out how we hope to express it, when we understand where to weave emotion throughout it, so many new things become possible. The Knight of Cups sees potential not only in projects but also people: every new connection is a chance to grow, every new community a place to engage. This is someone who finds magic and wonder in intimacy, who recognizes what it means to give voice to emotion, who puts their whole heart into every conversation, initiative, and dream. Like a deep-sea diver who is willing to traverse the darkest, most mysterious depths, the explorer of water moves through the world with a tender grace, an eagerness to share, a willingness to confide. They show their love through actions, intentions, ambitions.

While the knights of fire and air are often focused on a specific and tangible objective, the knight of water has a different goal: they want to be seen, appreciated, understood. Numerologically, as the twelfth cards of their suits all knights balance the energy of the Hanged One (12) and the Empress (3)—and in the suit of water, this manifests as a charming explorer who constantly, courageously takes the risk of vulnerability. The knight of cups shares their emotional abundance with joyful abandon and powerful expression. When it pays off it can make for incredibly vibrant and intense connections—but it also costs them to be so open and can leave them worn out or discouraged or even completely stagnant when their energy isn't reciprocated.

The Knight of Cups can get tangled up in the difficult emotions that manifest when their dreams do not come true, or feel fundamentally misunderstood if others aren't all in immediately. Letting others see our desires is a vulnerable thing, and this is someone that longs to be appreciated, supported, held. It can be so easy to tie our self-esteem to friendships and romantic connections, to feel the best about ourselves when we know that we are desired, to weigh our creative output against our broader value. But when the communities and partnerships that we pursue don't come to fruition, that loss can teach us so much about what we *truly* need. Passions can be both inspiring and harmful.

In Readings

The Knight of Cups asks us to pay attention when strong emotions come forward, and to be conscious and deliberate about what we are reaching for. Pleasure, connection, and love are beautiful, magical experiences, but they are not the only things that give us value. And if we find ourselves getting caught up in bold actions, able to see ourselves only through the eyes of those we desire, we can lose sight of our authentic self and forget what it is we actually want.

> JOURNAL PROMPT: *How can you be intentional about trusting your intuition? How is passion shaping your decisions and choices? Where might you be moving too fast, pressing too hard? How are you being vulnerable, and are you expecting more than is reasonable from another person or group of people? How can you balance your wishes with your needs? What can you give to yourself rather than demanding it from someone else?*

Queen of Cups

THIRTEEN & FOUR // Focus, pragmatism, independence, determination, organization, expression

WATER // Emotions, connections, love, intimacy, community intuition, associated with the heart

KEYWORDS // intuitive power · emotional experience · spiritual intimacy · faith · compassionate boundaries

The intuitive power that we have been cultivating continues to expand. We become known for our sensitivity, our artistry, our ability to explore and understand emotions in a way that feels deeply magical. We see things that others miss or ignore, and we have learned to navigate dreams and fantasies in a way that broadens and challenges, that gives us access to new layers of meaning. Others can see our heart, witness our magic, find hope and comfort in the wisdom and insight that we so effortlessly share. People look to us for understanding, and as we express empathy and care, as we lead with love, we fully embrace the gentle energy of the Queen of Cups.

. . .

When we learn to love our emotional self, when we have authentic compassion for other people, when we celebrate our tenderness, we can embrace our intuition as an extension of our magic. Emotion is not weakness, it is not a distraction or a defect. Being tapped into our heart center and knowing how to utilize our vulnerability can give us new layers of strength. The Queen of Cups has full control over emotional boundaries. They know when to let others in and when to protect their hearts from those that might take advantage of their kindness. Rather than letting their emotions drown them in a tidal wave of intensity, this queen is steady, certain, knows themselves intimately. This is someone with genuine empathy and compassion, who can hold space for complex emotions in both themselves and those they love, who can navigate heartache with grace and wisdom rather than immediately closing themselves off. I like to think of this queen as a diving instructor: operating with elegance and artistry, helping others move in a way that is fluid and graceful while still respecting the depth, power, and mystery of the water.

There is wisdom in recognizing when to ask for help and when to go it alone. Finding power in community and deep friendships, letting love flow and sustain, is a gift that we should not take lightly. The Queen of Cups understands the value in our past, in our stories, in our experiences and is willing to share that knowledge with other people, helping everyone around them to understand their emotions in a way that is empowering rather than suffocating. When we can explore the depths with other people, when we accept support instead of insisting on going it alone, we all benefit.

Like all queens and the number thirteen, the artist of water is a numerological combination of the inevitable release of Death (13) and the powerful, protective boundaries of the Emperor (4), and this blend gives us someone who celebrates the power of emotional boundaries, someone being deliberate about how much access to give to others. By leading with compassion, this artist can navigate the intuitive realms with confidence, demonstrating self-love in a way that feels achievable and admirable. And by respecting their own limits, the Queen of Cups can be truly tender, empathetic, and loving with those that they choose to share their full heart with.

In Readings

The Queen of Cups asks us to tap into our psychic gifts and inner wisdom, to reflect on how we feel and what that means. It can feel like strength to sweep our emotions under the rug, to deny vulnerabilities or desires or longings for connection—but when this card comes forward, it's an admonition to be honest with ourselves about what we hope for, to show ourselves and others authentic grace and compassion.

> JOURNAL PROMPT: *How often do you show yourself kindness? What lessons from your past might be relevant to your present, important for your future? Where might your emotional boundaries need reconsidering? How could forgiveness offer you relief?*

King of Cups

FOURTEEN & FIVE // Personal freedom, change, leadership, curiosity, knowledge, observation

WATER // Emotions, connections, love, intimacy, community intuition, associated with the heart

KEYWORDS // emotional intelligence · empathetic guidance · grace & sensitivity · compassionate expansion

Our powers of understanding and consideration have become well-known. We discover new opportunities for leadership, education, and community-building within this artistic and intuitive space. Rather than hiding from harsh or difficult feelings, we have learned to navigate them with deftness, knowing when to push back and when to let the water flow over and through us. We teach others to do the same and lead with kindness, sensitivity, and emotion, encouraging people to dive into their own depths rather than always skimming across the surface. This level of expertise and expression, this ability to withstand changing tides, is the self-assurance and gentle compassion of the King of Cups.

· · ·

Leadership and empathy are often painted as conflicting concepts rather than intentions that can work together. Some even view compassion or sensitivity as things that can derail us, influencing us to make cowardly or ineffective choices. Yet the King of Cups is not made weak by their ability to identify with others—instead, this is someone who allows their concern for broader situations or challenges to manifest as mercy, warmth, and tenderness. Leading with love does not always mean letting things go, but it does empower us to make decisions that bring a rich sense of community, collective healing, and deep grace. Like an experienced ship captain, this commander respects the power and strength of the water, navigating with ease, exploring new currents, and sharing the wisdom of their experience with everyone around them.

    The King of Cups understands that our intuition can help to guide us toward necessary change, creating safe spaces for other people to be vulnerable while simultaneously challenging systems that make us feel taken advantage of, harmed, or afraid. In carving out opportunities for authentic connection, in refusing to deny or suppress emotions, this ruler helps to shift the ways that we understand strong feelings and teaches others how to honor these sensations instead of trying to hide from them. With the energy of Temperance (14) and the Hierophant (5), this king is able to lean on tried-and-true methods while still balancing emotion with inspiration, diplomacy, perception, and deliberate growth.

This leader also knows how to disrupt the status quo with compassion. It's unfortunately rare to see people in authority offer genuine vulnerability, kindness, or grace, yet this king understands that showing empathy and care is not a weakness. Loving with dignity, with courage, with generosity, can completely alter the course of a project or ambition, can fully change the ways that we protect and attend to those that matter most. By being brave enough to do things differently, to value emotions instead of smothering them, we can build a new kind of world and imagine a different kind of future.

In Readings

The King of Cups can ask us what we teach others. Or to put it another way, what people are learning from us. The ways that we navigate our own emotions, intuitive impulses, relationships, desires, and personal needs can have a massive impact on those around us. And if we value tenderness, if we demonstrate mercy and empathy, if we are willing to express care and intimacy, we can develop new systems and frameworks for the ways that we define and enjoy community.

JOURNAL PROMPT: *Where might you feel emotionally stifled, and how could adjusting the systems you operate in shift that sensation? How can you hold space for all of your own emotions while also allowing others to do the same? Where are you disrupting the status quo, and how does vulnerability shift the ways that we engage with and understand other people?*

THE SUIT OF PENTACLES

EARTH

Resources, health, finances, senses, nature, health, legacy, associated with the body

Earth is the slowest-moving element, and the suit of pentacles considers all that grounds and protects us. This is a suit of abundance, responsibility, patience, diplomacy, structure, empowerment, discipline, and steady movement. The pentacles represent intentional, confident perseverance, the acts and choices that help us establish foundations for our lifelong dreams and ambitions. Earth and pentacles navigate the tangible world, exploring the daily acts and long-term ambitions that we invest in, the legacy that we work to establish. In understanding the resources that we activate, gather, and utilize, in practicing patience and steadfast devotion, we create lives that work for us, integrating structure and discipline into our passions, intellectual pursuits, and relationships.

As an element, earth is grounded, stable, solid; yet when volcanoes, earthquakes, and other massive transformative events occur, we see our world change on a permanent, powerful level. We often take rock and dirt and plant life for granted, yet these are the things that so often sustain us, settle us, soothe us. Earth is tied to the physical self: health, wealth, bodies, families, career, sensation, pleasure, homes, and movement. This is everything we touch and see and taste, the sensory experiences we enjoy or fear, the well-being that we strive for. Within this element we find pleasure and purpose, devotion and dedication, ambition and aspirations.

We see many of these concepts reflected in the suit of pentacles, cards that explore themes of taking up space, allowing ourselves comfort, pursuing goals that matter, understanding what we value, and building community. Generosity and reciprocity are ways that we can connect individual famine and fortune to the larger collective, highlighting mutual aid, networks of care, and structural support. The suit of pentacles tells the story of growth and tethers us to a particular future. But these cards are also about control and authority, about believing that we are capable of something, about tapping into resources like energy, time, space, inspiration, creativity, strength, money, and community in order to make our dreams come true. Within this suit we navigate challenges like stubbornness, stinginess, scarcity, illness, and an unwillingness to take risks. With the pentacles, we work to balance our desire to succeed with our fear of failure.

While the other suits deal with internal emotions, perceptions, and ambitions, the suit of pentacles focuses on what the rest of the world can see: our external efforts, investments, and legacies. Pentacles are about what we protect, what we devote ourselves to, the goals and objectives we pursue. Other people may not notice if we set a new goal, recognize a new truth, develop a new relationship—but they will perceive the ways that we pragmatically adjust our schedules, routines, finances, and resources in order to accommodate these shifts. The things that we value are the things that we defend and build upon, and with earth, we find what anchors us, what delights us, what makes us feel safe and secure.

• • •

As you move through the suit of pentacles and the element of earth, consider intention, cultivation, conservation. How do your desires take up space in the real world? What are you working to manifest, and how do your daily actions reflect those long-term goals? Where are you willing to take risks, and how do you decide what's worth a sensation of unpredictability? What brings you pleasure, comfort, and how do you integrate rest into your routines?

Ace of Pentacles

ONE // Motivation, confidence, independence, vision, trail blazing

EARTH // Resources, health, finances, senses, nature, health, legacy, associated with the body

KEYWORDS // intentional growth · a new opportunity · investing in the self · ambition · dreams of stability

A new opportunity has presented itself. After careful consideration, we make the decision to plant a seed for our future selves, to invest in ourselves in a way that will require dedication, effort, and care. We are dreaming of legacy, of abundance, of empowerment—and in taking this first step, in opening ourselves up to new possibilities, we invite in growth, potential, and expansion. This calculated invitation, this first effort toward a new kind of future, is the grounded optimism of the Ace of Pentacles.

• • •

Change does not always begin with a flash of inspiration, insight, or intuition. Sometimes we deliberately choose a path forward, make a decision about the future that we want to work toward, and take careful, intentional steps into the prosperous legacy that we long for. Growth comes in many forms, and with the Ace of Pentacles, we are not struck by sudden passion or truth or emotion, but instead with a spark of vision for the kind of life we will build for ourselves. Whether we decide to work toward a new career, start saving for a house, take on a physical challenge, or get in touch with our sensual side, the suit of earth speaks to pleasure, comfort, success, and stability, all things that take time, dedication, and focus to establish.

Think of the Ace of Pentacles like a carefully selected seed, one that we know will blossom and thrive if we plant and tend it. The ace of earth is a dawning realization, a slow but profound commitment to something new, a desire to protect ourselves and our legacy. Like all aces and ones, this first card of the suit represents a long-term goal that will impact your future—and with this suit of earth, it's investing in something that will allow you to care for yourself, creating systems of security and stability that reinforce everything else in your life. It's deciding to run a marathon, saving up to propose to someone you love, going back to school to get a new degree—something that will have a cost, but that will ultimately change the foundation of your world and will likely impact those around you at the same time.

This is investing in the self, putting down roots, making the choice to devote ourselves to a specific opportunity or effort. It's identifying the ways that our daily habits and behaviors reflect our deepest values, attending to the ways that we utilize our resources to pursue the things that matter. By taking responsibility for where we are and where we want to go, the Ace of Pentacles helps us recognize our role in our own happiness and take ownership of our personal growth.

In Readings

The Ace of Pentacles asks us to put our energy toward something new, to pay attention to the glimmer of hope or interest or stability that is growing within us. This isn't a rash decision or a quick fix but rather a careful, deliberate act to select a seed, bless it with magic and intention, choose a place to plant it, and commit to helping it thrive.

> JOURNAL PROMPT: *What are you ready to grow, to devote yourself to, to invest in? What new opportunity could change the shape of your life? How are you ready to take ownership of your happiness? What would make you truly happy, and how can you treat your future self to something beautiful, something pleasurable, something wonderful?*

Two of Pentacles

TWO // Sensitivity, intuition, psychic wisdom, choice, awareness, duality

EARTH // Resources, health, finances, senses, nature, health, legacy, associated with the body

KEYWORDS // multitasking · responsibility · delegating · deciding what matters · strategizing · synchronicity

Even as we plant our tender new kernel of hope, we still have existing responsibilities and projects to manage. It feels like growth is everywhere. At first we're able to handle everything with ease, juggling and flexing in order to stay on top of everything—but this kind of effort isn't sustainable, and we know that we have to make some decisions, have to prioritize and delegate, have to think not just about today but about all of our tomorrows. This need to shift and reorganize, to make changes that allow us to keep growing toward the life that we want, is the decisive action of the Two of Pentacles.

• • •

In choosing to begin a new long-term project, we start to make careful, necessary changes. That little seed needs to be placed in just the right location, must be tended and protected, needs regular care and consistent resources. And while it's a lot of extra work, this is an exciting time, when we're imagining all the resources we'll soon have access to, the expansion and growth and power that we'll eventually be able to harvest and utilize. Our new dream is taking shape in our minds—but those old tasks and responsibilities haven't gone anywhere. We're juggling the growth of this additional goal with our ongoing work, trying to carve out space in a busy life for this new pursuit. With the Two of Pentacles, we plot a strategy for the future and give ourself permission to pursue what we really want.

Twos always acknowledge our choices and efforts toward balance, for better or worse. No matter how well we are managing all of our tasks and duties, it's essential that we look at how our resources are being used, that we consider all of the places that our energy is being directed, that we choose what to set down and what to carry forward. Just because we're doing it all beautifully right now doesn't mean that we'll be able to keep up this pace forever. And rather than crashing and burning, or letting an important ball drop, this card urges us to be thoughtful, intentional, and deliberate in our decisions, to pursue balance with focus and determination rather than letting ourselves get swept up in projects and jobs. The Two of Pentacles wants us to make serious developmental choices, to stand at this crossroads of responsibility and consider how we will utilize our many resources.

In spite of the potential stress of this environment, there's a real sweetness to this card, as we celebrate what we've started, honor our progress, envision the ways that this new venture will mesh with the life we have already built for ourselves. But while we can feel that adjustments must be made and changes must happen, we also aren't anxious about the future. Things may feel unpredictable and slightly out of our control. But rather than being stressed out, we're invigorated, excited, energized. We know that the choices before us are positive ones, and that our goals are connecting and blending into the solid, wonderful life of our dreams.

In Readings

The Two of Pentacles urges us to be decisive, thoughtful, and focused—which may include saying no, setting up boundaries, or delegating certain obligations. You don't have to be in control of every single facet of your life, and there may be ways to share burdens, to put things on pause, to focus on your new dreams instead of getting lost in old patterns.

> JOURNAL PROMPT: *Where are you being stretched thin, and how can you make choices that give you more time, space, and resources for the things you want to invest in? What could someone else do? How can you live in the moment while still keeping your future in mind?*

Three of Pentacles

THREE // Innovation, creativity, expression, growth, manifestation

EARTH // Resources, health, finances, senses, nature, health, legacy, associated with the body

KEYWORDS // growth · abundant resources · collaboration & teamwork · manifestation · progress

Our resources are expanding. New opportunities keep emerging, and we find ourselves bringing in trusted friends and workers, people with additional assets that can help us develop with intention and purpose. We're starting to see real growth, even abundance, as our dreams become tangible and our ideas are made manifest. This expansive joy, this marked progress, this sense of momentum building, is the joyful creation of the Three of Pentacles.

• • •

When we commit to a path forward and intentionally activate our resources, momentum builds in a way that demands attention. With loyalty and devotion to our goals, with passionate creation and joyful collaboration, our personal ambitions merge with larger collective efforts. The Three of Pentacles tells us we are making measurable progress toward our goal, that the seed we planted is rooting and blossoming. This card is sharing the things that we love with the people that we love, seeing our desires and our practical efforts overlapping, recognizing that we are creating something useful and beautiful. Hope unfurls like flower petals, and we feel joy, satisfaction, wonder.

No matter the future that we are striving for, it can be tempting to hide our slow but real progress, wanting our successes to seem effortless, hoping to triumphantly reveal the finished, perfect product with a grand flourish before anyone sees the messy drafts or false starts. But the Three of Pentacles challenges that notion, reminding us that most don't succeed without people behind them, without helping hands, without endorsements and allies and encouragement. And as things continue to click into place, as we consistently pursue our passions and ambitions, we find real pleasure in these efforts, in letting others into our work, in accepting both praise and advice. A rising tide lifts all boats, and this card encourages us to bring fellow artists and builders along for the ride, to remember that what we are doing will benefit not only us as individuals but others as well.

The Three of Pentacles, as well as its broader numerological archetype of the Empress, can help us to recognize the wellspring of resources, energy, and power that we already have at our disposal and can remind us to relish every step forward rather than fixating on the finish line. This is empowering expression, a creation of accomplishment that reflects our dedication and determination. Focus is important but so is joy, and this card wants us to find fulfillment in process, to celebrate the little victories, and to be grateful for where we are right now. We may still feel far away from the finish line but every milestone is important—and taking pride in each step can make the entire journey more pleasurable, more satisfying.

In Readings

The Three of Pentacles makes space for both celebration and anticipation, encouraging us to take pleasure in what we are building while also continuing to expand in different directions. With this card we are reminded not just of the resources that we may recognize but also the skills, relationships, knowledge, education, or other things we have access to that we may not be fully taking advantage of.

> JOURNAL PROMPT: *Where are things coming together, and where is there room to grow? How are you managing your resources, and who or what might be available for more than you're aware of? What does collaboration look like, and how could the dream you're realizing help everyone?*

Four of Pentacles

FOUR // Structure, organization, systems, progression, foundations, stability

EARTH // Resources, health, finances, senses, nature, health, legacy, associated with the body

KEYWORDS // caution · holding back · controlling resources · fear · exercising restraint · thinking ahead

The plans that we've made have been fruitful, and we continue to invest energy into our vision of the future, building and planning. As we make new budgets and work to protect what we have already created, we feel a building tension between spending and hoarding. We may worry that we're overextending ourselves or don't have what we need to accomplish everything that we've been dreaming of. In putting limits on ourselves, in balancing payments with penny-pinching, we sit into the brittle tension of the Four of Pentacles.

• • •

In spite of the growth we've cultivated, the successes we've found, and the team we've assembled, we've slipped into a kind of survivalist mentality. By hoarding the resources we've gathered, by hesitating to utilize what we have for fear of running out, our progress may slow down, even stall out. The Four of Pentacles is a tricky card in that it can look like selfishness or stinginess from the outside, but often reflects an internal anxiety around scarcity, a desire for material discipline. The resources that we need are present—we genuinely have everything we need to move forward with our plans and dreams—and yet there's a sense of anxiety and concern, a frugal fixation on holding everything close instead of using it to further our ambitions.

It's not irrational to want to protect what we've built, to prioritize stability, to feel bound to the plan that we made early on. But when we find ourselves holding back from growth, when we get defensive or possessive over what we have, when every choice is filtered through a lens of lack, it can create a real disconnect. The Four of Pentacles reflects this tension of forgotten joy and collective growth. It reveals our hesitancy to share what we have with those around us, the fear that by continuing to invest in our work, we will lose what we already have. We may have all that we need right now—might have rows of flowers and fruits that are in full bloom—but what if we wake up tomorrow to a drought, a storm, a barren field?

Sometimes this card wants us to be more thoughtful about allocating and budgeting, to exercise restraint with our spending or saving, to think ahead and control our resources. Fours are not just about blind control but about exercising intention, being thoughtful about where we restrict and where we flow. More often than not, when the Four of Pentacles appears in readings it asks us to balance that craving for security with pleasure, freedom, growth, to have control over our resources. If we fixate only on limits, we can stunt our own expansion—but in trusting the plans that we've made, in honoring the foundations we have established, in loosening our grip on what we own, we often find new kinds of comfort, wonder, and power.

In Readings

This card encourages us to pay attention to the ways our personal work is intersecting with community movements or broader advances. Rather than just going through the motions, the Four of Pentacles asks us to continue putting our full self into our ambitions, to reconnect with what we love, to allow others to support us. Hoarding resources can limit opportunities, but we have a chance to release hesitation and believe in our ability to manage everything.

> JOURNAL PROMPT: *What do you really have, and why do you believe that it isn't enough? What are you restricting? How are you balancing growth with awareness? Where are you allowing yourself pleasure or comfort? How can you utilize your resources instead of just accumulating them? What do healthy boundaries around resources look like?*

Five of Pentacles

FIVE // Change, freedom, exploration, tension, growth, adventure, balance, transition

EARTH // Resources, health, finances, senses, nature, health, legacy, associated with the body

KEYWORDS // lack of resources · uncertainty · grief or illness · scarcity · refusing aid · difficulty · desperation

Our fears have materialized. We find ourselves without enough, and we feel desperate and afraid and alone. And while we may indeed be facing real grief, illness, or isolation, we may also be ignoring genuine help that's being offered, trying to push through our pain alone rather than letting others support us. This feeling of lack, this desire to grasp at anything we can find while keeping our worries hidden, this sensation of struggle is the empty regret of the Five of Pentacles.

• • •

There are times when asking for help feels impossible, even if we know that it's within reach. And if we don't know how to access what we need, we can end up feeling incredibly isolated, lost in our sorrow, uncertain of how to move forward. A card of struggle, illness, and melancholy, the Five of Pentacles often speaks to those moments of loneliness and pain, when we feel unsafe or displaced, when we need more than we have. Unlike the restless, restrained anxiety that we experienced with the Four of Pentacles, the five reflects actual scarcity, genuine hardship, material friction. We may not have lost an entire season's crop, but we have suffered a major setback, and our hope for the future has dimmed.

Like the other fives in the minor arcana, this card holds a sense of loss and worry, an uncertainty about the future, a tension between what we have and what we need. But also like other fives, there's a sense that all is not lost, and that if we can simply adjust our perspective and consider all of our options, the change in stability that we are undergoing can ultimately be a positive one. It may feel like we have to do something alone, like we cannot release our pain, like moving forward is impossible. In spite of the despair we're feeling, the Five of Pentacles tells us we also have more resources than we realize. We simply have to be willing to acknowledge that we need help, rather than continuing to suffer on our own.

Beyond recognizing the reality of our situation, the Five of Pentacles can also speak to a sensation of guilt or regret, a worry that we somehow brought this misfortune upon ourselves. If someone is devoted to the notion of their own bad luck, to their identity as a failure or a fraud, the Five of Pentacles can feel like a self-fulfilling prophecy, that negative assumptions have manifested into reality. And if we are in the habit of refusing help or hiding our troubles, it can make a bad situation worse, leaving us feeling isolated, desperate, or hopeless. The Five of Pentacles begs us to offer grace, to look at the present clearly instead of clinging to mistakes or grieving a painful, messy history.

In Readings

This card encourages asking for what we need and allowing the people that we love and trust to care for us. Sometimes this card simply acknowledges our grief and sorrow, making space for our suffering in a way that can be deeply comforting. But it also wants us to allow ourselves to heal, rather than ripping open those scars over and over.

JOURNAL PROMPT: *How are you suffering, and what are you lacking? Have you been offered help and denied it out of pride or inconvenience? What would it take for you to take the support that is being offered? How could you prioritize safety and healing instead of independence?*

Six of Pentacles

SIX // Harmony, nurturing, community, caretaking, movement, pride

EARTH // Resources, health, finances, senses, nature, health, legacy, associated with the body

KEYWORDS // generosity · reciprocity · expansion · caring for community · recognizing abundance

We've managed to strike a balance between limiting our resources and using what we have. We are finding joy in abundance, celebrating all that we have and even extending generosity to those who may be in need. Growth is everywhere and we're brimming with positivity and optimism, craving new methods of connection, seeing the fruits of our labors. In sharing what we have with those around us, in paying forward our good fortune and hard work, we step into the reciprocal spirit of the Six of Pentacles.

• • •

There can be real satisfaction in knowing that we have enough, a sense of pride in working through challenges and coming out the other side. On the heels of a genuine lack, we can celebrate the ways that we received what we asked for, take pride in knowing our limits and allowing others to lift us up. And like all of the tarot's sixes, the Six of Pentacles feels triumphant and joyful as we break free of struggles and honor a sensation of victory and pleasure. This is a long-awaited storm drenching the earth, new and joyful growth, an opportunity for a rich harvest.

Sometimes, this card shows up when it feels like we're still in the middle of a difficult situation, when we're still in a place of drought or scarcity. In this case, it can serve as a reminder that there are magic, comfort, and benevolence in both giving and receiving. Earth as an element is patient and responsible, grounded and attentive. And when we think about those attributes in combination with the number six's emphasis on abundance, generosity, and exploration, it leads us to ideas of mutual care, intentional service, being thoughtful when it comes to how we utilize and allocate our resources. This is expansion of community, making choices that serve the many instead of the few. Even when it feels like we are alone in the world, we are always connected to the people who love us, the people who have stood by our side through trials, the people who have celebrated our successes.

Reciprocity is a powerful rhythm, one that connects us to our allies. It contributes to systems of care. But this card can also remind us that there is no inherent morality in either giving or receiving, that shame has no place in this cycle. With the Six of Pentacles we are encouraged to be conscious of our relationship to generosity, to think about any expectations or assumptions we may have around giving, receiving, and sharing. There can be comfort in helping others, satisfaction in the role of caretaker, yet presenting someone with something does not mean we get to control how they utilize it. Investing in others can't come with strings.

In Readings

The Six of Pentacles reminds us that resources are energy, points of connection, powerful offerings. There's something so deeply satisfying about receiving a meal, helping someone while they're sick, giving or accepting assistance from someone we trust. It may be easy to offer help when someone is having a hard time, but the Six of Pentacles also encourages us to show up in victories, to celebrate the wins, to be as present for the good stuff as we are for the bad.

JOURNAL PROMPT: *What do you attach to generosity? What kinds of magic build when you ask and receive? How do you deepen connections when you extend compassionate care to others? Who encourages you when you feel down? What is your relationship with nurturing and being nurtured? How do you care for your family, friends, partners, communities through good times and bad?*

Seven of Pentacles

SEVEN // Intelligence, duality, movement, determination, protection, responsibility

EARTH // Resources, health, finances, senses, nature, health, legacy, associated with the body

KEYWORDS // acknowledgment · consideration · attention to detail · affirming goals · evaluation · authenticity

Our accomplishments are front and center, and we feel both joy and a hesitant kind of pride in our present. Now we reflect on where we started and appraise our position, asking ourselves if the path that we're currently on still feels right. We've chased our goals with purpose and intention, yet even in success we may feel it's time to make some changes, to shift in a new direction—or to correct course if we've gotten off track. This energy of assessment and awareness, this desire to move forward with renewed care for the destination, is the purposeful power of the Seven of Pentacles.

• • •

Growth has continued in earnest, and after finding opportunities to give back and support those who have provided resources to us, the Seven of Pentacles tells us it's now time for us to consider how far we've come, to reflect on our progress and look to our future responsibilities. By analyzing the choices we've made and the ways that our ambitions, resources, and dreams have shifted along the way, we can make any necessary adjustments. We can even commit ourselves to a new path if we so choose. Sometimes when we set a plan for the future, even after spending time planning and scheming, things still don't always come out exactly as we'd thought they would. And especially with earth, an element that moves slowly, the length of our journey may mean that we can gradually slip off track or decide to shift our end goal a bit. With the seven, we look at the full scope of our efforts and consider if the intentions that we set way back with the ace are still what we're working toward, and if we're still on track to meet them.

In addition to directional assessment and adjustment, the Seven of Pentacles also gives us a chance to rest and breathe, to celebrate how far we've come, to consider the personal growth we've experienced in the process of planting, tending, harvesting, and sharing. Sevens are often cards of advice and acknowledgment, looking for deeper meaning and spiritual messages. After the movement we experienced with the six, it can be helpful to consider how getting organized and keeping our eyes forward can help us stay focused and intentional during this last section of our work. How has our garden been growing? Do our aspirations still feel authentic? Are we satisfied with what we've accomplished? Do we love what we're doing? This is a chance to process, to contemplate, to grant ourselves flexibility instead of forcing ourselves to keep pursuing something we may no longer want or need. The Seven of Pentacles invites us on a quest of intention, letting us know that it's more than okay to interrogate our own needs, to make space for joy as well as stability.

In Readings

The Seven of Pentacles acknowledges both growth and desire, asking us to consider where we're clinging to old ambitions and where we may be craving change, expansion, even destruction. This card isn't about doubting what we've done or obsessing over the "right path"—instead it's about checking in with the self, about being as authentic and true to our needs as we possibly can.

JOURNAL PROMPT: *Where are you in your process, and how does it feel to reflect on the work you've already done? What does it feel like to be in your body right now, to acknowledge the resources you've gathered and created, to consider the road ahead? What are you protecting, and what do you feel responsible for? How is your work reflecting your longings?*

Eight of Pentacles

EIGHT // Power, momentum, discipline, assurance, control, practicality

EARTH // Resources, health, finances, senses, nature, health, legacy, associated with the body

KEYWORDS // craftsmanship · practice · mastery · learning & growth · focused effort · hard work · intention

After affirming that we're going where we want to go, that we have clarified our goals and have the resources and support that we need to achieve them, we step back into action. Growth is slow and steady, done with patience and diligence as we practice, learn, and improve. To build something that lasts takes time. It requires expertise and consistent effort. As we devote ourselves to our cause, as we develop the skills that we need to be a master of our craft, we embrace the focused energy of the Eight of Pentacles.

• • •

Sometimes we look at an accomplished musician, a gifted artist, a talented chef, a brilliant technician, a remarkable athlete, and we marvel at their abilities. We wish that we could be so skilled, that our hands and bodies could move with such confidence, that our minds could pick up patterns or languages or solve problems so effortlessly. And while we often see people at the height of their talents, celebrating all that they are capable of, what we don't always see are the days and weeks and months and years and decades of practice, determination, focus, commitment. We don't see the hours of rehearsals, the endless classes, the piles of books, the teachers and mentors and coaches and starter kits, the early mornings and late nights. We see the results of the Eight of Pentacles but rarely celebrate the process.

Prodigies and geniuses are unusual. For most of us mere mortals, we can't skip the years of practice and learning, of calluses and exhaustion, of putting the development of a skill before everything else in our lives. We can't skip the devotion or the faithfulness. Becoming a true expert in something does not happen overnight; it takes years and years of intention, dedication, and single-minded focus. Getting good at something takes work—and the Eight of Pentacles *is* that work. Eights are associated with power and purpose; they remind us to keep our eyes on the prize, to invest in our own future abundance. With the Eight of Pentacles, we let our natural gifts overlap with our biggest aspirations, pushing us to daily, dedicated effort.

Within this card we see both humility and hope—the ability to recognize where we need to go paired with the belief that we can achieve the goal that we've set for ourselves. After the clarity and refocusing of the Seven of Pentacles, the eight moves forward with powerful, genuine intention, and we put our whole hearts and souls into the objective we have identified. This can be a bit of a slog, the repetitive and unsexy part of the journey that usually gets thrown into a fast-forward montage in a movie: the training, the research, the falling down and getting back up. The Eight of Pentacles is pulling weeds, mixing fertilizer, researching seeds, gathering new tools. But on the other side of this consistent, steadfast diligence are power, pleasure, satisfaction. With the Eight of Pentacles we understand how our labor directly feeds into our success and move forward without doubts, without worries.

In Readings

This card is simple: do the work. In dedicating ourselves to a singular purpose, in waking up every day and choosing this path again and again, we build something truly incredible. We affirm to ourselves that what we are doing is important, that who we are becoming is brilliant. We do the hard work that we set out to do and establish a legacy.

> JOURNAL PROMPT: *What do you really want, and how hard are you really willing to work for it? What are you devoting yourself to, committing yourself to, determined to triumph over? What do you want to master? And how does the development of this skill transform who you are and what you believe that you are capable of?*

FINDING THE FOOL

Nine of Pentacles

NINE // Observation, personal responsibility, collective growth, expansion, clarity

EARTH // Resources, health, finances, senses, nature, health, legacy, associated with the body

KEYWORDS // independence · satisfaction & pride · self-assurance · recognition · stability · gratification

We have acted with purpose. We've been working so hard, have been careful and devoted. As we look at everything we have achieved, we feel an overwhelming sense of pride in ourselves, recognizing how we have grown and evolved along the way. Yes, we had help from our communities—but in this moment we celebrate the ways that we have invested in ourselves, that we have worked toward something that delights and comforts us. This rich sense of personal power and individual achievement is the dignity and magic of the Nine of Pentacles.

• • •

There are times when we shift our gaze from the steady effort we've been exerting to the horizon ahead of us and realize that we are so much closer to our goal than we realized. It can be a heady feeling, this excitement, this satisfaction, this absolute joy and pride in all that we have accomplished. We've made it so far, have put together something truly beautiful and valuable, and the consistent progress that we've made has brought us to a place of stability, comfort, wonder. The Nine of Pentacles is the recognition of our place in the world, an honor in how much we have grown, a contentment with the hard work we have put in. That little seed that we planted so long ago has flourished and borne fruit—and more so, we've taken that fruit and planted a rich garden, are able to share cuttings with friends and family, can use that plenty to build a promising, empowered future.

Luxury and abundance aren't only about access to beautiful, extravagant things—it's more personal than that. It's an understanding of wealth and prosperity and comfort that isn't simply financial. Nines are both independent and service-oriented, and the Nine of Pentacles explores the things that have true value, the contentment we feel when we have enough and we don't have to worry about scarcity anymore. It's the joy in being able to give and give without fearing that we'll run out. There are richness and wisdom in security, in knowing that what we have cannot be taken from us, in recognizing purposeful evolution instead of seeing everything as random or happenstance. With the Nine of Pentacles we reap the rewards of a long and sustained commitment and celebrate the prosperous life that we have built, the stability that we have found, the opportunities that continue rolling in. Beyond the pleasure in our present, we also trust ourselves to navigate any future challenges, to be able to continue caring for ourselves, to know that we are capable and resourceful.

In Readings

The Nine of Pentacles asks us to recognize our path from past to present and to acknowledge the ways that our consistent, devoted efforts have ensured a beautiful future. Our hard work is paying off and it's beautiful. We have done something good, something wonderful, and this is a moment to step back from that work and smile at all that we now have.

> JOURNAL PROMPT: *How are you commemorating your efforts, remembering who you once were and celebrating who you are now? Which experiences, relationships, encouragements have shaped this journey? How often do you let yourself feel pride over your accomplishments? What does it mean to be solitary and present in your joy?*

Ten of Pentacles

TEN & ONE // Unity, vision, pride, independence & community together, trail blazing, confidence

EARTH // Resources, health, finances, senses, nature, health, legacy, associated with the body

KEYWORDS // deep satisfaction · legacy · community strength · bountifulness · reciprocity & care

Personal fulfillment is a powerful thing, but after celebrating our achievements, we open up to our community, invite everyone in to enjoy the abundance that we have found. Everything that we've been working toward is now at our finger-tips, and beyond just creating a safe and stable life for ourselves, we have also established a legacy, something that will endure beyond us. We feel incredible satisfaction in all that we have accomplished. We are able to give generously and receive with joy—and this deep pleasure, this collective contentment, is the rich gratification of the Ten of Pentacles.

• • •

Success can have many definitions and can be such an intimate and personal thing to pursue. But with the Ten of Pentacles, we embrace triumph and pride, feel relief and serenity as we look back at all that we have accomplished. Not only have we built a comfortable, pleasurable life for ourselves, we have also invested in interdependence, created spaces of collective joy and security, established a community garden that will keep producing and expanding season after season. In the Ten of Pentacles, we see our dreams not only coming true but also being exceeded.

The idea of pulling ourselves up by our bootstraps, of doing every single thing alone, is a capitalist myth. In reality, almost everyone needs help and advice and encouragement to get where they are. They need access to resources and education, a sense of safety and comfort, a push to get moving, someone to catch them if they fall. We may have received help but that only makes us stronger, reminds us that we have people that we can rely on and that people in turn may rely on us. In the same way, when we already have stability, we can take new, deliberate risks—and tens, while they signal completion, also point us right back to another beginning, offering us a foundation to build upon.

As tied to the physical world as the element of earth is, the Ten of Pentacles feels connected to the other suits in a very special way. A safe and comfortable home may mean chosen family and strong, supportive community, like we see in the suit of cups. A major achievement or victory may link to personal passions and vision, like we explore in the suit of wands. A powerful choice or decisive step forward might mean clarity or a richer exploration of truth, like we discover in the suit of swords. The physical world of pentacles is not necessarily any simpler than these other planes, but it can be grounding and stabilizing, helping us create spaces that give us the room to dive deeper in other areas. When these most important needs are filled—clothing and shelter and safety, comfort and support and stability—we're able to start reaching for those other goals. Without the grounding support of earth, we may not be able to go anywhere else. And as we look back on our work, we take such pride in knowing that we have helped to establish community resources that will last beyond our lifetime.

In Readings

The Ten of Pentacles serves as a reminder to stay grounded in the things that we value and to continue investing in the people and concepts and work we cherish. Communities are so important, and by allowing our legacy to be for the many instead of the few, we can create new systems of protection, new structures of power. We are not operating in a vacuum, so this is also a chance to share our bounty with others, to extend love and care and support to those that have offered them to us, to reconnect with the community that has never left us.

> JOURNAL PROMPT: *What goals have come to fruition, and how are you honoring both your work and the power of the collective? What have you vowed to protect, and how is that protection a piece of your legacy? In building a better life for yourself, how can you, in turn, empower those that are still in earlier stages of their own journeys?*

Page of Pentacles

ELEVEN & TWO // Healing, choice, intentionality, sensitivity, intuition, psychic wisdom, duality

EARTH // Resources, health, finances, senses, nature, health, legacy, associated with the body

KEYWORDS // observation · thoughtfulness · careful movement · gentle assessment · pragmatic questioning

A desire to build something lasting has been slowly growing within us. We deliberately open ourselves up to new experiences, exploring and experimenting, observing and questioning. Our natural sensuality is balanced by a rich desire for responsible awareness, and we move with grace, patience, and purpose, even if we aren't sure exactly what we want our legacy to be. As we venture out into the world, as we seek to gather resources and share them with others, we step into the careful curiosity of the Page of Pentacles.

• • •

Sometimes when we discover a new dream within ourselves, we immediately worry about potential mistakes and feel pressure to do everything correctly the very first time. We become so fixated on a specific future, so concerned about succeeding, that we forget to take pleasure in the process and miss the possibilities of discovery that come from mistakes. The practical Page of Pentacles teaches us about finding ease in movement, tells us to devote ourselves to our work without getting frustrated about how long the journey may take. As a child of earth, the Page of Pentacles is not afraid of experiences and knows that sometimes, getting lost in the woods can lead to delightful and important discoveries. This is someone who wants more for themselves and for their community, who longs to set something in motion even if they aren't sure what they may ultimately accomplish.

Like the other pages of the minor arcana, this student of earth is curious, inquisitive, unrestrained by convention or expectation. Yet this page is guided by a deep sense of responsibility, wanting to utilize their natural resources in the best possible way, eager to get the full value out of their efforts while also making a difference in the world. They are able to be deeply present even while considering what their work is building to, imagining the many pathways forward that they could follow, paying attention to the impact that their movements can have. And while there's still a spirit of play here, a desire to experiment and observe, it's tempered by a thoughtful desire for discovery, a need to grow in a way that is sustainable. This page doesn't want to wildly fling seeds far and wide, to see which ones grow and which ones die, to leave their dreams to chance—instead they want to choose one seed with care and deliberation, nurture it through its life cycle, patiently anticipate its harvest.

In numerology the tarot's pages, as the eleventh cards of their suits, balance the clarity of Justice (11) with the intuitive awareness and quiet observation of the High Priestess (2). With the student of earth this translates to careful observation, thoughtful navigation, tender interrogation. This is slowly building a dream, letting details fall gently into place rather than obsessing over a very narrow definition of legacy or victory or prosperity. The Page of Pentacles trusts their senses, learning by touch and feel and taste. They explore with awareness, honoring their cravings, recognizing the natural ebbs and flows that surround them. And by being humble enough to grow as they go, by being deeply engaged with every physical act, the Page of Pentacles reminds us to take pleasure in our work, play, and breakthroughs.

In Readings

This figure encourages us to recognize where we are changing our behavior in a way that invites expansion, to be aware of the shifts that may be occurring within and around us. In imagining all that we can accomplish through hard work and intention, new doors may be opening. And rather than talking ourselves out of trying, this page wants us to embrace curiosity, to be open to failure.

> JOURNAL PROMPT: *How do you understand and prioritize pleasure? What new longings are you discovering within yourself? What does it feel like to give your body what it needs? How much easier do you move and breathe when you're pursuing goals that are yours alone? And in being true to yourself, how do you open up new possibilities for connection?*

Knight of Pentacles

TWELVE & THREE // Expansion, manifestation, growth, abundance, creativity, experimentation

EARTH // Resources, health, finances, senses, nature, health, legacy, associated with the body

KEYWORDS // responsibility · steadfastness · determination · persistence · inflexibility · pragmatic exploration

We have clarified our ambitions, know what we want to accomplish, and fix our eyes on the future. We're moving with determination and resolution toward our big, beautiful goal. It feels more important to go at a steady pace than to rush forward, and although we are eager to prove our value, we refuse to be pressured or hurried along. Focused as we are, sometimes we get a bit headstrong, a bit attached to our own path, a bit reluctant to hear other ideas. This need for safety and comfort, this effort to balance stubbornness with security, this powerful sense of attention and calm, is the quiet confidence of the Knight of Pentacles.

• • •

In planting a seed, we commit to a particular path of growth, declare to the earth and the rain and the sun that we intend to cultivate something specific. And in attending to this seed's needs, in devoting ourselves to its care, we invest in that growth, put our own love and effort into this ongoing process. This knight is a person who sets a course and is determined to follow it in spite of obstacles, challenges, or unexpected shifts along the way. Just as a rock climber is deliberate and cautious with every movement—unable to rush their progress but knowing that they'll eventually reach an epic and incredible destination—the Knight of Pentacles relishes every step of the progress, refusing to be pressured into another path.

Discipline is a powerful skill, and consistent forward motion can be wildly effective in reaching our goals. We take pride in our abilities and our devoted, methodical efforts. Yet we need to balance that pride with a willingness to try something new, to learn as we go, to trust our bodies and instincts if something feels off. We may believe that what we are doing needs to be done, but is there really only one way to accomplish our goal? The challenge of the Knight of Pentacles is in recognizing where we are in a particular journey and being able to shift our perspective, resources, or efforts in order to continue progressing. If we just keep doing something that isn't effective, we may destroy our own accomplishments. If we keep watering a plant that's drowning, if we keep using a fertilizer that isn't actually offering the necessary nourishment, that plant will die. Flexibility can be a challenging skill to learn, but it also empowers us to adjust, to find new gifts, to mature as a person.

From a numerological perspective, knights balance the energy of the Hanged One (12) and the Empress (3). Just as they find joy in the process of growth and exploration, they may also get hung up on obstacles, getting frustrated by stagnation or tangled up in complex choices. There's wisdom in carefully monitoring every step, but there's also joy to be found in shifting landscapes, changing horizons, new viewpoints. Instead of measuring progress only by analytical means, instead of devoting themselves to only one method of expression, the Knight of Pentacles invites us to show ourselves generosity in experience, to allow ourselves to find satisfaction in different ways. Adapting to shifting goals or circumstances is not a weakness.

In Readings

The Knight of Pentacles asks us to examine where we are being steadfast and where we're simply being stubborn. There's magic to a steady pace, beauty to discover in slow and patient movement—but sometimes it's necessary to shake things up, blaze a new trail, activate different resources. If you're so obsessed with your ultimate goal that you're missing the scenery along the way, consider how you can incorporate more pleasure into your efforts.

JOURNAL PROMPT: *How do you plot a course, adjust to complications or difficulties, understand success? What helps you to balance dignity with discovery? How can you show yourself generosity and flexibility in your work, and how does that provide space for a different kind of satisfaction? When are you methodical, and how does that energy serve you?*

Queen of Pentacles

THIRTEEN & FOUR // Focus, pragmatism, independence, determination, organization, expression

EARTH // Resources, health, finances, senses, nature, health, legacy, associated with the body

KEYWORDS // daily pleasures · sensuality · observation · diligence · control · satisfaction · pragmatic boundaries

Fortitude and ambition fill us. We move through the world with poise, self-confidence, and intention, taking charge when necessary and delegating when possible. We know our value, understand our power, recognize the many resources that we have at our disposal. Others value our observations, trust our experience, respect our boundaries. And while the people we work alongside and teach may admire us, may strive to be like us, we have a kind of poise and grace that cannot be imitated. This personal assurance, this ability to guide and inspire, is the captivating magic of the Queen of Pentacles.

• • •

When we act in alignment with our values, when we understand what we want and devote ourselves to getting it, we can find so much pleasure in our daily efforts. There's a sense of powerful satisfaction in the Queen of Pentacles, a recognition of how well-balanced and beautifully cultivated their days are. Like an herbalist and teacher who weaves education with professional growth, this is someone who recognizes the value in every facet of who they are, who shares important wisdom with their community while also guiding them away from danger. In keeping our biggest goals in focus without letting ourselves get overwhelmed by ambition, by finding joy in the present even while establishing security for our future, we can relish every stage of progress, celebrate every achievement.

Stabilizing growth with recovery takes consistent effort—we have to truly see the value in all of the parts of the generative cycle. The Queen of Pentacles takes pleasure in every portion of their days and celebrates the joy in being clear about what they want, setting clear parameters for different aspects of life. This is someone who is fully present wherever they are, who creates frameworks of protection and creation and discovery that function as anchors for grounding. Abundance doesn't just come out of nowhere; it requires nurturing, attention. As a pragmatic and sensual ruler, the Queen of Pentacles refuses to compromise and chooses instead a few goals at a time. They are organized in how they tackle and execute each one.

All queens understand systems, but this artist of earth is truly a master of them. A numerological combination of the inevitable release of Death (13) and the powerful, protective boundaries of the Emperor (4), this ruler knows when to say *no*. Setting limits and restrictions helps us protect all that we truly care about, and in many ways, that is the biggest lesson of the Queen of Pentacles. Instead of jumping at every possible opportunity, this ruler is able to focus their energy and insights on the things that matter most to them, creating limits and rules for themselves that help protect their energy and their empathy. This isn't a selfish choice but rather a kind one—this queen knows their time and experience are important, and values them accordingly. In being truthful about how much they can take on, this queen also teaches everyone around them to do the same, empowering others to put their energy toward the interests and ideals that they hope to grow and delegating responsibilities that they can't or won't take on to those that can. This queen can be truly charitable in protecting their resources and is pragmatic in spending them.

In Readings

The Queen of Pentacles is often a reminder that we have more power and influence than we realize, and that we are fully capable of being in charge in a way that is dignified, respectful, and efficient. Rather than letting others walk all over us, we can stand firm in our needs and desires, can create balance between work and play, can utilize our resources in a healthy and satisfying way.

JOURNAL PROMPT: *How are you being present in work, play, rest, discovery, connection, dreaming? Where do you find joy, and how do you incorporate pleasure into your daily routines? How do you understand restriction, and how do boundaries allow you to be deeply, intentionally generous?*

King of Pentacles

FOURTEEN & FIVE // Personal freedom, change, leadership, curiosity, knowledge, observation

EARTH // Resources, health, finances, senses, nature, health, legacy, associated with the body

KEYWORDS // generosity · care · responsibility · organization · intentionality · pragmatic expansion

Our natural aura of responsibility, patience, and generosity has made us a valuable mentor. We find others coming to us more and more, seeking help, guidance, and resources, wanting to create legacies for themselves and their loved ones. While we may not be known for taking big risks, our calm demeanor and deep sense of community create rich stability, helping others feel safe, cared for, and protected. This ability to lead with pragmatism, maturity, and benevolence, paired with a mindful desire to shelter those we care for, is the thoughtful, attentive energy of the King of Pentacles.

• • •

There is strength in the many. Community care and collective action require multiple viewpoints on organization, distribution, responsibility, and stewardship. Good leaders recognize the value of individual contributions as well as the potential for cooperative transformation. With the King of Pentacles, we consider the ways that assets, energy, and ideas combine to create spaces of safety, comfort, and abundance. Think of this king like a hydroponic farmer: inventive, resourceful, taking a centuries-old profession and making it modern, accessible, sustainable. This kind of work takes time but it also has a real, lasting impact, shifting the ways that we grow and distribute assets, allowing old systems to transform into new, more functional ones.

Many of us have found security within institutions, even if they aren't perfect or equal. So much of our lives is defined by organizations and establishments; we have been following pathways that were founded long ago. Yet we may have more power than we realize, more strength than we utilize—something that the King of Pentacles never forgets. This is a leader who finds deep satisfaction in making the world better, who sees generosity as imperative for community prosperity. All kings help to build frameworks for strong and stable futures, but the King of Pentacles is particularly interested in protecting those under their leadership, ensuring that everyone has access to what they need. Empowering others to build and supporting their efforts, from planning to creation to long-term sustainability, are both important to this king. And as an architect of earth, as someone devoted to ideas of legacy, this figure can serve as a patron or bene-factor, intentionally creating spaces of safe experimentation and rich investment.

Each king holds the energy of Temperance (14) and the Hierophant (5). With the King of Pentacles, we see the ways that a desire for moderation and a comfort with tradition can shape the upgrades we make. This ruler of earth may be a bit more stubborn and reluctant to take chances than other kings—but they are also someone who understands long-term investments, who believes in the importance of established, lasting legacy. And while history is important, old protocols are not the only way, are not rules that we have to cling to at any cost. With care, deliberation, and intention, improvements can be made that make life better for the many, rather than just the few.

In Readings

The King of Pentacles can urge us to think about the extended implications of our choices and to be conscious of how our actions may play out in the future. This is a reminder that you do not need to apologize for taking up space or having needs. This king serves as an invitation to take pleasure in the things that you are good at, to establish boundaries to protect and preserve the things that matter, to invest in systems of change that will make things more abundant and secure for everyone.

> JOURNAL PROMPT: *How are you taking care of your resources? Where can you be generous and share what you have with those who are in need? What in your physical world could use more attention, and how can you step into your power in a way that lets you define your own parameters of success, legacy, and stability?*

PART THREE

The Journey Never Ends

TAKING YOUR JOURNEY DEEPER

The journey through the tarot is not a linear one, nor is it a journey that we take only one time. Remember that the Fool is the beginning and the end, the hidden in-between, dancing through empty spaces and affirming our completeness. The Fool never stops being zero, never stops filling in the gaps between milestones with desire, wonder, curiosity. Each time you work through this book, each time you revisit a section or work more closely with a particular card, you will deepen your awareness, your insight, your capacity for transformation. Answers often inspire new questions, resolutions naturally lead us to new inspirations, and embracing the energy of the Fool empowers you to build a life of questioning. As you grow, you will continue to want *more*.

And there is more—so much more. Beyond working with tarot through readings, correspondences, and cycles, we can combine the insights of the cards with additional tools; we can also tap into the magic and energy of the cards through personal spiritual and creative practices. The following pages offer suggestions for deeper connection, side paths that you can wander down on this journey of transformation and self-discovery.

Tarot & Spirituality

What feels holy to you? What feels sacred?

Reading tarot can help us forge connections with larger forces, bigger energies, those mysterious and unknown sources. In considering your own beliefs, in clarifying the magic that feels present when working with the cards, your spirituality naturally becomes part of the equation. Pulling cards is already an introspective and contemplative practice; but with intentionality, we can use tarot for prayer, rituals, mantras, spells, and other outpourings of faith, letting the cards provide insight, wisdom, and structure for our spiritual work.

Meditation with tarot can be the simplest place to start, as this practice in many ways overlaps with the ritual of reading cards. By spending dedicated time with an archetype—either one that is drawn at random or one that is specifically chosen—we allow our own energy to mingle and blend with the energy of these cards. This can help us to sharpen our focus and step into a particular mindset or intention with purpose. An important decision may have you reaching for the contemplation of the High Priestess or the sharp perceptions of Justice, while a big shift could inspire you to work with Strength, Temperance, or the Star. On a day of rest, you may want to work with the Four of Swords, and in a time of celebration you may reach for the Ten of Pentacles or the Three of Cups. Spending time in meditation with these cards—and expanding that practice to include journaling or setting up a simple altar—can help you identify with these concepts in new ways and make them more intimate, more personal. How do you connect with specific cards using the gifts of your mind, heart, and soul?

In the same way, **prayer and mantras** can be interwoven with tarot work. In seeking connection or guidance with larger forces, divine beings, or energies, we can deepen those spiritual relationships and find new meaning within our readings. Readings and meditations can feel like communion, spreads become a new kind of sacrament, our whispered hopes and dreams become offerings. If you already have a religious practice or work with particular gods or spirits, consider using tarot as part of your rituals. And if you don't, try writing simple mantras to accompany cards whose energy you want to explore or embody, statements of purpose or exploration that help you embody these concepts. What would it look like to reimagine archetypes as deities? How could the cards provide different kinds of answers? What lessons do these archetypes have to impart, and how could working with specific cards help you clarify your own objectives or ambitions?

For many, tarot offers a natural method for **divination**, also known as fortune-telling. There are many methods for this practice that vary in precision and complexity. As your own relationship with the cards grows, digging into the power of tarot and its ability to forecast events can help you clarify what you believe about readings. Many books have been written on tarot as a method of divination, and I have included some of these in the bibliography. Divination can be very general or wildly specific depending on the kinds of timings that you use. *Organic* and *relative* timings are based around completing a challenge, moving through a situation, or taking a risk in order to reach a new stage of growth, whereas *seasonal* and *predictive* timings use astrological and numerological correspondences to establish more specific seasons, dates, and even times of day for when something will or will not happen. Do you believe that the tarot can offer us a window into future events, emotions, or connections? How do you think about your personal role in your own fate, and where can tarot offer clarity in your ongoing growth?

Spellwork is another way that we can engage with the tarot on a spiritual level. Individual archetypes or groups of cards can be an inspiring way to clarify purpose when engaging in the sacred arts and can help us layer new meanings into our plans and resolutions. Even the simplest healing spell can be boosted by incorporating the Star or Strength. When we tap into our magic for abundance, connection, willpower, confidence, courage, or any number of other intentions, bringing in the clarity of these cards can make our spells stronger, more sharply attuned to our goals. Using the cards even in our smaller rituals can be a joyful experience, making daily offerings and intimate spiritual moments feel deeper, clearer. Try lighting candles or making honey jars with specific cards in mind, or add a relevant archetype into the components of your next spell. How does choosing cards for different kinds of spellwork illuminate or intensify your practice?

An important spiritual practice that I want to highlight is **ancestor work**. Connecting to the people in our past is one of the most ancient forms of magic, and using major arcana archetypes as well as the minor arcana court cards can be a beautiful way to explore our heritage and to understand lineage in new ways. Tarot can offer gateways of understanding to blood relatives and chosen families but can also help us tap into the energies of ancestors of place, time, and intention. And if you're interested in pursuing a relationship with a specific ancestor or spirit guide, utilizing spreads and systems can be an accessible starting point, giving you both structure and freedom to make personal, poignant connections. Whom do court cards or major arcana archetypes remind you of in your own life, or your past? How could integrating ancestry work with the tarot help expand your perspectives on both your own heritage as well as the cards themselves?

The more you work with the tarot, the more you'll find it offers many different bridges to spirituality. Utilize different practices in your own personal way to build rituals that speak to who you are and what you crave. Consider how you already work with your cards, and how you let the lessons, truths, and perceptions that your readings offer intersect with your other routines, habits, and rituals. Do you consider every tarot reading spiritual? How do you translate the lessons that the tarot offers into your own personal ceremonies and sacraments?

Tarot & Creativity

What does it mean to be creative, innovative, expressive? How does art teach us about ourselves?

The imagery, concepts, and mythology attached to tarot have inspired artists for centuries. And whether you consider yourself an artistic person or not, everyone has a little spark of creativity inside of them, one that is not always nurtured or nourished in our capitalistic society. Tarot can be a brilliant way to tap into that creativity and to make intentional rituals around it in our daily lives.

Looking at the cards and gaining **inspiration** through them are the simplest place to start and can serve as the driving force or framework for all kinds of projects. Studying the layers of meaning and symbolism within a card can send you off into dozens of possible directions, inspiring you to write stories, poetry, or songs. The images can move you into tactile realms of drawing, sculpting, collaging, or painting. Tarot can be captured in performance art, photography, and so many other forms of expression—and combining different mediums can even facilitate entirely new creations. You don't have to have any natural skill or talent in order to try this out for yourself—don't think of it as something that you have to show to anyone else, but instead as a natural outpouring of expressive magic that flows through you. What would it mean to make space for creativity without judgment? How much could you learn about your relationship with a card by trying to draw it or write about it, and then studying the results later?

In exploring inspiration with the cards, you may feel called to create a full **deck** of your own. This can be an intensive and personal project, one that transforms your understanding of each card. Again, this doesn't have to be something that you show to anyone else, or something that you try to sell or monetize; but it can be a long-term project that you revisit when you're wanting to spend intensive time with a specific card. The simple practice of digging into meanings and translating these archetypes through your own lens of experience and artistry can dramatically deepen your connection to these cards and help you see things in them that you may not have even been conscious of. What are your favorite cards to work with, and what do the images that sit in your mind's eye for these archetypes reveal about you and your relationships to these cards? How could you translate that onto paper, language, music, or another medium? How many different versions of these cards can you imagine?

Creativity doesn't always have to be about designing something new. You might find that putting together **collections** is a simple but powerful method of connecting with various tarot archetypes and energies. Curating musical playlists, compiling photographs or pieces of art, or creating personal correspondences can all be effective ways of learning to find these archetypes in our everyday lives, and being intentional about connecting with them in different ways. In translating the energy and experiences of the cards through different mediums of sound, place, and space, we find new messages, hear new truths, create new opportunities for expansion and discovery. Try gathering songs, poems, film or television shows, recipes, perfumes, plants, crystals, and images that remind you of different cards. I love to make playlists for different archetypes and to curate vision boards for various elements, card groupings, or intentions. Which songs would you choose for the Hierophant? What might a page's Pinterest board look like? Which scents remind you of the suit of swords? How can you allow existing art to deepen your relationships with the cards? How could creating collections of objects, media, or experiences help you tap into that specific energy when you need it?

Expanding on this idea, sensory **experiences** offer their own methods for creativity and discovery. In thinking about the smells, tastes, sounds, and tactile sensations of different cards, we put ourselves into the energy of the tarot, creating immersive experiences for ourselves. Which scents remind you of Temperance? How does it feel to sit in the Sun's warm glow, the Moon's pale light? What meal might embody the fortitude of the Chariot, the passionate strength of the

Queen of Wands, the collaborative joy of the Three of Pentacles? Pay attention to the moments when different cards reveal themselves in your physical world, in your daily experiences, and make a catalog for them that you can refer back to and constantly expand. How could sitting in these energies with intention deepen your own tarot practice? How can you seek out specific archetypes in the world?

Creativity can help us create our own series of tarot correspondences, bridging works, experiences, and sensory connections with these archetypes—but this doesn't have to look only one particular way. Creativity does not have to mean *only* artistry. In expanding the lenses that we use to view and understand these cards, in letting the tarot inspire us in different ways, in seeing where our studies lead us creatively, so many new doorways can be opened. What does creativity mean to you, and how do you experience the tarot in inventive and innovative ways?

Tarot & Occult Esoterica

Tarot has natural correspondences with astrology and numerology, and lends itself beautifully to spiritual and creative practices. But there are so many other ways that we can use tarot, far too many to explore in this book. I highly encourage you to play around with the following tools, rituals, and exercises, and to see what resonates with you, what inspires you, what pushes you to expand your appreciation of these cards and their meanings. In making space for new kinds of correlations and relationships, in inviting the tarot into other areas of your life, you can find so many new layers of magic. See what feels good for you as well as what pushes your boundaries. You may surprise yourself with what you want to pursue.

There are a number of spiritual and occult tools that play well with tarot cards, and you may find that combining different tools for different needs offers you a lot of flexibility in your regular readings. Many readers find value in pulling cards from other decks, like **oracle**, **Lenormand**, or **angel** card sets, as these decks include keywords, prompts, and imagery outside of the tarot's 78-card structure. **Runes** (stones carved with the runic alphabet) can be pulled in conjunction with tarot cards, offering broader themes, concepts, and wisdom to consider. **Pendulums** (a small weight on a chain) and **dice** can provide clarity in decision-making and when paired with tarot can provide additional nuance when making complex choices or analyzing different possibilities. **Crystals** (stones with distinctive energetic properties) are excellent companions to tarot when it comes to meditation, spells, and setting intentions. **Sigils** (a magical symbol, often created by an individual practitioner) help us clarify and express our intentions, and can give us simple ways of combining the energies of multiple cards. And more accessible **household items** and **sacred tools** such as candles, incense, plants, herbs, tinctures, essential oils, and teas work beautifully with tarot archetypes, particularly as part of daily work and rituals. Tarot can absolutely stand on its own, but if you already work with different tools or have been interested in learning about something new, integrating these into your tarot practice can give you a great place to start, as well as expanding the ways that you already use the cards.

The tarot can also be useful for working with the **moon**. Many witches and practitioners of the sacred arts follow the moon's monthly cycles of growth, manifestation, celebration, release, and rest—and in working with the different archetypes that correspond with these phases, we can use the tarot to tap into the moon's magic and learn to work with it in more individual and unique ways.

New moon: Fool // desire, curiosity, new beginnings

Waxing crescent moon: High Priestess // observation, planning, intuitive wisdom

First quarter moon: Magician // creativity, activation, confidence

Waxing gibbous moon: Wheel of Fortune // movement, opportunities, luck

Full moon: Sun // abundance, celebration; and Moon // discovery, desire

Waning gibbous or disseminating moon: Star // healing, optimism, trust in the self

Last quarter moon: Judgment // forgiveness, awakening, revelations

Waning crescent moon: Hermit // wisdom, spirituality, service

A simple moon altar can help you be more in tune with lunar cycles; pulling the cards for the moon's phase and astrological sign together can help you work with multiple archetypes at once. Learn to see the moon through these shifting lenses. You can even introduce other cards from both the major and minor arcana that capture the overlapping energies between these cards, giving you deeper insights into how to work with the moon during different periods of its cycle. The more you work with the moon, the more you might feel comfortable creating your own correspondences and finding cards that reflect your personal energy level during each phase.

. . .

Tarot offers us opportunities for powerful self-exploration, reflection, and awareness. We can use the cards to **understand ourselves** more deeply and even to expand on the person that we thought we were. Tarot naturally encourages introspection, but in using these cards we can also explore our own identity, sexuality, gender, relationship and community needs, desires, and dreams, opening up new ways of looking at our physical, spiritual, and emotional selves. There is so much capacity for acceptance and growth through consistent readings, and if we let them, the cards can help us drastically expand our concepts of who we are, what we are capable of, and what our bigger and brighter purpose could be. Consider pulling cards that represent different aspects of yourself, that reflect where you are in your various cycles. Which archetypes, court cards, pips do you see in yourself? If you were to describe yourself or tell your personal story using only tarot cards, which ones would you choose? How might the cards you choose change at various points in your life, and what might laying those out and tracing patterns help you discover about yourself?

You can also harness the power of the tarot in **daily activities**. Using exercise, rest, movement, work, play, and exploration to intentionally connect with different energies can be a useful reminder to be present, expand your viewpoints, and be rooted in your current experience. How might you harness your inner Page of Swords, Knight of Cups, Queen of Pentacles, King of Wands? Which activities give you new appreciation for the Emperor, the Lovers, the Hanged One? How can trying new things or introducing new hobbies into your routines help you deliberately cultivate specific kinds of insights?

While tarot is absolutely not a substitute for **therapy**, readings can be deeply therapeutic. They can help us understand ourselves more deeply, as well as learn to express ourselves with new clarity and depth. Reading with a therapist, a partner, or a trusted friend can open up unique lines of communication, giving us language and context for our emotions, experiences, desires, and needs. Consider what it feels like to be in a Magician state, a Hermit state, a Temperance state. How might this kind of framework help you explore your feelings in another way? And how does thinking about your current positioning as part of a larger cycle give you a different perspective on what you're moving toward, and what you're leaving behind?

This is in no way an exhaustive list, but rather an offering of permission and encouragement. Tarot can find purchase anywhere in our lives, anywhere we invite it in and interact with it. Experiment with the structures, disciplines, practices, and tools that I've offered here, but don't be afraid to try your own methods, to write your own correspondences, to play with your own rules. How can you make space for tarot in many different aspects of your life? What would it mean to not limit tarot to just readings but to start seeing its magic everywhere?

TAROT SPREADS

Spreads are a beautiful way to create a framework for readings, helping you give shape and purpose to your questions. You can use these spreads with a specific topic or concern in mind, or you can use them for more general readings. Be open to whatever the cards may want to discuss.

There are literally thousands and thousands of tarot spreads out in the world: some are classics that are practically considered sacred, and others are deliberately irreverent, silly, expansive, or flexible. Some have very open positions, while others are incredibly detailed. To use a spread, shuffle the cards well and simply pull one card for each position in the layout, then interpret the card through that lens. I tend to go through each card invidually, and then look at the entire picture, but you may find it preferable to get a general sense of all of the full reading first and then look at each card one at a time.

To be very clear: you do not have to use spreads in your readings. It is perfectly acceptable, and sometimes preferable, to pull a few cards and have a conversation with them. It's also absolutely fine to tweak any spread (yes, even the classic ten-card Celtic Cross) to suit your needs, as long as you do so *before* pulling cards and not afterwards. This is *your* journey, *your* reading, *your* transformation, so do what you like with it.

At their best, tarot spreads help to provide clarity, establishing specific points of truth, insight, and advice that can give shape to your questions and offer pointed, specific answers. I personally like spreads that use two, three, and four cards better than massive spreads with eight, ten, twelve, or more cards—but I encourage you to play around with different formats and sizes, and to see what resonates for you personally.

Some spreads can be used entirely on their own, while others work best in response to a specific question or situation. I like to figure out what I'm looking for from the cards, choose my spread, then shuffle the cards with this query in mind. I take my time until the cards feel well mixed and I'm ready to draw, and then I place a card in each position and go through them one at a time. You may find patterns within the reading, so pay attention to similarities in suit, element, number, function, advice, or emotion—these broader themes can add additional layers of meaning to your reading and help give an overall functionality to the spread.

Below, you'll find spreads for each of the twenty-two major arcana archetypes. You can use these to tap into the energy of the cards or as a starting point to connect with minor arcana cards that share the same numerological or astrological correspondences. (For example, if you're struggling with the Four of Cups, you may find that using the Emperor spread offers some new insights on boundaries, protection, and goal-setting.) When using these, I like to pull out the specific card whose energy I am working to explore, connect with, or embody, and place it at the top of my reading space before pulling cards with the remaining 77 cards in the deck.

This section also includes two- and three-card spreads. Two-card spreads are great for quick and dirty insights, especially if you're trying to make a decision, figure out a blockage, or overcome an obstacle. Three-card spreads offer a bit more nuance and depth, creating opportunities for additional advice or perspective. Feel free to use these suggestions as starting points: the sky is the limit.

Archetype Spreads

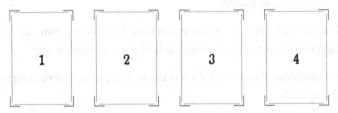

| 1 | 2 | 3 | 4 |

Fool: a dream / a potential risk / a first step / a glimpse at who you might become

Magician: a magic that I already possess / a way that it manifests / something that my magic craves / a way to use my magic to its fullest potential

Priestess: an area of my life that would benefit from stillness / a way that my wisdom is revealing itself / something my intuition wants me to realize / a method for tapping into personal truth

Empress: a gift to offer / wisdom to receive / an expression to celebrate / a way to nourish the self

Emperor: a reminder of my power / a place to implement more structure / a goal to refine / a resource to utilize

Hierophant: a tradition that offers stability / a habit to build or expand / an idea to explore / a community to seek

Lovers: a new experience or adventure to pursue / an aspect of self to celebrate / an insight into an existing partnership or community / a way to find joy in the present

Chariot: an insight into the path ahead / a boundary that is ready to be broken / a victory to celebrate / a way to maintain control

Strength: a place to be patient / a way to express wildness / a reminder of your power / an expression of your wisdom

Hermit: a glimpse of your light / a truth about your shadow / something to surrender / something to ponder

Wheel: an insight into your current position / something you can control / something you cannot control / a way to find peace in your present

Justice: a reminder of your truth / a way to use your power / something to clarify / something to do

Hanged One: something to observe / a truth to breathe into / a way to show yourself grace / something that is changing

Death: something that is ending / a way to find power in this transformation / something to take from this experience / a self-care practice to remember

Temperance: something that is growing / a way to tap into new magic / an unexpected lesson / a method for finding peace

Devil: a place to exercise less control / a place to exercise more control / something to pay closer attention to / a way to reclaim power

Tower: something to release / something to remember / a new freedom that is being revealed / a way to care for yourself in this time of transformation

Star: something that is true / something that is important / something that has been revealed / something to pursue

Moon: a fantasy to indulge / a fear to examine / a mystery to explore / a dream to embrace

Sun: a success to acknowledge / something to celebrate / a gift to give yourself / a way to be present

Judgment: someone you used to be / someone you are becoming / a possibility that's within reach / a rule to break

World: an achievement to celebrate / an evolution to acknowledge / a personal change to recognize / a way to rest

Two-Card Spreads

```
┌─────────┐   ┌─────────┐
│         │   │         │
│    1    │   │    2    │
│         │   │         │
└─────────┘   └─────────┘
```

truth / dare

red light / green light

if / then

expand / restrict

yes / no

situation /advice

perception / reality

give / take

want / need

obstacle / insight

pro / con

pursue / avoid

work / play

inner world / outer world

known / unknown

fear / hope

above / below

Three-Card Spreads

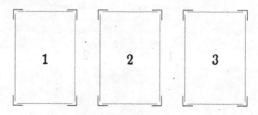

stop / start / continue

challenge / insight / action

needs / wants / fears

you / another person / the relationship

what to hold on to / what to let go of / what to remember

past / present / future

morning / afternoon / evening

body / mind / spirit

idea / knowledge / action

desire / conflict / resolution

identity / community / purpose

situation / action / outcome

you / current path / potential

idea / process / objective

option 1 / option 2 / a way to choose

choice / pro / con

problem / solution / advice

release / receive / retain

red light / yellow light / green light

present / desired future / how to get there

a seed to plant / a method for tending / what you'll harvest

tomorrow / next week / next month

obstacle / fear / solution

idea / reality / potential

an existing pattern / a potential shift / a new horizon

how I see me / how others see me / a truth about me

strength / weakness / passion

light / shadow / a necessary shift

RESOURCES FOR FURTHER STUDY

The works listed below have been incredibly useful for me in my own practice, as well as helping me develop the techniques and interpretations explored in this book. I highly encourage you to continue your studies with these books and articles, and to make education an ongoing part of your tarot work.

Books

Basile, Lisa Marie. *The Magical Writing Grimoire*. Beverly, MA: Fair Winds Press, 2020.

Constantino, Victoria. *Tarot by the Moon*. Woodbury, MN: Llewellyn Publications, 2021.

Crispin, Jessa. *The Creative Tarot*. New York: Atria Books, 2016.

Dore, Jessica. *Tarot for Change*. New York: Penguin Life, 2021.

Elizabeth, S. *The Art of the Occult*. London: White Lion Publishing, 2020.

Greer, Mary K. *Archetypal Tarot* (previously published as *Who Are You in the Tarot?*). Newburyport, MA: Weiser Books, 2021.

———. *Tarot Constellations: Patterns of Personal Destiny*. Hollywood, CA: Newcastle Publishing, 1987.

———. *Tarot for Your Self*. Newburyport, MA: Weiser Books, 2019.

———. *21 Ways to Read a Tarot Card*. Woodbury, MN: Llewellyn Publications, 2006.

Hendrickson, Nancy. *Ancestral Tarot*. Newburyport, MA: Weiser Books, 2021.

Hundley, Jessica. *The Library of Esoterica: Tarot*. Cologne, Germany: Taschen, 2020.

Kenner, Corinne. *Tarot and Astrology*. Woodbury, MN: Llewellyn Publications, 2011.

Konraad, Sandor. *Numerology: Key to the Tarot.* Atglen, PA: Schiffer Publishing, 1997.

Jodorowsky, Alejandro. *The Way of Tarot: The Spiritual Teacher in the Cards.* Rochester, VT: Destiny Books, 2009.

Matzner, Andy. *The Tarot Activity Book.* CreateSpace, 2013.

Muller, Brittany. *The Contemplative Tarot.* New York: St. Martin's Essentials, 2022.

Nicholas, Chani. *You Were Born for This.* New York: HarperOne, 2021.

Place, Robert M. *The Tarot: History, Symbolism, and Divination.* New York: TarcherPerigree, 2005.

Pollack, Rachel. *Rachel Pollack's Tarot Wisdom.* Woodbury, MN: Llewellyn, 2008.

——— *Seventy-Eight Degrees of Wisdom.* Newburyport, MA: Weiser Books, 2019

Reed, Theresa. *Astrology for Real Life.* Newburyport, MA: Weiser Books, 2019.

———*Tarot: No Questions Asked.* Newburyport, MA: Weiser Books, 2020.

———*Twist Your Fate.* Newburyport, MA: Weiser Books, 2022.

Reed, Theresa, and Shaheen Miro. *Tarot for Troubled Times.* Newburyport, MA: Weiser Books, 2019.

Saussy, Briana. *Making Magic.* Boulder, CO: Sounds True, 2019.

Scolnick, Rebecca. *The Witch's Book of Numbers.* San Antonio, TX: Hierophant Publishing, 2022.

Snow, Cassandra. *Queering the Tarot.* Newburyport, MA: Weiser Books, 2019.

Snow, Cassandra, and Siri Vincent Plouff. *Lessons from the Empress.* Newburyport, MA: Weiser Books, 2022.

Tea, Michelle. *Modern Tarot.* New York: HarperOne, 2017.

Wen, Benebell. *Holistic Tarot.* Berkeley, CA: North Atlantic Books, 2015.

Wintner, Bakara. *WTF is Tarot?* Salem, MA: Page Street Publishing, 2017.

Woods, Mecca. *Astrology for Happiness and Success.* Avon, MA: Adams Media. 2018.

Worth, Liz. *The Power of Tarot.* Lulu Publishing, 2019.

Articles

"Exploring the Arcanas through Astrology" series for *Hermit's Mirror*

"Fools, Hermits, and Devils: Tarot as a Spiritual Discipline" by Brittany Muller for *Earth & Altar*

"Fool's Journey: How to Get the Most from a Tarot Reading" by Beth Maiden for *Autostraddle*

"Fool's Journey: The Language of Numbers in the Minor Arcana" by Beth Maiden for *Autostraddle*

"4 Ways to Interpret Reversed Tarot Cards" by Gina Wisotzky for *Incandescent Tarot*

"How to Expertly Shuffle Your Tarot Cards" by Meg Jones Wall for *Astrology Answers*

"How to Read Tarot Intuitively with the Five Senses" by Kimberly M. for *Fables Den*

"Intuitive Tarot vs. Reading by the Book" by Flora Green for *Green Witch Living*

"Numerology 101 Zine" by Rebecca Scolnik

"Numerology and Tarot: How to Find Your Tarot Birth Card" at *Numerologist*

"Ritual & Honey: Seeking Lineage in Ancestral Reverence" by Asali Earthwork

"Short Tarot Meditations to Deepen Your Practice" by Jean Linder for Kellee Maize

"A Song for Every Card in the Major Arcana" by Tiana Traffas for *Wayfinder Tarot*

"Tarot 101: A Beginner's Guide" by Steff Yotka for *Vogue*

"Tarot as Witness" by Beth Maiden for *Little Red Tarot*

"Tarot beyond the Visible" by M. M. Meleen for *Llewellyn*

"Tarot by the Mouthful" series by Theresa Reed and Kyle Cherek

"Tarot Mythology: The Surprising Origins of the World's Most Misunderstood Cards" by Hunter Oatman-Stanford for *Mental Floss*

"Tarot Reversals: Visual Cues" by Diana Rose Harper

"Timing Events Using Tarot and Astrology" by Catherine Chapman for *Tarot Elements*

"Unlocking Archetypes Tarot Study" by Meg Jones Wall

"A Visual History of Tarot Cards" by Vivian Li for *MODA* at UChicago

"Yoga Tarot Challenge" by Queen Tiye Tarot

ACKNOWLEDGMENTS

Thank you to all of the queer tarot writers, readers, artists, and deck creators that have come before me, and that will come after me. I am endlessly inspired by the visions of these archetypes that are out in the world, the hundreds of creatives that have helped me and so many others to find ourselves within these complex and wonderful cards. Your work is more powerful than you know, and I am so wildly grateful for all of it.

Thank you to the Instagram community, especially #queertarot. I have found so much love, joy, connection, magic, and wisdom among the readers and writers on this platform, and it's been such a privilege to share knowledge, ideas, and community over the years.

Thank you to Jill Marr, my brilliant agent, who has believed in this project since the beginning and has never wavered in full support for me. You gave me the confidence to keep pursuing this project, to fight for it to be published, and I am so wildly grateful for your knowledge, experience, and encouragement.

Thank you to Peter Turner, who recognized early on the importance of this book, and thank you to Kathryn Sky-Peck, who knew exactly what to do with this project to make it the best book possible. Thanks to the entire team at Weiser for believing in me and my work. It's been such a dream to see this book come to life, and it would not have been possible without your vision and resources.

Thank you to my patrons and newsletter subscribers for reading my words consistently, for engaging with my ideas and dreams, and for providing the financial support that I needed to finish so many projects. It's been such a gift to grow along with you, to share my delights and sorrows, to know that my words were reaching people even in my darkest moments. Your support has given me the confidence to keep going, keep writing, keep trying new things.

Thank you to my brilliant and patient therapist, Maggie Field, who has never failed to listen to my concerns, support my dreams, and honor my journey. You helped me identify my place in this world and gather the confidence to pursue it. I truly believe that you saved my life, and I am so appreciative of the work that we have done together.

Thank you to Stephen Wall, for many years of love, patience, adventures, support, and encouragement. You have always been one of my biggest cheerleaders and stood by me through so many personal transformations. I am deeply grateful for our friendship and for your continued presence in my life.

Thank you to my friends and creative communities, for being endlessly positive in your encouragement and excitement. To my queer gaming groups and questing companions Smita Patankar, Mel Lusk, H. Shafran, Michelle Marchese, Nic Sam, Jeanna Kadlec, Heather Hogan, Valerie Anne Liston, A. E. Osworth, Hannah Fairchild, Rachel Madsie Flynn, Jenny Ashman, and Michael Walker: the worlds that we have built and explored together have manifested some of the most special times of my life and have truly helped me to find a confidence, power, and strength within myself that I never knew were possible. Thank you for celebrating my efforts, finding joy in my mistakes, and being so wildly generous in your friendship. I love you all so dearly, and you have enriched my life more than I can possibly say. To my writing group of Siri Plouff, Cassandra Snow, Diana Rose Harper, and Asali Earthwork, thank you for always bringing kind words, for sharing your wisdom and insights, for making my work better, and for reminding me of why my voice matters. And to Kendra Clarke and Marisol Sternke, for being there through thick and thin.

Thank you to my chosen sisters Barbara Baggs and Christine Anckner, along with the rest of my GC crew, for loving me for nearly twenty years. You've watched me reinvent myself so many times and have never failed to show up for me, and I don't know where I would be without your friendship.

Thank you to Heather Hogan, who not only has stood by my side through thick and thin but has also been endlessly positive and profoundly encouraging. You set so many things in motion, from tarotscopes and writing for Autostraddle to discovering so many new facets of myself. Your belief in me, in my vision and talent, in my ability to be my fullest and truest self has been one of the greatest gifts that I have ever received. This book simply would not exist without you.

And lastly, thank you to Jeanna Kadlec. You are constantly teaching me, encouraging me, supporting me, and sometimes scraping me off the floor when I've forgotten myself. Thank you for never losing sight of who I am, for building me up, for sticking with me, for cheering me on, and for somehow always knowing exactly what I need to hear. *Joy is not made to be a crumb*, and you remind me of that every single day. I love you.

TO OUR READERS